Digital Techniques for Heritage Presentation and Preservation

Jayanta Mukhopadhyay • Indu Sreedevi •
Bhabatosh Chanda • Santanu Chaudhury •
Vinay P. Namboodiri

Editors

Digital Techniques
for Heritage Presentation
and Preservation

 Springer

Editors
Jayanta Mukhopadhyay
Indian Institute of Technology Kharagpur
Kharagpur, India

Indu Sreedevi
Delhi Technological University
Delhi, India

Bhabatosh Chanda
Indian Statistical Institute Kolkata
Kolkata, West Bengal, India

Santanu Chaudhury
Indian Institute of Technology Jodhpur
Jodhpur, India

Vinay P. Namboodiri
Indian Institute of Technology Kanpur
Kanpur, Uttar Pradesh, India

ISBN 978-3-030-57909-8   ISBN 978-3-030-57907-4   (eBook)
https://doi.org/10.1007/978-3-030-57907-4

This Springer imprint is published by the registered company Springer Nature Switzerland AG.
The registered company address is: Gewerbestrasse 11, 6330 Cham, Switzerland

Preface

Cultural heritage keeps a record of the history of humankind and its legacy and is often expressed as either tangible or intangible cultural heritage. On one hand, we discover new sites, excavate artifacts, document findings, and archive and classify them, linking them to our existing knowledge. On the other hand, existing information as well as knowledge is being lost, artifacts damaged, and traditions and practices ignored. It is important now more than ever to preserve tangible cultural heritage considering its demolition due to changes in climatic conditions, increase in pollution levels, and manmade disasters. In addition, most of the intangible heritage is vanishing due to changes in lifestyle and lack of interest. Efforts are therefore being made to archive and preserve it digitally for transfer to future generations.

A major goal of this book is to contribute to the management of heritage objects in digital space, called *digital heritage (DH)*, with new computer-based approaches in the areas of reconstruction of heritages, recognition, restoration, presentation, and classification of DH. The contributions of this book to DH management are divided into three parts: (1) classification and retrieval of heritage data in various domains, (2) recognition and reconstruction of DH artifacts using computer-based techniques, and (3) applications of modern tools in digital heritage.

Part I consists of five chapters. The chapter titled "Introduction to Heritages and Heritage Management: A Preview" presents a brief introduction to digital heritage and its development and management using computer-based tools. The most important and abundant carrier of information since ancient times are manuscripts on various subjects written in different languages and scripts. A detailed survey of different techniques of categorization of monolingual and multilingual text documents based on different criteria like language and subject domains is given in the chapter titled "Language-Based Text Categorization: A Survey." One of the heritage practices that originated in ancient India and continues even today is Yoga. This is a physical and mental exercise that is often related to traditional Hindu philosophy. The chapter titled "Categorization and Selection of Crowdsourced Images Towards 3D Reconstruction of Heritage Sites" describes a technique of categorizing Yoga Asanas, or poses, using 3D landmark points as features. The classification techniques employed are kNN, SVM, and deep neural networks such as AlexNet, VGGNet, and ResNet. Another important work is archiving images of heritage artifacts such as buildings, sculpture, and paintings for future reference and retrieval. Many researchers are working on building a suitable retrieval system. To test such systems, an appropriate and standard dataset is of utmost importance. The chapter titled "IHIRD: A Data Set for Indian Heritage Image Retrieval" presents the development of an extensive image dataset of Indian heritage monuments like sculptures and paintings that can be used in archival-and-retrieval systems of heritage images. The dataset is referred to as the Indian Heritage Image Retrieval Dataset (IHIRD). The archived images are expected to be retrieved in many different ways. A useful way of retrieving an image from the archive may be based on the supplied pattern present in the image. In the case of a temple image, this pattern may be an artifact (e.g., a figurine or a wheel), or in the case of a manuscript page image, it may be a specific word used in a particular period of time. An efficient method for object (text and artifacts) spotting in an image based on Wave Kernel Signature (WKS) using SIFT features as key points is proposed in the chapter titled "Object Spotting in Historical Documents." Text is spotted using a two-step search technique while artifacts are spotted using normalized cross-correlation.

Part II consists of four chapters. This part mostly discusses restoration and reconstruction of degraded images of old manuscripts, monuments, etc. As mentioned earlier, manuscripts are a major carrier of information from ancient times. Deep learning models being useful computational tools are very popular nowadays for solving computer vision-related problems. However, the requirement of large amounts of training data makes this technique unsuitable for application to heritage artifact preservation. The chapter titled "Text Extraction and Restoration of Old Handwritten Documents" proposes a novel method for the restoration of old degraded handwritten documents using deep neural networks with minimal training data. The performance of the proposed method is evaluated and compared with other state-of-the-art techniques. An important means for preserving and archiving three-dimensional heritage objects like buildings, monuments, towers, and statues is 3D reconstruction of the objects from 2D images. The next three chapters deal with different aspects of digital heritage preservation. The chapter titled "Categorization and Selection of Crowdsourced Images Towards 3D Reconstruction of Heritage Sites" explains how heritage images are selected from unstructured heritage image data for 3D reconstruction and how the heritage image data is cleaned up and categorized. 3D reconstruction focuses on texture preservation. For various datasets, the results of 3D models of the proposed pipeline are compared with the state-of-the-art methods. When one considers 2D images available on the Internet for 3D reconstruction, the resource is much more heterogeneous in terms of size, resolution, focal length of camera, lighting, and so on. Selecting the right set of images is a big challenge. A pipeline that selects a suitable set of Internet-sourced images of heritage sites for 3D reconstruction is described in the chapter titled "Deep Learning-Based Filtering of Images for 3D Reconstruction of Heritage Sites." These methods are quite universal in nature and are applicable to many different sites. On the other hand, the chapter titled "Improving Landmark Recognition Using Saliency Detection and Feature Classification" presents the graph-based visual saliency (GBVS) network using convolutional neural networks (CNN) to recognize and classify Indian landmark images and architectural styles. GBVS is combined with other models to make ensemble model architecture, which is used in the classification.

Finally, in Part III, there are three chapters. This part describes the applications of modern tools in heritage-related tasks which are traditionally done by human experts. This kind of approach is becoming more and more inevitable as experts are rarely available. We have presented work on three different topics, namely, evaluation of Indian classical dance, studies on commonality in the geometric structure of temples in large geographical regions, and knowledge on various types of plants. The chapter titled "*Bharatanatyam* Dance Transcription Using Multimedia Ontology and Machine Learning" describes machine learning-based dance transcription that uses labanotation (akin to music transcription using musical notes). This is done using parsable XML representations of a dance video that are generated to annotate performances and for dance synthesis. Events and/or activities of a dance are related to an ontological model. In the chapter titled "Evolution and Interconnection: Geometry in Early Temple Architecture," a framework for obtaining architectural geometric models of early temples from their digital reconstruction is explained thoroughly. The features from these geometric models provide new knowledge and mathematical understanding of heritage monuments as well as cultural links over a vast region in Southeast Asia. The chapter titled "Computer Vision for Capturing Flora" discusses various computer vision-based tools for collecting, delivering, analyzing, and having an integrated knowledge on plants. The challenges associated with this task are also discussed.

This book has been motivated by the great enthusiasm of the research community in this field during the 2nd Workshop on Digital Heritage (WDH) in association with the Indian Conference on Computer Vision, Graphics and Image Processing (ICVGIP), which was held in December 2018 in Hyderabad. In fact, the chapters are an extended version of research outcomes presented at that workshop. We are thankful to the organizers of the workshop, all the authors for their contributions, reviewers of the chapters, and also all those who have been involved in the publication of this book.

Kharagpur, India   Jayanta Mukhopadhyay
Delhi, India   Indu Sreedevi
Kolkata, WB, India   Bhabatosh Chanda
Jodhpur, India   Santanu Chaudhury
Kanpur, India   Vinay P. Namboodiri
July 2020

Acknowledgments

The proceedings have been made possible by the sheer efforts and teamwork of the organizing committee of the 11th Indian Conference on Computer Vision, Graphics and Image Processing (ICVGIP-2018). First and foremost, we thank the organizing committee for allowing us to conduct the 2nd Workshop on Digital Heritage (WDH) under ICVGIP-2018. We are greatly indebted to the WDH organizing committee for making the workshop a success. Much appreciation goes to the team of reviewers whose efforts resulted in the selection of the best research papers for the oral presentation at the workshop and for the proceedings. We are grateful to the keynote speakers who graced the workshop with their rich experience in their respective areas of expertise. Special thanks to all the authors for their valuable contribution and cooperation in preparing the manuscript. Lastly, we thank the students, staff, and faculty members of the International Institute of Information Technology (IIIT), Hyderabad, for hosting the WDH-2018.

Organization

Program Co-chairs

Indu Sreedevi   Delhi Technological University, Delhi
Jayanta Mukhopadhyay   IIT Kharagpur

Program Committee

A. Rajagopalan   IIT Madras, India
Andreas Georgopoulos   NTUA, Greece
Arindam Biswas   IIEST, Shibpur, India
Ayesha Chaudhary   JNU, Delhi, India
Bhabotosh Chanda   ISI Kolkata, India
Chaluvaraju   Kannada University, Hampi, India
Dipti Prasad Mukherjee   ISI Kolkata, India
Gaurav Harit   IIT Jodhpur, India
Joan Anton Barcelo   UAB, Spain
Meera Natampally   SSA, India
Murali Mohan   DST, India
Parag Cahudhuri   IIT Bombay, India
Partha Bhowmick   IIT Kharagpur, India
Ramesh Agarwal   JNU, Delhi, India
Sanjoy Saha   JU, India
Subhasis Chaudhuri   IIT Bombay, India
Uma Mudenagudi   KLE Technological University, Hubballi, India

Contents

Part I
Classification and Retrieval of Heritage Data

Introduction to Heritages and Heritage Management: A Preview

Enock Osoro Omayio, Indu Sreedevi, and Jeebananda Panda

Abstract This chapter introduces heritage as a concept that acts as a bridge between the past and the present and one that brings pride from the past to the present. Heritages are classified based on various criteria, such as tangible versus intangible, natural versus cultural, portable versus immovable, and domain specific, among others. The management of heritages is a multidisciplinary and multisectoral undertaking. Stakeholders ranging from historians to archeologists, governments, scientists, and international organizations are playing an active role in heritage management and preservation. Of these groups, the contribution of scientists is most visible, especially in the development of scientific approaches, computer-based techniques, and information and communications technology (ICT) tools and platforms employed in the management, processing, sharing, conservation, and preservation of heritages, particularly digital heritages (DH).

Keywords Heritage · Digital heritages (DH) · Information and communications technology (ICT) · United Nations Educational, Scientific and Cultural Organization (UNESCO)

1 Introduction

Heritage is something that has historical, scientific, political, religious, or cultural significance and is of importance to groups of people, communities, countries, institutions, organizations, or individuals. The heritage of these entities is valued and protected in every possible way, since they trace history and connect it to the present. Heritages differ from place to place, from culture to culture, or from country to country. They come in many forms and classes, ranging from historical manuscripts to books, physical structures, natural sites such as mountains, traditions, cultures,

E. O. Omayio · I. Sreedevi (✉) · J. Panda
Department of Electronics and Communication Engineering, Delhi Technological University, Delhi, India
e-mail: s.indu@dce.ac.in; jpanda@dce.ac.in

© Springer Nature Switzerland AG 2021
J. Mukhopadhyay et al. (eds.), *Digital Techniques for Heritage Presentation and Preservation*, https://doi.org/10.1007/978-3-030-57907-4_1

and art, among others. The origin of the present is traced in the richness of heritages across the globe, and they have economic and aesthetic values and spearhead sustainable development and innovation. Some heritages are irreplaceable once destroyed. Globally, heritages are agents of social and international cohesion and integration. They are remembrances of the past achievements of man [1].

2 Classification of Heritages

Heritages are classified based on the following criteria:

1. Tangible and intangible heritages: Heritages can be physical or nonphysical. Physical heritages include manuscripts, natural sites, artwork, and museums, among others. Intangible heritages are nonphysical, for example some forms of culture, such as cultural dance or language.
2. Natural and cultural heritages: Natural heritages exist without any human involvement. They include physical sites such as mountains, rivers, and vegetation. Cultural heritages are in existence through the active involvement of groups of people, societies, communities, institutions, and organizations. They reflect the way of life of those who created them and value them. Examples are structures, monuments, manuscripts, artwork, and books.
3. Portable and unportable heritages: Portable heritages can be moved from one place to another, for example manuscripts, letters, artwork, and historical items. Unportable or fixed heritages cannot be moved from place to place. They are explored where they are located. Examples include mountains, rivers, caves, and forests, among others, though with virtual heritage technology, such unportable heritages can be remotely/virtually viewed or toured.
4. Domain-based heritages: Heritages fall into various domain classes, such as art, science, politics, business, governance, religion, linguistic, security, sport, and culture.
5. Heritage classification based on status or level: Heritages are classified depending on the extent or level to which they are significantly recognized. The various level-based classes are global, national, regional, local, institutional, and personal heritages. Global heritages have the global features of cultural and natural value, such as the heritages listed by the United Nations Educational, Scientific and Cultural Organization (UNESCO) in the World Heritage List [2]. National heritages are recognized by respective countries only and have relatively less recognition compared to global heritages. Regional heritages are valued and recognized by some parts or regions of a country. Local heritages are recognized within a society or community. Institutional heritages are recognized and protected by institutions and organizations such as schools, colleges, industries, government departments and ministries, and companies, among others. Personal heritages are created, valued, recognized, and protected by individuals or families.

3 Mapping of World Heritages

All countries, communities, and organizations have heritages unique to them. Some are minor and localized while others are major and spectacular. Governments all over the world, through their respective ministries and departments, have put considerable efforts toward the conservation and promotion of heritages within their territories. Various nongovernmental and international organizations have joined in these efforts to recognize and conserve various heritages across the globe. Among other organizations, UNESCO is at the forefront in identifying and listing cultural and natural heritages around the world. This helps create global awareness of various heritages across the world. As of July 2020, there were 1121 heritages in the UNESCO World Heritage List divided into three categories: cultural (869), natural (213), and mixed (39). The heritages in the list are distributed among 167 countries. The leading countries with the highest number of listed heritage sites are China (55), Italy (55), Spain (48), Germany (46), France (45), India (38), Mexico (35), the UK (32), Russia (29), Iran (24), and the USA (24) [2]. For some time now, there have been multidisciplinary efforts from fields such as ICT, computer science, engineering, chemistry, physics, mathematics, and social sciences, which are geared toward the better management of heritages.

4 Digital Heritage

Digital heritages (DH) are resources acquired by information and communications technology (ICT) tools for the purpose of knowledge and information. Such heritages cover the areas of education, entertainment, culture, science, administration, politics, art, religion, agriculture, medicine, and security, among others. DH resources include texts, images, audio, software, databases, graphics, and artworks, among others. The main merit of DH is to move heritages from their physical and analogue form to electronic or digital form such that they can be easily managed, maintained, stored, accessed, and shared among stakeholders and end users. Heritage in physical form is obtained using ICT tools in analogue form and/or directly converted to digital form, as shown in the DH system in Fig. 1. DH can be further subjected to computer-based processing for better management and other usages. With advancement in ICT tools, it is now conveniently possible to remotely view, manage, and tour heritages without physically being there. DH has revolutionized the management of natural and cultural heritages.

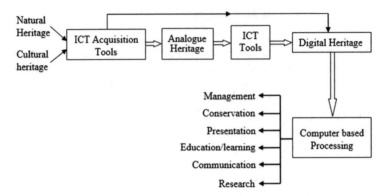

Fig. 1 Digital heritage system

5   Public, Classified, and Personal Digital Heritage

Public heritage is created by individuals, organizations, groups, and institutions and is accessible and used by the general public. Classified digital heritage is created by institutions or groups and is not accessed by the public. It is confidential and is only for official use, and access is granted to authorized people only. Examples of classified digital heritage are medical records, government records, and security systems' intelligence data. Personal digital heritage is created by individuals and is for personal use only, such as personal photos.

6   Science and Digital Heritages

Science and its subdisciplines have contributed significantly to the management of heritages of all forms such as analogue forms of heritage, DH, and physical heritage (natural or cultural). This multidisciplinary approach has significantly contributed to heritage management aspects such as acquisition, documentation, analysis, presentation, communication, and conservation. In acquisition and documentation of heritages, ICT methods such as photographing and manual taping are used. Other heritages such as architecture are preserved using engineering methods such as AutoCAD [3, 4].

7   Computer-Based Processing of Digital Heritage

1) *Digital Reconstruction (DR) of Digital Heritage*

Digital reconstruction is a computer vision task where the shape and appearance of an object are reproduced when information such as depth is supplied. The main aim of DR is to preserve the original physical form, appearance, geometry, color, and texture of a heritage item that is damaged, lost, or interfered with in any way. DR also helps multiple end users avail DH conveniently through virtual museums and communication technologies such as the Internet. Some information on heritages such as dimensions, geometry, and texture is easier to obtain from the DR output [5].

Examples of where DR has been used to obtain a digital model of natural and cultural heritages are the digitization of statues by Michelangelo [6], the restoration of Buddha statues [7], a project by Rushmeier [8] in establishing virtual museums created from the DR of artifacts from ancient Egypt, and a project by Allen et al. [9] involving the creation of a digital model of the Cathedral of Saint-Pierre in Beauvais, France. In all these DR tasks, ICT tools such as depth sensors, laser scanners, and digital cameras have been used to obtain information to create 2D or 3D models of heritages.

2) *Image Processing and Computer Vision*

These areas are especially used in enhancement, noise filtering, recognition, and classification of heritages.

3) *Artificial Intelligence (AI)*

AI is mostly applied in heritages for enhancement, recognition, virtual reconstruction, classification, and clustering. In this book, AI methods have been specifically applied in heritage restoration, recognition, filtering, and enhancement.

4) *Virtual Heritage*

ICT tools in conjunction with concepts from other disciplines, such as psychology, engineering, computer science, chemistry, physics, and mathematics, have successfully enabled remote viewing and experiencing tangible and physical heritage without physically being where they actually are. Heritages are virtually viewed.

5) *ICT and Realities*

The reality of an environment can be represented in one of three domains: augmented reality (AR), virtual reality (VR), or mixed reality (MR).

(a) *Augmented Reality (AR)*

This is a technology-based enhancement of reality by superimposing on it additional digital content such as text, lines, graphics, and images so as to provide a better outlook, view, or understanding. In AR, computer-based processes such as computer vision, image processing, speech recognition, and object recognition are used to generate virtual digital information integrated with the real-world environment to give it a better look. An example of where AR is applied is during games (such as soccer or cricket) where game analyzers use AR to superimpose virtual lines on the pitch to better illustrate a point. In the medical field, AR is used to obtain a 3D view of body organs for deep studies and diagnostic tasks. In all these

AR tasks, viewing is done through helmet visors, AR glasses, computer screens, or smartphones with AR apps.

(b) *Virtual Reality (VR)*

This is a computer-based simulation of the real world. VR can be a complete animation of a real-world environment or images of the real world infused into a VR platform. With VR, one can interact with the world environment as if it were real, where the platform running the VR system responds to the user's actions, such as the movement of the eyes, head, and hands, and gives varying displays accordingly. This stimulates the body senses, especially the hearing and visual senses. VR gives a feeling of actually touring the site being virtually viewed via screens, smartphones, VR viewers, and other VR-viewing platforms. With VR, you can tour places you have never been to or places that are otherwise impossible or risky to tour, such as the inside of an active volcano, the surface of the sun, distant planets, and stars. VR is applied in the fields of exploratory science, astronomy, medicine, and virtual museums.

(c) *Mixed Reality (MR)*

This is a combination of the aspects of both AR and VR, that is, both real-world and computer-simulated virtual environment are integrated together.

8   Threats to Digital Heritage

As long as DH is far better than heritage in analogue form, it faces some dangers. Being supported and created by scientific technologies, DH is threatened by the rapid growth of new technologies, hardware, and software where there is incompatibility between old and new technologies. Another threat is concerned with the methods of maintenance and preservation, some of which are costly and need skills training before use. There is a lack of legislation regarding the management of DH, especially in the areas of cyber theft and crime [10]. Incompatibility between technologies hinders sharing and integration of DH. This is evident especially where DH created or acquired by one ICT tool may not be accessed or handled by another ICT tool if it is run by a different system. Issues of transparency and integrity impact virtual heritage, especially where a DH item, for some reason, is manipulated using modern technologies so as to look different from the actual physical item on the ground. There is a lack of standard formats and methods for heritage conservation. Various science scholars have different interests that bring disharmonious approaches to heritage management. Insufficient capacity-building for digital heritage preservation and lack of collaborative and mutual approaches in multidisciplinary-based heritage conservation often hinder the work of better heritage management.

9 Motivation for Digital Heritage

Digitization is a systematic and efficient scientific method for the management of cultural and natural heritages. As shown in Fig. 1, the digitization process involves conversion of the actual heritage to electronic form using ICT tools such as digital cameras, video cameras, and scanners. Electronic heritage can either be in analogue or digital form. Heritages in analogue form are converted to digital formats. The digital form of actual heritage is referred to as digital heritage (DH). A major advantage of DH is its easier heritage management, such as processing, retrieving, archiving, concurrent sharing by many people, digital reconstruction, virtual viewing, and contribution to research and education. The management of DH relies heavily on computer-based processing techniques such as digital reconstruction (DR), artificial intelligence (AI), and virtual heritage and computer-based representations of DH such as augmented reality (AR), virtual reality (VR), and mixed reality (MR), among others. Digital heritage management is a wide research area with many computer-based techniques. There is no single technique in any one domain of DH management that is universally suitable for all application areas. Various computer-based techniques and approaches are domain and application specific, that is, a technique suitable for one application may not be suitable for another. For example, a technique for 3D architectural reconstruction of monuments such as temples may not be suitable for a similar task with natural heritages such as rivers.

References

1. Sullivan, A.M.: Cultural heritage & new media: a future for the past. J. Marshall Rev. Intell. Prop. Law. **15**, 11 (2016)
2. UNESCO World Heritage. UNESCO World Heritage Centre-World Heritage List. https://whc.unesco.org/en/list/. Retrieved 6 July 2020
3. Fischer, A., Manor, A.: Utilizing image Processing Techniques for 3D reconstruction of laser-scanned data. CIRP Ann. Manuf. Technol. **48**(1), 99–102 (1999)
4. Fontana, R., Greco, M., Materazzi, M., Pampaloni, E., Pezzati, L., et al.: Three dimensional modelling of statues: the Minerva of Arezzo. J. Cult. Herit. **3**(4), 325–331 (2002)
5. Gomes, L., Bellon, O.R.P., Silva, L.: 3D reconstruction methods for digital preservation of cultural heritage: a survey. Pattern Recog. Lett. **50**, 3–14 (2014)
6. Levoy, M., Pulli, K., Curless, B., Rusinkiewicz, S., Koller, D., Pereira, L., Ginzton, M., Anderson, S., Davis, J., Ginsberg, J., Shade, J., Fulk, D.: The Digital Michelangelo Project: 3D scanning of large statues. In: Proceedings of the Conference on Computer Graphics and Interactive, Techniques, pp. 131–144 (2000)
7. Ikeuchi, K., Oishi, T., Takamatsu, J., Sagawa, R., Nakazawa, A., Kurazume, R., Nishino, K., Kamakura, M., Okamoto, Y.: The great Buddha project: digitally archiving, restoring, and analyzing cultural heritage objects. J. Comput. Vision. **75**(1), 189–208 (2007)
8. Rushmeier, H.: Eternal Egypt: experiences and research directions. In: International Workshop on Recording, Modeling and Visualization of Cultural Heritage, pp. 22–27 (2006)

9. Allen, P.K., Troccoli, A., Smith, B., Stamos, I., Murray, S.: The Beauvais Cathedral Project. Conference on Computer Vision and Pattern Recognition Workshop, IEEE. (2003). https://doi.org/10.1109/CVPRW.2003.10004
10. Charter on the Preservation of the Digital Heritage. 32nd session of the General Conference of UNESCO, 17 October 2003. https://unesdoc.unesco.org/ark:/48223/pf0000179529.page=2

Language-Based Text Categorization: A Survey

Enock Osoro Omayio, Indu Sreedevi, and Jeebananda Panda

Abstract Language-based text classification has attracted interest over the years, especially in the fields of business, tourism, hospitality industry, international relations circles, sports, and social media. This chapter surveys various techniques for language-based text classification that have been developed over the years for application in different areas. Classification is performed on multilingual and mono-lingual text documents. Monolingual documents are classified based on the subject of the contents, whereas multilingual documents are classified based on language. The main techniques used are statistical methods (like regression models, KNN, decision trees, and Bayesian methods) and machine learning methods like neural networks, support vector machines, and deep learning classifiers. Classification performance among these techniques is comparatively evaluated.

Keywords Convolution neural networks · Decision tree · K-Nearest neighbor · N-Gram · Support vector machine · Text classification

1 Introduction

A huge amount of heritage is in text format. These text documents, besides being kept as heritages, are also used as records of past events in administration and governance, sports, medicine, politics, science, literature, history, arts, and religion, among others. Most of them are in hard copy form. They suffer from degradation due to environmental and storage conditions, vandalism, and unauthorized inter-ference like alterations. In addition, it is a challenge to store, access, process, and manage these text documents. All these downsides of hard copy text documents have prompted their digitization using information and communications technology (ICT) devices. The digitized text documents are comparatively easier to store,

E. O. Omayio (✉) · I. Sreedevi · J. Panda
Department of Electronics and Communication Engineering, Delhi Technological University, Delhi, India
e-mail: s.indu@dce.ac.in; jpanda@dce.ac.in

© Springer Nature Switzerland AG 2021
J. Mukhopadhyay et al. (eds.), *Digital Techniques for Heritage Presentation and Preservation*, https://doi.org/10.1007/978-3-030-57907-4_2

11

access, use, share, and manage. With the huge amount of digital text documents originating from individuals, organizations, learning institutions, governments, and cultural and heritage centers, there is a huge demand for their automatic management with respect to analysis, processing, retrieval, and presentation. A crucial task in analyzing text documents is categorization. Text categorization is a task of classifying documents based on their contents into some predefined categories or classes [1, 2]. Text documents fall into two main classes, i.e., monolingual and multilingual. Monolingual documents are written in one language only, whereas multilingual documents are written in more than one language per document. Multilingual documents can further fall into two subclasses: homogeneous or mixed multilingual documents. In homogeneous multilingual text documents, a corpus consists of a collection of text documents written in different languages, but each document is written in one language only. In mixed multilingual documents, a single text document is written in more than one natural language.

1.1 Monolingual Text Categorization

Classification of monolingual text documents is domain based. Various domains under which monolingual text documents fall include business, sports, arts, science, history, education, politics, governance, agriculture, religion, and medicine, among others. According to [3], there are three approaches to monolingual text categorization:

1. Single-label versus multi-label text classification. Single-label classification is where an input document is assigned to only one category, whereas multi-label classification is where an input document is assigned to more than one category.
2. Category pivoted versus document pivoted. For category-pivoted classification, each document $d \in D$ is assigned to a specific class $c \in C$, whereas in document-pivoted classification, a category $c \in C$ is found under which a given document $d \in D$ falls.
3. Hard categorization versus soft categorization. In hard categorization, a classifier firmly assigns a category to a document, whereas in soft categorization, a system ranks various possible category assignments and it is left to the user to decide the class/category to assign to the document. Therefore, soft categorization is a semi-automatic process where users have the final decision on the category to assign a given text document input. It is a user-driven process. Therefore, the user contributes to classification accuracy.

1.2 Multilingual Text Classification

Categorization of multilingual text documents is mainly language based. Therefore, the main task is to automatically identify the languages of the texts in the input documents.

1.2.1 Automatic Language Identification

Automatic language identification is the task of automatically detecting a language or languages of the contents of text documents. Documents can be monolingual or multilingual. An obvious assumption made in the language identification process is that the language used in a given document is a natural language (i.e., one of the known languages) whose training data is obtainable. Thus, a document's language is selected from language of training sets. Most natural language processing (NLP) techniques assume documents to be monolingual and any other language is seen as noise. This leads to decreased language identification performance [4]. Figure 1 shows a framework for language identification for text documents. The training corpus consists of labeled text documents. The corpus has documents written in many languages, which are modeled as a stream of characters.

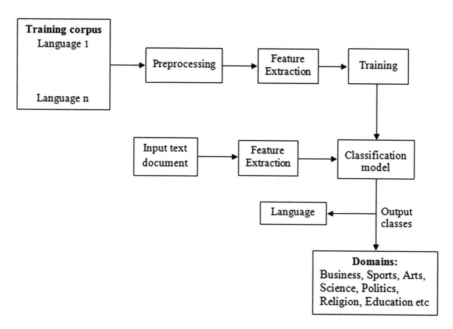

Fig. 1 Framework for automatic language identification

1.2.2 Preprocessing

This is the first step in text classification task where word segmentation and removal of stop words are carried out. Stop words are removed so as to make the classification process more accurate and robust. For deep learning methods, words are represented in vector form for more efficient classification [5].

1.2.3 Feature Extraction

Features are descriptive attributes that give essential information about an object or entity. They are used to distinguish one object from another. Extracted features for text documents are used to distinguish one class from another. The various features used for text categorization and language identification are stop words, morphology and stemming, phrases, collocations, controlled vocabulary, and mutual information [6, 7], document frequency (DF), information gain (IG), mutual information (MI), CHI statistics, term strength (TS), bag of words (BOW), and compound features (C-features) [1]. Of these traditional feature extraction methods, BOW is used to represent a text document by using single terms as keywords. BOW improves the scalability, efficiency, and accuracy in text classification. Whereas traditional BOW consists of single keywords to represent text documents, compound-feature (C-feature) extraction method for making BOW, proposed by [1], consists of two terms that co-occur in a text document. An example of C-feature is (student, course) where the keywords represent a document for student information. Shang et al. [8] proposed a novel feature selection method based on Gini index theory. In their method, Gini index algorithm is designed to reduce the dimensionality of feature space so as to improve classification efficiency while maintaining classification accuracy.

The size of feature vector for text classification is usually very big and varies from language to language depending on the richness of its morphology. Languages with large morphologies require a large-size feature vector and vice versa. The size of training set to be used increases with the size of feature vector (number of features). For efficient training, the size of feature vector is scaled down.

Feature extraction from text documents is followed by feature representation and selection. Feature representation of text documents helps remove redundant words from a text document, hence enabling a text document to be represented in a clear word format [9–12]. Various methods are used to reduce the number of features, such as stop words, morphology and stemming, phrases, collocations, controlled vocabulary, and mutual information [7]. Stop words are short function words and occur very frequently in a document. They are removed from feature vector. In morphology and stemming, full and inflected words are reduced to their root form. For example, the words *driving*, *driver*, *driven*, and *drove* are represented in their reduced root form *drive*. Stemming algorithms like N-gram stemming are used. Phrases are a group of words of syntax and semantics and can be identified using algorithms like finite state grammar [6]. Collocations are terms that co-occur often in various text categories which can be used to classify the text documents. Controlled Vocabulary are pre-defined keywords unique for some categories. Mutual Information (MI) is a measure of relevance that is used to measure a close relationship between two variables [7]. Finally, dimension reduction is performed to have a relatively small feature size that will be used in the final text classification step. Dimension reduction helps create an efficient learning process in classification tasks and also saves storage space [13].

1.2.4 Learning/Training Phase

During the learning phase, the classification model that is used to predict the language of a new text document presented to it is trained. The training corpus used consists of multilingual text documents. The documents are modeled as a stream of characters [14, 15]. After learning has taken place, the system is presented with a new text document where its features are extracted and fed to the trained classification model. The model gives a score of the new text document which is compared with the scores of the text documents in training corpus. The training corpus consists of text documents whose language of text contents are known. Comparison is carried out using a selected algorithm. Then one of the languages of the text documents in the training corpus is assigned to the new document using some pre-set criteria. Factors that determine language identification performance are size of input text, size of training dataset, classification features used, language identification algorithm used, and similarities in languages [16–19]. The performance of a language identification system increases with the size of input text document and the use of different sizes of training sets. During the language identification process, a language that is not in the training set is seen as noise. This leads to decreased language identification performance [4].

In most language identification methods, common words like determiners, conjunctions, and prepositions are used as indicators of a specific language [20, 21]. Training corpora for monolingual documents are readily available, whereas there are no standard corpora for multilingual documents. Therefore, the language for multilingual documents is identified using monolingual corpora/data [22]. This explains the reason behind most work on language identification being based on monolingual documents [23].

1.3 Language and Document Models

The language model consists of features that represent specific characteristics of a language included in the training corpus. The document model is similar to the language model, only that it is obtained from an input document whose language is to be determined. During the language identification process, the document model is statistically compared with the language model by calculating the distance between the two models. The language model that gives minimum distance for a given input document is taken as the language of the document [14, 24]. There are mainly two language modeling methods, i.e., word-based and N-gram methods. The word-based method is further divided into two classes, i.e., frequent word and short word methods. In the frequent word method, the words used to generate language models are the ones with the highest frequency in the text corpus. The short word method uses words of specific set lengths (4–5 letters). Short words are usually determiners, conjunctions, and prepositions which again are language specific. The N-gram method uses continuous N-character slice of strings of words whose size is determined by the value of N. The beginning and end of words are marked with an underscore (_) or space [14]. Researches that have employed the N-gram method for modeling languages are [16, 25–27]. Graph-based N-gram method, which is an improved form of N-gram method, is also used. In this method, occurrences of N-grams are determined and arranged so that a graph language model is created on labeled data. This method is used by Tromp and Pechenizkiy [28] in graph-based N-gram approach (LIGA) for language identification. The nodes are the N-grams and the edges are the transitions from one character (e.g., 3-gram) to the next. The weights of nodes are the frequency of trigrams, while the weights of edges capture the transition from one 3-gram to the next.

1.4   Applications of Language Identification

Text categorization has been employed for various tasks like making text documents more comprehensible, indexing text documents for information retrieval, and classifying memos and emails, among others. It is also used to assign category labels to new documents, web page search engines, text filtering, and natural language processing such as in finding the meaning of a word in a text [29]. Identification of multilingual documents has various applications, for example, pre-filtering data to improve the quality of input data and obtaining linguistic data from the web and documents [30, 31]. Detection of multilingual documents can also be used to mine bilingual texts for statistical machine translation from online resources [32–34]. It can be used in web page application and query searches [15, 35–38], building minority language corpora [31, 39, 40], text categorization [1, 41–43], searching names in a phonebook using voice input [20] and multilingual speech recognition [44], and making of crawler, which is a large-scale multilingual web [45]. In addition, language identification in multilingual documents is used by security agents in fighting global terrorism where communications (in diverse languages) among suspicious terrorist-minded subjects are monitored and then necessary security measures are taken [46].

1.5   Supervised Learning Methods for Text Categorization

Machine learning methods commonly used in text classification and automatic language identification tasks are naïve Bayes, K-nearest neighbor (KNN), support vector machine (SVM), decision tree (DT), and neural networks (NN). They are briefly explained below.

1.5.1   Naïve Bayes Method

It is a probabilistic method that is based on the Bayes theorem [47]. It classifies a text document using posterior probability that a text document D_i belongs to a certain category C_i. In this classification method, the posterior probabilities of text documents belonging to all predetermined classes are calculated. A text document is assigned to a class for which its probability is highest. More details on this can be found in the work by [48]. Patil and Pawar [49] used naïve Bayes (NB) to categorize websites and achieved an accuracy of 80%. Other text classification tasks using NB in a modified form are [50, 51].

1.5.2   K-Nearest Neighbor

In this technique, an input data object is assigned to a category depending on the categories of its K-nearest neighbors. All categories containing K neighbors are scored with respect to the input object (x). The category with the highest score is assigned to the input object/text document. The downside of the KNN technique is in choosing the K value. A detailed explanation is found in [52]. This method has been employed by [53] for text categorization. In other instances, a modified form of KNN has been used, like in the works of [54, 55].

1.5.3   Support Vector Machine

SVM is a statistical method of classification proposed by Cortes and Vapnik [56]. It is a binary classifier. Linear classification with SVM is done using hyperplanes optimized by maximum margin between support points (boundary points of two categories). For nonlinear classification, kernels are used to map data to a higher-order dimension so that it becomes linearly separable. Text classification researches where SVM classifier has been used include [57–59]. In [58], LibSVM is used to categorize cricket sports news. According to [59], SVM outperforms NB and KNN in text classification.

1.5.4   Decision Tree Classifier

It consists of roots, branches, and nodes. Branches connect the nodes. The root is the top node. During classification tasks, one starts from the root. At every node, subset discriminatory features are used to split input data objects to various lower nodes. This goes on until the bottom nodes (leaf nodes) are reached. Leaf nodes are categories of input objects. More details are discussed in [60]. Selamat et al. [61] used DT for language identification in Arabic documents.

1.5.5   Neural Networks

The architecture of neural networks is an imitation of the mechanisms of the human brain. Various neurons that make up the neural network system are activated by input signals. Their response depends on the magnitude of the input signal and the activation function it uses in making decisions. Common classifiers used are artificial neural networks (ANN) and deep learning networks like convolution neural networks (CNN). CNN were first proposed by Kim [62]. Deep learning has been used by [63] for text classification. Other text classification tasks that employ deep learning classifiers are TextRNN [64] and TextRCNN [65]. TextRCNN is a combination of TextRNN and CNN.

1.5.6   Performance Measures

To compare various text classification systems, the evaluation metrics used are recall (R) and precision (P), F-measure, and recognition accuracy. Recall and precision metrics are calculated using Eqs. (1) and (2), respectively. F-measure combines recall and precision as shown in Eq. (3). It measures a trade-off between recall and precision.

$$R = \frac{k}{N} \times 100 \qquad (1)$$

$$P = \frac{k}{N - u} \times 100 \qquad (2)$$

$$F1 = \frac{2PR}{P + R} \times 100 \qquad (3)$$

where k is the number of text documents that are correctly classified, u is the number of text documents not classified, and N is the total size of test data.

2 Related Work

Related researches carried out have been divided into two: text categorization of monolingual text documents based on content and multilingual text categorization based on the language of the text.

2.1 Categorization of Monolingual Text Documents

Text documents have been categorized using a new method utilizing learning vector quantization (LVQ) classifiers as proposed by [66]. LVQ are based on modified proximity measure. The features used are term frequency-inverse document frequency (TF-IDF) and bag of words. The F-score of the new method is 92%, surpassed only by SVM with radial basis function (RBF) kernel having an F-score of 94%. Cosine similarity has been used to classify Arabic text documents. Vector space model (VSM) and latent semantic indexing (LSI) were used to extract textual features. Singular value decomposition (SVD) method is used to extract textual features based on LSI. The training corpus used consists of 4000 documents of 10 classes. LSI showed an accuracy of 83.5% [67].

Machine learning approaches such as NB, KNN, and SVM have been used for categorizing web text documents written in various languages. The features used are term frequency-inverse document frequency (TF-IDF), bag of words, and WordNet. Text documents that have been categorized with these methods are Nepalese news stories, Arabic web text documents, and Turkish, Malay, and Indian languages like Assamese, Bangla, Gujarati, Hindi, Kannada, Malayalam, Oriya, Punjabi, Tamil, Urdu, Telugu, and Marathi [1, 7, 41, 42, 48, 68–83]. Decision tree and centroid algorithms have also been used to categorize text documents [41]. Cosine similarity and Euclidean distance measures have been used to categorize Bangla text documents to subject domains. These distance measures are used with the vector space model (VSM) based on the TF-IDF feature. The recognition accuracy obtained is 95.8% and 95.2% for cosine similarity and Euclidean distance, respectively [84]. The two distances have also been used by other researchers to classify English text documents [85, 86]. Supervised learning- and ontology-based classification methods have been used to classify Marathi text documents to predefined classes: festival, sports, tourism, literature, movies, etc. The classifiers used are naïve Bayes (NB), modified K-nearest neighbor (MKNN), and support vector machine (SVM) [87].

The vector space model (VSM) has been used to categorize Marathi documents based on subject domain. The features used are extracted by the label induction grouping (LINGO) technique. The overall accuracy attained is 95.83% [88, 89]. Modified LINGO has also been used to categorize Marathi documents. Feature extraction was done by the single value decomposition (SVD) method. Principal component analysis (PCA) is used to improve the results. The performance achieved is 64% compared to 46.2% (F-measure) for ordinary LINGO with SVD [90]. Naïve Bayes has been used to categorize Assamese text documents into subject classes like sports, politics, law, and science. Multinomial and multivariate Bernoulli models were used. BOW was used for feature representation of the documents. A total of 200 documents were used for training and testing. The dataset used was sourced from three newspapers (*Amar Asom*, *Asomiya Pratidin*, and *Khabor*) for the years 1999 and 2000. The performance measures used are precision, recall, and F-measure. A precision of 94.41% and recall of 94.68% are reported [91]. Supervised learning algorithm has been used by [92] for representing and categorizing Indian language text documents. Documents are preprocessed by tokenization, removal of stop words, and stemming. The training corpus used comprises 300 text documents. The features used are term frequency (TF), document frequency (DF), inverse document frequency (IDF), and TF-IDF weighting. The classifiers used are decision tree (C.45), naïve Bayes (NB), and K-nearest neighbor (KNN) classifiers. The performances of C.45, NB, and KNN were 97.3%, 93%, and 97.67%, respectively.

A rule-based knowledge tool was used to classify Hindi verbs from a syntactic perspective. An accuracy of 99.9% was achieved [93]. Nidhi and Gupta [80] used existing classification algorithms like naïve Bayes and centroid-based techniques for Punjabi text classification. A hybrid approach to classify text documents was used where the algorithms were combined and where one technique is used to extract features and the other used as a classifier. Keyword extraction technique has been used by [78] to categorize text documents using the bag of words feature. Other features used are TF-IDF and WordNet. The classifiers used and their respective classification accuracies are KNN (94.47%), naïve Bayes (87.09%), and decision tree (98.47%). Tamil documents were categorized by [94] using Advanced Back Propagation Algorithm (ABPA). The performance achieved was 94.33% compared to ANN's back-propagation algorithm (93.33%) and VSM (90.33%).

Text categorization was performed by [95] using the rule reduction (RR) technique. RR involves three steps: creation of tokens, token feature recognition, and alpha token categorization. In the work by [96], eager learning and KNN were used for the classification of text documents. These methods improved the failings of traditional KNN algorithms that involve many calculations. They enhance the efficiency and accuracy of categorization and their performance is 92.31% (F-score). These methods have a reduced computational cost compared to traditional KNN. Improved K-nearest neighbor (IK-NN) algorithm [29] has been proposed to classify documents based on language. Multilingual documents were used. Rajan et al. [3] used VSM and artificial neural network (ANN) to perform text classification of the Dravidian classical language, Tamil. ANN achieved a classification accuracy of 93.3% for Tamil document classification. Thabtah et al. [97] have used naïve Bayesian algorithm based on Chi-square features to categorize Arabic text data. The dataset used is the Saudi Press Agency (SPA) dataset by [98], which consists of 1562 Arabic documents from 6 categories, i.e., economic, cultural, political, social, sports, and general. A similar approach was adopted by [99] in categorizing Arabic text documents except that the corpus used was obtained from online Arabic newspaper archives like *Al-Jazeera*, *Al-Nahar*, *Al-Hayat*, *Al-Ahram*, and *Al-Dostor*. The macro-averaged F-measure obtained was 88.11%.

A categorization technique based on variable precision rough set was used to categorize Chinese text documents into five classes: environment, computer, economy, education, and transportation. The performance achieved was 84.69% [100]. In [101], Chinese text documents were categorized by candid covariance-free incremental principal component analysis (CCIPCA) and the sequential minimization optimization (SMO) method. The dataset used was TanCorpV1.0, which consists of 12 categories. The vector space model (VSM) was used for feature extraction. The performance attained was 47.1% for Macro-F1. Xu [102] has proposed a text categorization technique based on pattern aggregation (PA), latent semantic analysis (LSA), and Kohonen network (TCBPLK). This method uses PA and LSA to construct the vector space model (VSM) of text documents. There are six categories of text documents, i.e., physical, education, finance and economics, traffic, medicine, and church. The average precision obtained is 92%. An N-gram-based algorithm has been used for Bangla text classification. Prothom-Alo news corpus classification performance increased as the value of n increased from 1 to 3. For values of $n = 3$ and 4, the performance decreased. Trigrams achieved the best performance in most cases of normalized frequencies being 100% [103]. In [104], Chinese text documents have been classified by a method called proximal support vector machine (PSVM). The dataset used was image segmentation data from the UCI KDD Archive. PSVM is faster to train compared to SVM. An average precision of 88.4% was achieved.

2.2 Multilingual Text Categorization

This class of text documents is classified based on language. Its main task is to automatically identify the language of the document's text content. Various techniques have been proposed for this task. Most of them are based on supervised learning methods like SVM, KNN, and DT, among others. The performance of such methods is good. In [105], a system is developed that distinguishes Slavic languages by using a cascade classifier approach. The training dataset used is the Discriminating Similar Languages Corpus Collection (DSLCC) 2.0 [106]. The features used in these models are character N-grams (where n is in the range of 2–5). The best performance achieved is 96.20%. An approach using language-dependent phonotactic features and prosodic information has been developed for automatic language identification (LID) for seven Indian languages: Bengali, Hindi, Telugu, Urdu, Assamese, Punjabi, and Manipuri. A multilayer feed-forward neural network (NN) is used for language identification. The accuracy obtained for both phonotactic and prosodic systems is 72% and 68%, respectively [107].

A data-driven method called language identification by neural networks (LanideNN) has been proposed by [108]. It is based on bidirectional recurrent neural networks. The languages keep changing in text documents covering 131 languages. A character sliding window slides over the document while assigning a language to each character. The datasets used are Wikipedia, EUROGOV (with texts in Western European languages) and TCL (Thai Computational Linguistics) Laboratory, ALTW2010 shared task, and WikipediaMulti. The best results for monolingual and multilingual texts are 95.5% and 96%, respectively. Naïve Bayes has been used for language identification of text chatbots. Lexicon-based classifier is also used to distinguish the specific local South African language in a text. Categories of 11 South African languages are used. The dataset used is the NCHLT Text Corpora. The best result achieved is an accuracy of 95.2% [109]. Selamat and Akosu [110] have proposed a lexicon-based method for language identification for languages whose training size is small. The language of a new input document is identified by comparing its words with a list of words of language models in the dataset. The language of model with maximum number of words from the input document is assigned to the document. The accuracy obtained is 93%.

In [111], contextual entropy (CE) is used for language identification of short texts from Twitter messages. The Twitter texts were written in six different languages. The entropy of a text is calculated for different word distributions and then assigned to a predetermined category with the largest entropy. The method is simple and easy to code and no training is required. With 50% of training data used, CE attained an accuracy of 99.2%. Lui et al. [112] proposed a method for identifying different languages and their proportions in multilingual documents. The documents are represented as byte N-gram sequences, which can be function words, common suffixes [113], or grammatical word classes [114]. Yadav and Kaur [115] used Bayesian classifiers for the identification of 11 Indian languages together with English in corrupted text documents. The N-gram technique was used to represent languages, and distance measure-based metrics were used to correct corrupted text documents. The corpus used was obtained from the web. Verma and Khanna [116] have used K-means clustering and SVM in language identification of speech signals of three languages: English, Hindi, and Tibetan. Mel-frequency cepstral coefficients (MFCCs) were used to extract the features of languages involved, and SVM classifier was used for final classification. An accuracy of 81% was obtained.

Three under-resourced languages of South Africa (Tshivenda, Xitsonga, and Sepedi) have been identified using support vector machines (SVM) and naïve Bayes (NB) classifiers. Multinomial naïve Bayes posted the highest classification accuracy [117]. Milne et al. [118] employed two approaches for language identification, i.e., baseline approach and trigram method on long and short documents having four languages: English, German, Spanish, and French. In baseline method, a language profile is created using the most frequent words, whereas in trigram method, trigrams are used to build the language profile. The profiles of input document and languages are statistically compared, and the language assigned to the document is one with the highest frequency of common words/trigrams. The minimum description length (MDL) method has been proposed for text segmentation by language. The text documents used were written in more than 200 languages and taken from the Universal Declaration of Human Rights (UDHR) and Wikipedia (Wiki). In this method, a multilingual text document is segmented to monolingual segments of each language. The MDL of each text segment is calculated, and its respective language determined through dynamic programming using minimization of cross entropy. Mean match statistics (MMS) and prediction by partial matching (PPM) are used to calculate cross entropy. The performance was higher for UDHR than for Wiki since the content of Wikipedia is broader. A related work using minimum cross-entropy method and PPM model was undertaken by [119] for language identification of Chinese and English text documents. Classification by genre used newsgroups data and posted a highest accuracy of 94.2%. The best result in segmentation of documents to various languages is 99.5% accuracy. In [120], inverse class frequency (ICF) has been used to improve centroid-based classification in addressing language identification problems. This method is a vector space-based classifier. Centroid vector is constructed with a central value that represents each class. The language of a new document is obtained by calculating its similarity to each centroid using cosine similarity measure. The language class with the highest similarity value is the one assigned to the new input document. The European Corpus Initiative/Multilingual Corpus (ECI/MCI) with 27 languages was used. An accuracy of 97.1% was achieved with ICF as a weighting factor.

Distance measurement, Boolean, and optimum profile methods have been used for language identification [121]. The distance measurement method uses the approach given by [14]. The Boolean method is based on the work of [122]. The matching rate between training and testing profile is used. The language of the document is the one whose matching rate has the highest value. The downside of this method is misclassification where two or more languages have the same N-gram frequency. A graph-based approach for language identification (LIGA) has been employed for natural language identification for short and poorly written text documents. It is an N-gram-based approach. In LIGA method, the words are arranged in order and then a graph model created on labeled data. The graph has vertices and edges. The labels of vertices represent the words of a certain language, whereas the weights of vertices represent the frequency of words. The weights of edges represent the arrangement of words, hence the grammar of a certain language. The system allows learning both elements of grammar and N-gram frequencies. The advantage of LIGA is that overfitting is less pronounced. The performance of LIGA is 95–98% compared to 87–93% for N-grams [28].

Selamat [27] has used an improved N-gram method to identify the languages of documents from the web. Both original N-gram and modified N-gram approaches are used. The original N-gram approach is based on the work by [14], which is based on the rank-order statistic of N-gram profiles where the distance between training and testing data is computed. The data with the minimum distance is chosen as the language of the document. Chew et al. [123] employed an improved N-gram method for language identification of web pages in Asian languages. The training corpus used consists of 1660 web pages, spanning 182 languages from Asia, Africa, America, Europe, and Oceania. The algorithm attained a language classification accuracy of 94.04%. Wavelets and artificial neural networks (ANN) have been combined in language identification and classification of English and Arabic languages. They are used in web searches where the language of the query by the user is first identified as either English or Arabic. Wavelet transforms are used as a feature vector and the feed-forward artificial neural network used as a classifier. Three wavelet filters are used, i.e., Haar, Bior 2.2, and Bior 3.1, where Haar filter posted the best performance of 76.9% [124]. An approach combining N-gram statistics and Wikipedia has been used in [125] to identify the language of multilingual documents written in more than 250 languages. First, the input text document is segmented to N-gram units and then the language of each unit determined using the language versions of Wikipedia. The advantage of this joint approach is that a single language corpus (English) is used for all languages to be identified.

Ceylan and Kim [36] worked on language identification and classification of queries of Yahoo Search Engine from 10 different Western languages over 3 months. The models used for language identification were trained on Europarl Collection [126]. The features used are character-based N-gram, word-based unigram, and affix information. The language models used and their performances are as follows: statistical model (N-gram), accuracy (82.2%), knowledge-based method (70.3%), morphology feature (26%), and rank-order method (65.2%). These models were also used with decision tree classifier where the highest accuracy attained is 85.6%. Also, Mayer [127] has worked on language identification for multisite Internet domains (tweets and emails) created by users using the dataset of emails in seven languages (English, German, Italian, French, Spanish, Dutch, and Polish). The local geometric approach has been used to identify a language in an Indian text document with three languages, i.e., English, Hindi, and Kannada. Top and bottom profile features are extracted from the text lines of the documents and their values computed. The feature values are computed and compared with the values stored in the knowledge base, and the correct language is identified using a rule-based classifier. An average language identification performance of 95.4% is attained [128]. Modified N-gram has been proposed by [122] in which the Boolean rate strategy is used to compare the training and testing N-gram profiles. The Boolean rate is 1 if the training and testing profiles match, and 0 if not. The match rate is obtained for all N-grams in the training and testing sets. The language with the highest match rate is taken as the language associated with the document. An improved N-gram method uses N-gram frequency of testing profile and feature position of training profile. The language selected is one where the document has the maximum N-gram frequency and minimum feature position. Rehurek and Kolkus [129] proposed a new method that constructs language models based on word relevance. This method addressed the limitations of N-gram and Markov model approaches when used for language classification of text documents from the web. The limitations include difficulty in language identification of short and multilingual texts. The method was also used to segment multilingual text document to segments of different languages. N-gram and dictionary methods were employed. The highest accuracy obtained was 98.4%. An algorithm based on feature value profiles has been used to identify the language of documents with three languages, i.e., Kannada, English, and Hindi. The profile features of the text lines used are top and bottom profile features. *Coeffprofile* feature is calculated for each of the three languages. *Coeffprofile* value and rule-based classifier are used to determine the language of the input document. A language identification accuracy of 96.6% was realized [130]. In [61], decision tree (DT) and ARTMAP models have been proposed for language identification of Arabic documents. DT identifies significant letters of a language in documents, whereas ARTMAP identifies the Arabic script in documents. The classification performance for Arabic and Persian text documents is 98.33% and 99.17%, respectively. However, the method may not work with other languages.

Bilcu and Astola [131] proposed a hybrid method for bilingual language recognition. They used a multilayer perceptron (MLP) neural network and decision rule to identify a language (English or French) from a text document. This method employs neural network for text-to-phoneme (TTP) mapping which is used in language recognition. It outperformed other existing MLP and hybrid methods with an accuracy of 87% when 90% of the training dataset was used. Other methods used for language identification are neural network-based scalable method by [132], which can be scaled to meet the pre-set memory requirements of target systems like mobile phones with a performance of 93.35% with a much-reduced memory requirement. Prager [26] developed the LINGUINI system to identify multiple languages and their proportions in one document. It is based on vector space model (VSM) and cosine similarity. The best classification accuracy obtained is above 99%. Combrinck and Botha [133] used the statistical approach for language identification with a focus on discrimination between different language models. The corpus used contained 12 languages (Afrikaans, English, Sepedi, Xhosa, Zulu, Tswana, Swazi, German, Italian, French, Spanish, and Portuguese). The classifier achieved 100% classification. The short word approach with trigrams has been used in classifying text documents in 10 languages, i.e., Danish, Dutch, English, French, German, Italian, Norwegian, Portuguese, Spanish, and Swedish. In this method, the sentences are tokenized. All words with five characters and below and trigram occurrences are counted. When generating N-gram-based language models, punctuation marks were not removed. The language models consisted of trigrams with a frequency of 100 and above. The method did better in classifying languages with an accuracy of 99.9%, especially where the input documents have more than 15 words [25]. Souter et al. [134] used frequent word approach in identifying languages. In this method, nine languages are used, i.e., Friesian, English, French, Gaelic, German, Italian, Portuguese, Serbo-Croat, and Spanish, which had been extracted from the Oxford Text Archive at Oxford University. Hundred frequent words were identified per language and their probability calculated using the training sets. A classification accuracy of 91% was obtained.

2.3 Way Forward

From the survey discussed, the main challenge is the availability of a standard corpus that can be used for common evaluation of language identification and classification tasks. Standard corpora need to be created for four different levels: (1) Multilingual structurally dissimilar languages. This corpus consists of language using alphabets of different structures, e.g., Chinese, Arabic, Hindi, English, among others. (2) Multilingual structurally similar languages, i.e., languages using alphabets with the same structure, e.g., English, Spanish, and German, among others. (3) Monolingual corpus. (4) Short text corpus. Evaluation based on the complexity of text categorization should be included in such future systems. Neural network-based systems that automatically learn language features are needed as only a few are available. Such systems have promising performance.

3 Conclusion

A number of research papers have been examined in this survey on text document classification based on language and subject domain. Documents with both monolingual and multilingual texts have been considered. Monolingual text documents are categorized based on domains like business, sports, art, science, and medicine with the best categorization rated at 99.9%. Multilingual text documents are categorized based on language. The language is automatically identified using various classifiers like ANN, Bayesian classifiers, decision tree classifiers, minimum distance method, and rank-order statistic technique. The highest language classification accuracy achieved is 99.8%. A summary of various text classification techniques is given in Tables 1 and 2.

Table 1 Performance for monolingual text documents

Author, year	Method used	Work done and identification accuracy
Dhar et al. [84]	CS, ED, RF	Categorized Bangla text documents to subject domains. Best CS—95.8% and ED—95.2%
Al-Anzi and AbuZeina [67]	VSM, CS, LSI	Classified Arabic text documents. 83.5%
Sahani et al. [89]	LINGO, SVM	Categorized Marathi text document to domain classes. 95.83%
Gogoi and Sarma [91]	NB	Categorized Assamese text documents to subject classes; bag of words was used to represent features. 94.41%
ArunaDevi and Saveetha [1]	C-feature and NB, KNN, and VSM	Used C-feature to categorize Tamil text documents. Good identification
Dixit and Choudhary [93]	RBK	Classified Hindi verbs. 99.9%
Mandal and Sen [48]	DT (C4.5), KNN, NB, SVM	Assessed the efficiency of four supervised learning methods in categorizing Bangla online text documents. SVM—89.14%, NB—85.22%, KNN—74.24%, DT—80.65%
Patil and Game [81]	NB, KNN, centroid, modified KNN	Classified Marathi text documents. Good
Nidhi and Gupta [80]	NB, centroid algorithm, hybrid	Classified 184 Punjabi text documents. F-scores: hybrid (80%), centroid (66%), NB (57%)
Ali and Ijaz [68]	NB and SVM	Classification of Urdu documents. 93.34%
Rajan et al. [3]	VSM and ANN	Categorized Tamil documents. ANN—93.3%, VSM—90.33%
Mansur et al. [103]	N-Gram	Classified Bangla text documents. 100%
Raghuveer and Murthy [7]	NB, KNN, and SVM	Categorized top 10 Indian languages (Assamese, Bengali (Bangla), Gujarati, Hindi, Kannada, Oriya, Malayalam, Punjabi, Tamil, and Telugu). SVM—86.7%
Kim et al. [75]	NB	Classified text documents from Reuters 21578 corpus and 20 newsgroups corpora. 84.6%
Patil and Bogiri [88]	LINGO	Categorized Marathi documents. 78.2%

Table 2 Performance for multilingual text documents

Study/author	Method used	Work done and identification accuracy
Kocmi and Bojar [108]	LanideNN	Language identification by sliding character window over text. Monolingual—95.5%, multilingual—96%
Duvenhage et al. [109]	NB	Language identification for text documents written in 11 South African languages. Accuracy—95.2%
Selamat and Akosu [110]	Lexicon based	Language identification based on word length for 15 languages. Accuracy—93%
Chavez et al. [111]	CE	Categorized Twitter texts written in six languages. Accuracy—99.2%
Takci and Güngör [120]	Centroid based and CS	Classified language in documents of ECI/MCI corpus consisting of 27 languages. Accuracy—97.1%
Mayer [127]	Frequency table of extreme two words	Language identification for short documents from multisite Internet domains like tweets. Seven languages used. Over 90% accuracy
Milne et al. [118]	Baseline and trigram method	Worked on documents having four languages: English, German, Spanish, and French. Good
Yamaguchi and Tanaka-Ishii [135]	MDL	Text segmentation of documents from UDHR and Wikipedia by language using PPM and MMS. Over 90% accuracy
Ng and Selamat [121]	Boolean and optimum profile methods	Language identification by employing distance measurement
Chew et al. [123]	Improved N-gram	Language identification of web pages in Asian languages. Accuracy—94.04%
Tromp and Pechenizkiy [28]	LIGA	Graph-based approach for language identification of Twitter messages. Accuracy between 95 and 98%
Al-Dubaee et al. [124]	Wavelets and ANN	Language identification and classification of English and Arabic languages. Accuracy—76.9%
Vijaya and Padma [130]	Rule-based classifier	Used feature value profiles to identify language of document with three languages (Kannada, English, and Hindi). Accuracy—96.6%
Padma et al. [128]	Local geometric approach and RBC	Identified a language in an Indian text document with three languages (English, Hindi, and Kannada). Accuracy—95.4%

Reference	Method	Description
Teahan [119]	CE, PPM	Identified multilingual documents by segmentation to labeled monolingual segments. Classification—94.2%, Lang Id—99.5%
Ceylan and Kim [36]	N-Gram and DT	Language identification and classification of queries of Yahoo Search Engine from 10 different languages over 3 months. Accuracy—85.6%
Selamat et al. [61]	DT and ARTMAP	Language identification for Arabic documents. Decision tree and ARTMAP models used. Arabic—98.33%, Persian—99.17%
Bilcu and Astola [131]	ANN, MLP, and DT	Hybrid methods for bilingual language recognition from English and French word text documents. Best accuracy—87%
Tian and Suontausta [132]	ANN and TTP mapping	Language recognition from documents by scalable ANN method. Less memory required. Accuracy—93.35%
Prager [26]	VSM % cosine similarity	Uses LINGUINI system to identify multiple languages and their proportions in a document. Accuracy—over 99%
Cavnar and Trenkle [14]	N-Gram	Identification of eight languages in documents. Accuracy—99.8%

References

1. ArunaDevi, K., Saveetha, R.: A novel approach on Tamil text classification using C-feature. Int. J. Scientif. Res. Dev. (IJSRD). **2**(5), 343–345 (2014)
2. Swamy, M.N., Hanumanthappa, M.: Indian language text representation and categorization using supervised learning algorithm. Int J Data Mining Techn Appl. **2**, 251–257 (2013)
3. Rajan, K., Ramalingam, V., Ganesan, M., Palanivel, S., Palaniappan, B.: Automatic classification of Tamil documents using vector space model and artificial neural networks. Expert Syst Appl. **36**, 10914–10918 (2009)
4. Alex, B., Dubey, A., Keller, F.: Using foreign inclusion detection to improve parsing performance. In: Joint Conference on Empirical methods in Natural Language Processing and Computational Natural Language Learning (EMNLP-CoNLL 2007), Prague, pp. 151–160. (2007)
5. Tom, Y., Devamanyu, H., Soujanya, P., Erik, C.: Recent trends in deep learning based natural language processing. Comput Intell Mag. **13**(3), 55–75 (2018). https://doi.org/10.1109/MCI.2018.2840738
6. Murthy, K.N.: Universal clause structure grammar. PhD thesis, Department of CIS, University of Hyderabad (1996)
7. Raghuveer, K., Murthy, K.N.: Text categorization in Indian languages using machine learning approaches. In: Proceedings of IICAI, pp. 1864–1883 (2007)
8. Shang, W., Huang, H., Zhu, H., Lin, Y., Qu, Y., Wang, Z.: A novel feature selection algorithm for text categorization. Expert Syst Appl. **33**(1), 1–5 (2006). https://doi.org/10.1016/j.eswa.2006.04.001
9. Khan, A., Bahurdin, B.B. and Khan, K.: An overview of E-documents classification. IPCSIT. **3**, 544–552. IACSIT Press, Singapore (2011)
10. Lee, L.W., Chen, S.M.: New methods for text categorization based on a new feature selection method and new similarity measure between documents. In: Ali, M., Dapoigny, R. (eds.) Advances in Applied Artificial Intelligence. IEA/AIE 2006. Lecture Notes in Computer Science, vol. 4031, pp. 1280–1289. Springer, Berlin (2006)
11. Manomaisupat, P., Abmad K.: Feature selection for text categorization using self organizing map. In: 2nd International Conference on Neural Network and Brain, vol. 3, pp. 1875–1880. IEEE (2005)
12. Wang, Y., Wang X.J.: A new approach to feature selection in text classification. In: 4th International Conference on Machine Learning and Cybernetics, vol. 6, pp. 3814–3819. IEEE (2005)
13. Yan, J., Liu, N., Zhang, B., Yan, S., Chen, Z., Cheng, Q., Fan, W., Ma, W.: Optimal orthogonal centroid feature selection for text categorization. In: International Conference on Research and IR, pp. 122–129. ACM SIGIR, Barizal (2005)
14. Cavnar, W.B., Trenkle, J.M.: N-gram based text categorization. In: 3rd Symposium on Document Analysis and Information Retrieval (SDAIR), pp. 161–175. Las Vegas, USA (1994)
15. Kikui, G.: Identifying the coding system and language of on-line documents on the internet. In: 16th International Conference on Computational Linguistics (COLING 1996), pp. 652–657. Kyoto, Japan (1996)
16. Dunning, T.: Statistical identification of language. Technical Report MCCS 940-273, Computing Research Laboratory, New Mexico State University (1994)
17. Murthy, K.N., Kumar, G.B.: Language identification from small text samples. J Quant Linguistics. **13**(1), 57–80 (2006)
18. Padro, M., Padro, L.: Comparing methods for language identification. J. Procesamiento del Lenguaje Natural **33** (2004)
19. Poutsma, A.: Applying Monte Carlo techniques to language identification. In: Proceedings of Computational Linguistics in the Netherlands, pp. 179–189. Rodopi (2001)

20. Hakkinen, J., Tian, J.: N-gram and decision tree-based language identification for written words. In: Workshop on Automatic Speech Recognition and Understanding, pp. 335–338. IEEE, Madonna di Campiglio Trento, Italy (2001)
21. Tian, J., Hakkinen, J., Riis, S., Jensen, K.: On text-based language identification for multilingual speech recognition systems. In: 7Ih International Conference on Spoken Language Processing, pp. 501–504. Denver, USA (2002)
22. Lui, M., Baldwin, T.: Cross-domain feature selection for language identification. In: 5th International Joint Conference on Natural Language Processing (IJCNLP 2011), pp. 553–561. Chiang Mai, Thailand (2011)
23. Hughes, B., Baldwin, T., Bird, S., Nicholson, J., MacKinlay, A.: Reconsidering language identification for written language resources. In: 5th International Conference on Language Resources and Evaluation (LREC 2006), pp. 485–488. Genoa, Italy (2006)
24. Bashir, A., Sung-Hyuk, S., Charles, T.: Language identification from text using n-gram based cumulative frequency addition. In: Student/Faculty Research Day (2004). CSIS, Pace University, S. 12–1 (2004)
25. Grefenstette, G.: Comparing two language identification schemes. In: Proceedings of Analisi Statistica dei Dati Testuali (JADT), pp. 263–268. Rome, Italy (1995)
26. Prager, J.M.: Linguini: language identification for multilingual documents. In: 32nd HICSS-32, pp. 1–11. Maui, Hawaii (1999)
27. Selamat, A.: Improved N-grams approach for web page language identification. In: Nguyen, N.T. (ed.) Transactions on CCI V, LNCS, vol. 6910, pp. 1–26 (2011)
28. Tromp, E., Pechenizkiy, M.: Graph-based n-gram language identification on short texts. In: 20th Machine Learning conference of Belgium and The Netherlands, pp. 27–34 (2011)
29. Rani, K., Satvika.: Text categorization on multiple languages based on classification technique. Int. J. Comput. Sci. Inf. Technol. (IJCSIT) 7(3), 1578–1581 (2016)
30. Abney, S., Bird, S.: The human language project: building a universal corpus of the world's languages. In: 48th Annual Meeting of the Association for Computational Linguistics, pp. 88–97 (2010)
31. Scannell, K.P.: The Crubadan Project: Corpus building for under-resourced languages. Building and exploring web Corpora. In: 3rd Web as Corpus Workshop, pp. 5–15. Louvainla-Neuve, Belgium (2007)
32. Ling, W., Xiang, G., Dyer, C., Black, A., Trancoso, I.: Microblogs as parallel corpora. In: 51st Annual Meeting of the Association for Computational Linguistics, 1, 176–186. Association for Computational Linguistics, Sofia, Bulgaria. https://www.aclweb.org/anthology/P13-1018.pdf (2013)
33. Nie, J.Y., Simard, M., Isabelle, P., Durand, R.: Cross-language information retrieval based on parallel texts and automatic mining of parallel texts from the web. In: 22nd International ACM-SIGIR Conference on Research and Development in Information Retrieval (SIGIR), pp. 74–81. Berkeley, USA (1999)
34. Resnik, P.: Mining the Web for bilingual text. In: 37th Annual Meeting of the Association for Computational Linguistics, pp. 527–534. College Park, USA (1999)
35. Bosca, A., Dini, L.: Language identification strategies for cross language information retrieval. Working Notes of the Cross-Language Evaluation Forum (CLEF) (2010)
36. Ceylan, H., Kim, Y.: Language identification of search engine queries. In: Proceedings of the Joint Conference of the 47th Annual Meeting of the ACL and the 4th International Joint Conference on Natural Language Processing of the AFNLP, pp. 1066–1074. Singapore (2009)
37. Liu, J., Liang, C.: Text categorization of multilingual web pages in specific domain. In: 12th Pacific-Asia Conference on Advances in Knowledge Discovery and Data Mining, pp. 938–944. Osaka, Japan (2008)
38. Martins, B., Silva, M.J.: Language identification in web pages. Proceedings of the 2005 ACM Symposium on Applied Computing, pp. 764–768. Santa Fe, USA (2005)

39. Bergsma, S., McNamee, P., Bagdouri, M., Fink, C., Wilson, T.: Language identification for creating language-specific Twitter collections. In: 2nd Workshop on Language in Social Media (LSM2012), pp. 65–74. Montreal, Canada (2012)
40. Ghani, R., Jones, R., Mladenic, D.: Building minority language corpora by learning to generate web search queries. Knowl. Inf. Syst. **7**(1), 56–83 (2004)
41. Bolaj, P., Govilkar, S.: A survey on text categorization techniques for Indian regional languages. IJCSIT. **7**(2), 480–483 (2016)
42. Nadimapalli, V., Raju, G., Vidya, R.V., Sukavasi, B., Chava, S.R.K.: Automatic information collection & text classification for Telugu corpus using K-NN. Int J Res Comput Appl Manag. **1**(9), 88–93 (2011)
43. Selamat, A., Omatu, S.: Web page feature selection and classification using neural network. Inf Sci. **158**(1), 69–88 (2004). https://doi.org/10.1016/j.ins.2003.03.003
44. Li, H., Ma, B., Lee, C.H.: A vector space modeling approach to spoken language identification. IEEE Trans. Audio Speech Lang. Process. **15**(1), 271–284 (2007)
45. Callan, J., Hoy, M.: ClueWeb09 Dataset. http://boston.lti.cs (2009)
46. Garg, A., Gupta, V., Jindal, M.: A survey of language identification techniques and applications. J. Emerging Technol. Web Intell. **6**, 388–400 (2014). https://doi.org/10.4304/jetwi.6.4.388-400
47. Chen, J., Huang, H., Tian, S., Qu, Y.: Feature selection for text classification with Naïve Bayes. Expert Syst. Appl. **36**, 5432–5435 (2009)
48. Mandal, A.K., Sen, R.: Supervised learning methods for Bangla Web document categorization. Int J Artif Intell Appl (IJAIA). **5**(5), 93–105 (2014). https://doi.org/10.5121/ijaia.2014.5508
49. Patil, A.S., Pawar, B.: Automated classification of web sites using Naive Bayesian algorithm. In: International MultiConference of Engineers and Computer Scientists, pp. 14–16 (2012)
50. Jiang, L., Cai, Z., Zhang, H., Wang, D.: Naive Bayes text classifiers: a locally weighted learning approach. J. Exp. Theor. Artif. Intell. **25**, 273–286 (2013)
51. Yuan, Q., Cong, G., Thalmann, N.M.: Enhancing Naive Bayes with various smoothing methods for short text classification. In: 21st International Conference Companion on World Wide Web, pp. 645–646 (2012)
52. Yang, Y., Liu, X.: A re-examination of text categorization methods. In: 22nd Annual International ACM SIGIR Conference on Research and Development in Information Retrieval, pp. 42–49 (1999)
53. Bijalwan, V., Kumar, V., Kumari, P., Pascual, J.: KNN based machine learning approach for text and document mining. Int. J. Database Theory Appl. **7**, 61–70 (2014)
54. Li, B., Yu, S., Lu, Q.: An improved k-nearest neighbor algorithm for text categorization. In: 20th International Conference on Computer Processing of Oriental Languages, pp. 12–19. Shenyang, China (2003)
55. Suguna, N., Thanushkodi, K.: An improved K-nearest neighbor classification using Genetic Algorithm. Int J Comput Sci Issues. **7**, 18–21 (2010)
56. Cortes, C., Vapnik, V.: Support-vector networks. Machine Learn. **20**, 273–297 (1995)
57. Liu, X.L., Ding, S., Zhu, and Zhang, L.: Appropriateness in applying SVMs to text classification. Comput Eng Sci. **32**, 106–108 (2010)
58. Zakzouk, T., Mathkour, H.: Text classifiers for cricket sports News. In: International Conference on Telecommunications Technology and Applications ICTTA, pp. 196–201 (2011)
59. Zhijie, L., Xueqiang, L., Kun, L., Shuicai, S.: Study on SVM compared with the other text classification methods. In: 2nd International Workshop on Education Technology and Computer Science (ETCS), pp. 219–222 (2010)
60. Quinlan, J.R.: Induction of decision trees. Machine Learn. **1**, 81–106 (1986)
61. Selamat, A., Ching, N.C., Mikami, Y.: Arabic script web documents language identification using decision tree-ARTMAP model. In: International Conference on Convergence Information Technology, IEEE Conference, pp. 721–726. IEEE (2007)
62. Kim, Y.: Convolutional neural networks for sentence classification. EMNLP. **1**, 1746–1751 (2014)

63. Cai, J., Li, J., Li, W. and Wang, J.: Deep learning model used in text classification. In: International Computer Conference on Wavelet Active Media Technology and Information Processing (ICCWAMTIP), pp. 123–125. IEEE (2018). https://doi.org/10.1109/ICCWAMTIP.2018.8632592

64. Liu, P., Qiu, X., Huang, X.: Recurrent neural network for text classification with multi-task learning. IJCAI. (2016)

65. Siwei, L., Liheng, X., Kang, L., Jun, Z.: Recurrent convolutional neural networks for text classification. In: 29th AAAI Conference on Artificial Intelligence, 3(3), 2267–2273 (2015)

66. Temel, T.: High-accuracy document classification with a new algorithm. Electronics Lett. 54(17), 1028–1030 (2018)

67. Al-Anzi, F.S., AbuZeina, D.: Toward an enhanced Arabic text classification using cosine similarity and Latent Semantic Indexing. J. King Saud Univ. Comput. Inf. Sci. 29, 189–195 (2017)

68. Ali, A.R., Ijaz, M.: Urdu text classification, FIT. CIIT, Abbottabad, Pakistan (2009)

69. Alsaleem, S.: Automated Arabic text categorization using SVM and NB. Int. Arab J. e-Technol. 2(2), 124–128 (2011)

70. Alshalabi, H., Tiun, S., Omar, N., Albared, M.: Experiments on the use of feature selection and machine learning methods in automatic Malay text categorization. In: 4th International Conference on Electrical Engineering and Informatics (ICEEI 2013), vol. 11, pp. 748–754. Procedia Technology (2013). https://doi.org/10.1016/j.protcy.2013.12.254

71. Chy, A.N., Seddiqui, M.H., Das, S.: Bangla News classification using Naive Bayes classifier. In: 16th International Conference on Computer and Information Technology, pp. 366–371. Khulna, Bangladesh (2014)

72. Fatih, A.M., Diri, B.: Automatic Turkish text categorization in terms of author, genre and gender. In: Natural Language Processing and Information Systems, pp. 221–226. Springer, Berlin (2006)

73. Hao, P., Ying, D., Longyuan, T.: Application for web text categorization based on support vector machine. International Forum on Computer Science-Technology and Applications, pp. 42–45 (2009)

74. Kava, KS, and Desai, N.P.: A survey on text categorization of Indian and non-Indian languages using supervised learning techniques. Discovery, 43(198), 118-124 (2015).

75. Kim, S.B., Han, K.S., Rim, H.C., Myaeng, S.H.: Some effective techniques for Naïve Bayes text classification. IEEE Trans. Knowl. Data Eng. 18(11), 1457–1466. IEEE (2006). https://doi.org/10.1109/TKDE.2006.180

76. Kourdi, M.E., Bensaid, A., Rachidi, T.: Automatic Arabic document categorization based on the Naïve Bayes algorithm. In: Workshop on Computational Approaches to Arabic Script-based Languages, Association for Computational Linguistics, pp. 51–58. Geneva (2004)

77. Kumar, G.B., Murthy, K.N., Chaudhuri, B.: Statistical analysis of Telugu text corpora. Int. J. Dravidian Lang. 36(2), 71–99 (2007)

78. Menaka, S., Radha, N.: Text classification using keyword extraction technique. Int J Adv Res Comput Sci Softw Eng (IJARCSSE). 3(12), 734–740 (2013)

79. Murthy, K.N.: Automatic categorization of Telugu news articles. Department of Computer and Information Sciences, University of Hyderabad, Hyderabad (2003). doi:202.41.85.68.

80. Nidhi, Gupta, V.: Punjabi text classification using Naïve Bayes, centroid and hybrid approach. In: 4th International Workshop on Computer Networks & Communications, pp. 245–253 (2012). https://doi.org/10.5121/csit.2012.2421

81. Patil, M., Game, P.: Comparison of Marathi text classifiers. ACEEE Int. J. Inf. Technol. (2014)

82. Shinde, S., Joeg, P., Vanjale, S.: Web document classification using support vector machine. In: International Conference on Current Trends in Computer, Electrical, Electronics and Communications, pp. 688–690. IEEE, Mysore, India (2017). https://doi.org/10.1109/CTCEEC.2017.8455102

83. Thakur, S., Singh, V.: A lexicon pool augmented Naive Bayes Classifier for Nepali Text. In: 7th International Conference on Contemporary Computing (IC3), IEEE, pp. 542–546 (2014)

84. Dhar, A., Dash, N. and Roy, K.: Classification of text documents through distance measurement: an experiment with multi-domain Bangla text documents. In: 3rd ICACCA, pp. 1–6. IEEE (2007)
85. Khamar, K.: Short text classification using K-NN based on distance function. Int. J. Adv. Res. Comput. Commun. Eng. **2**, 1916–1919 (2013)
86. Vinoth, R., Jayachandran, A., Balaji, M., Srinivasan, R.: A hybrid text classification approach using KNN and SVM. Int J Adv Found Res Comput (IJAFRC). **1**, 20–26 (2014)
87. Bolaj, P., Govilkar, S.: Text classification for Marathi documents using supervised learning methods. Int. J. Comput. Appl. (IJCA). **155**(8), 6–10 (2016). https://doi.org/10.5120/ijca2016912374
88. Patil, J.J., Bogiri, N.: Automatic text categorization: Marathi documents. In: International Conference on Energy Systems and Applications (ICESA 2015), pp. 689–694 (2015). https://doi.org/10.1109/ICESA.2015.7503438
89. Sahani, A., Sarang, K., Umredkar, S., Patil, M.: Automatic text categorization of Marathi language documents. Int J Comput Sci Inf Technol. **7**(5), 2297–2301 (2016)
90. Narhari, S.A., Shedge, R.: Text categorization of Marathi documents using modified LINGO. In: International Conference on Advances in Computing, Communication and Control (ICAC3). IEEE (2017). https://doi.org/10.1109/ICAC3.2017.8318771
91. Gogoi, M., Sarma, S.K.: Document classification of Assamese text using Naïve Bayes approach. IJCTT. **30**(4), 182–186 (2015)
92. Swamy, M.N., Hanumanthappa, M., Jyothi, N.M.: Indian language text representation and categorization using supervised learning algorithm. In: International Conference on Intelligent Computing Applications, pp. 406–410 (2014). https://doi.org/10.1109/ICICA.2014.89
93. Dixit, N., Choudhary, N.: Automatic classification of Hindi verbs in syntactic perspective. Int. J. Emerging Technol. Adv. Eng. **4**, 2250–2459 (2014)
94. Kanimozhi, S.: Web based classification of Tamil documents using ABPA. Int. J. Scient. Eng. Res. (IJSER). **3**(5), 1–6 (2012)
95. Devasena, C.L., Hemalatha, M.: Automatic text categorization and summarization using rule reduction. In: International Conference on Advances in Engineering, Science and Management (ICAESM), pp. 594–598. IEEE (2012)
96. Dong, T. Cheng, W., Shang, W.: The research of KNN text categorization algorithm based on eager learning. In: International Conference on Industrial Control and Electronics Engineering, pp. 1120–1123 (2012)
97. Thabtah, F., Eljinini, M.A.H., Zamzeer, M., Hadi, W.M.: Naïve Bayesian based on chi square to categorize Arabic data. In: 11th International Business Information Management Association Conference (IBIMA) Conference on Innovation and Knowledge Management in Twin Track Economies, pp. 930–935. Cairo, Egypt (2009)
98. Al-Thubaity, A., Almuhareb, A., Al-Harbi, S., Al-Rajeh, A., Khorsheed, M.: KACST Arabic text classification project: overview and preliminary results. In: 9th IBMIA Conference on Information Management in Modern Organizations (2008)
99. Mesleh, A.M.A.: Chi square feature extraction based SVMs Arabic language text categorization system. J. Comput. Sci. **3**(6), 430–435 (2007)
100. Wang, M.Y., Liu, T.: Method of Chinese text categorization based on variable precision rough set. In: 3rd Symposium on Intelligent Information Technology Application Workshops, pp. 26–29 (2009). https://doi.org/10.1109/IITAW.2009.12
101. Li, X.F., He, H.B., Zhao, L.L.: Chinese text categorization based on CCIPCA and SMO. In: 7th International Conference on Machine Learning and Cybernetics, pp. 2514–2518. Kunming (2008)
102. Xu, J.S.: TCBPLK: a new method of text categorization. In: 6th International Conference on Machine Learning and Cybernetics, pp. 3889–3891. Hong Kong (2007)
103. Mansur, M., UzZaman, N., Khan, M.: Analysis of N-gram based text categorization for Bangla in newspaper corpus. In: International Conference on Computer and Information Technology (ICCIT), pp. 25–31 (2007)

104. Zhou, J.G., Wang, K., Wu, J., Yan, P.L., Wu, M.: A method of Chinese text categorization based on proximal support vector machine. In: 4th International Conference on Machine Learning and Cybernetics, pp. 1615–1619. Guangzhou (2005)

105. Kosmajac, D., Keselj, V.: Slavic language identification using cascade classifier approach. In: 17th International Symposium INFOTEH-JAHORINA (2018). East Sarajevo, Bosnia-Herzegovina. https://doi.org/10.1109/INFOTEH.2018.8345541

106. Tan, L., Zampieri, M., Ljube, N., Tiedemann, J.: Merging comparable data sources for the discrimination of similar languages: the dsl corpus collection. In: Proceedings of the 7th Workshop on Building and Using Comparable Corpora (BUCC), Reykjavik, Iceland, pp. 11–15 (2014)

107. Madhu, C., George, A., Mary, L.: Automatic language identification for seven Indian languages using higher level features. In: International Conference on Signal Processing, Informatics, Communications and Energy Systems (SPICES), pp. 1–6. IEEE (2017)

108. Kocmi, T., Bojar, O.: Lanide NN: multilingual language identification on character window. In: 15th Conference of the European Chapter of the Association for Computational Linguistics (ACL), vol. 1, pp. 927–936 (2017)

109. Duvenhage, B., Ntini, M., Ramonyai, P.: Improved text language identification for the South African languages. In: Pattern Recognition Association of South Africa and Robotics and Mechatronics International Conference (PRASA-RobMech), pp. 214–218. Bloemfontein, South Africa (2017)

110. Selamat, A., Akosu, N.: Word-length algorithm for language identification of under-resourced languages. J King Saud Univ Comput Inf Sci (JKAUCIS). **28**, 457–469 (2016)

111. Chavez, E., Garc, M., Favela, J.: Fast and accurate language detection in short texts using contextual entropy. Res. Comput. Sci. **90**, 351–358 (2015)

112. Lui, M., Lau, J.H., Baldwin, T.: Automatic detection and language identification of multilingual documents. Trans. Assoc. Comput. Linguistics. **2**, 27–40 (2014)

113. Giguet, E.: Categorisation according to language: a step toward combining linguistic knowledge and statistical learning. In: 4th International Workshop on Parsing Technologies (IWPT-1995), Prague, Czech Republic (1995)

114. Lins, R.D., Goncalves, P.: Automatic language identification of written texts. In: ACM Symposium on Applied Computing (SAC 2004), pp. 1128–1133. Nicosia, Cyprus (2004)

115. Yadav, P., Kaur, S.: Language identification and correction in corrupted texts of regional Indian languages. In: International Conference Oriental COCOSDA held jointly with Conference on Asian Spoken Language Research and Evaluation (O-COCOSDA/CASLRE), pp. 1–5 (2013)

116. Verma, V.K., Khanna, N.: Indian language identification using k-means clustering and support vector machine (SVM). In: Students conference on Engineering and systems (SCES), pp. 1–5. IEEE (2013)

117. Sefara, T.J., Manamela, M.J., Malatji, P.T.: Text-based language identification for some of the under-resourced languages of South Africa. In: International Conference on Advances in Computing and Communication Engineering (ICACCE), pp. 303–307 (2016)

118. Milne, R.M., O'Keefe, R.A., Trotman, A.: A study in language identification. In: Proceedings of the Seventeenth Australasian Document Computing Symposium, pp. 88–95. Dunedin, New Zealand (2012)

119. Teahan, W.J.: Text classification and segmentation using minimum cross-entropy. In: 6th International Conference "Recherche d'InformationAssistee par Ordinateur" (RIAO'00), pp. 943–961. Paris, France (2000)

120. Takçi, H., Güngör, T.: A high performance centroid-based classification approach for language identification. Pattern Recogn Lett. **33**, 2077–2084 (2012)

121. Ng, C., Selamat, A.: Improving language identification of web page using optimum profile. In: Zain, J.M., et al. (eds.) ICSECS 2011, Part II, CCIS 180, pp. 157–166 (2011)

122. Choong, C., Mikami, Y., Marasinghe, C., Nandasara, S.: Optimizing n-gram order of an n-gram based language identification algorithm for 68 written languages. Int. J. Adv. ICT for Emerging Reg. **2**(2), 21–28 (2009)

123. Chew, Y.C., Mikami, Y., Nagano, R.: Language identification of web pages based on improved N-gram Algorithm. IJCSI. **8**(3), 47–58 (2011)
124. Al-Dubaee, S. A., Ahmad, N., Martinovic, J., Snasel, V.: Language identification using wavelet transform and artificial neural network. In: International Conference on Computational Aspects of Social Networks (2010)
125. Yang, X., Liang, W.: An N-Gram-and Wikipedia joint approach to natural language identification. In: 4th International Universal Communication Symposium, IEEE (2010). https://doi.org/10.1109/IUCS.2010.5666010
126. Kohen, P.: Europarl: a parallel corpus for statistical machine translation. Machine Translation Summit X, pp. 79–86. Phuket, Thailand (2005)
127. Mayer, U.F.: Bootstrapped language identification for multi-site internet domains. KDD'12, pp. 579–585. Beijing, China (2012)
128. Padma, M.C., Vijaya, P.A., Nagabhushan, P.: Language Identification from an Indian Multilingual Document Using Profile Features, pp. 332–335. ICCAE (2009)
129. Rehurek, R., Kolkus, M.: Language identification on the web: extending the dictionary method. In: 10th International Conference of Computational Linguistics and Intelligent Text Processing, (CICLing), pp. 357–368. Mexico City, Mexico (2009)
130. Vijaya, P.A., Padma, M.C.: Text line identification from a multilingual document. In: International Conference on Digital Image Processing ICDIP, pp. 302–305 (2009)
131. Bilcu, E.B., Astola, J.: A hybrid neural network for language identification from text. In: 16th Conference of Signal processing society workshop on machine learning for signal processing, pp. 253–258. IEEE (2006)
132. Tian, J., Suontausta, J.: Scalable neural network based language identification from written text. In: International Conference on Acoustics, Speech and Signal Processing, vol. 1, pp. 1–48. IEEE, Hong Kong, China (2003). https://doi.org/10.1109/ICASSP.2003.1198713
133. Combrinck, H.P., Botha, E.C.: Text-based automatic language identification. In: 6th Annual Symposium of the Pattern Recognition Association of South Africa (ASPRASA), Gauteng, South Africa (1995)
134. Souter, C., Churcher, G., Hayes, J., Hughes, J., Johnson, S.: Natural language identification using corpus-based models. Hermes J Linguistics. **13**, 183–203 (1994)
135. Yamaguchi, H., Tanaka-Ishii, K.: Text segmentation by language using minimum description length. In: Proceedings the 50th Annual Meeting of the Association for Computational Linguistics, vol. 1, pp. 969–978. Jeju Island, Korea (2012)

Classification of Yoga Asanas from a Single Image by Learning the 3D View of Human Poses

Chirumamilla Nagalakshmi and Snehasis Mukherjee

Abstract In this chapter, we propose a technique for the classification of yoga poses/asanas by learning the 3D landmark points in human poses obtained from a single image. We apply an encoder architecture followed by a regression layer to estimate pose parameters like shape, gesture, and camera position, which are later mapped to 3D landmark points by the SMPL (Skinned Multi-Person Linear) model. The 3D landmark points of each image are the features used for the classification of poses. We experiment with different classification models, including k-nearest neighbors (kNN), support vector machine (SVM), and some popular deep neural networks such as AlexNet, VGGNet, and ResNet. Since this is the first attempt to classify yoga asanas, no dataset is available in the literature. We propose an annotated dataset containing images of yoga poses and validate the proposed method on the newly introduced dataset.

Keywords Yoga asana · 3D human pose · 3D landmark points · Human mesh recovery

1 Introduction

Yoga poses (asanas) have become popular during the last couple of decades as a useful aid to fight against increasing stress in daily life. Proper skill and regular practice of appropriate yoga asanas can help people stay healthy, both mentally and physically, by regularizing blood flow, pulse rate, and hormone secretion in the body. Regular practice of yoga asanas also enhances activeness, flexibility, ability to concentrate, and various other features related to the human body and personality.

C. Nagalakshmi · S. Mukherjee (✉)
Indian Institute of Information Technology, Sri City, Chittoor, India
e-mail: snehasis.mukherjee@iiits.in

© Springer Nature Switzerland AG 2021

J. Mukhopadhyay et al. (eds.), *Digital Techniques for Heritage Presentation and Preservation*, https://doi.org/10.1007/978-3-030-57907-4_3

Proper guidance is necessary for a healthy practice of yoga asanas due to various reasons. Specific physical or mental exercises are required for specific physical or psychological problems. Only proper guidance can enable yoga practitioners to get the maximum benefit from their practice. Moreover, improper practices of yoga asanas may not provide the expected betterment to the human body or mind; sometimes improper yoga practices may lead to damages to the physique. However, with the increased popularity of yoga practices, getting a skilled yoga trainer has become challenging. In this scenario, an online system is necessary to train people on yoga asanas, given the unavailability of trained yoga experts.

This study is an attempt at making a first step toward building an online system to provide training on yoga asanas. We propose a system to classify yoga asanas from images of the performances of various asanas. The proposed system applies an autoencoder CNN to extract the 3D landmark points and constructs the 3D representation of the pose of the performer with the landmark points. The 3D poses are learned by a classifier for the classification of the yoga asana.

A single 2D view of a performer performing a yoga pose cannot capture the minute variations in poses across different yoga asanas. Hence, a 3D view is required. Recently, several methods have been proposed in the literature for single-view 3D reconstruction of human poses, which enables more accurate classification of yoga asanas compared to classifying based on 2D images.

The proposed method first applies Histogram of Oriented Gradient (HOG) features to localize the performer in the image. The preprocessed image after localization of the performer is passed to an autoencoder followed by a regression layer, which estimates the parameters. The estimated parameters are mapped to 3D landmark points by an SMPL (Skinned Multi-Person Linear) model. The estimated 3D landmark points are used as features for classifying the yoga asana. We apply different existing classifiers on the extracted landmark points and compare the results.

In this chapter, our contributions are twofold. First, we introduce a challenging dataset consisting of images of performances of different yoga asanas. This dataset can be used for classifying yoga asanas from images of yoga performances. Second, this study makes the first attempt to apply a CNN-based 3D pose reconstruction model to classify yoga asanas from images. Next we discuss some methods available in the literature for 3D human pose reconstruction from images.

2   Related Work

Reconstruction of a 3D shape of human pose from an image is an active area of research in the field of computer vision and graphics [15]. There are two parallel ways for 3D human pose reconstruction found in the literature: reconstruction from multiple views of the object and reconstruction from a single image.

2.1 Multiple-View 3D Human Pose Estimation

The process of generating a 3D representation of human pose from multiple images relies either on images taken from multiple cameras from different viewpoints [1, 5, 12, 13, 18] or on images captured at different time stamps, of the same scene [2, 3, 17]. Inertial sensors are used in [12, 18] for generating multiple views of a scene. In [13], a marker-based method is proposed for generating a 3D view of the human. However, these approaches are expensive. A part-based HOG descriptor is used in [5] to extract the probability distributions of the body parts. The body parts are connected in a tree graph structure and the dependency structure of the parameters of the model by a Bayesian network. Dynamic programming is used to discretize the state space. Amin et al. [1] projected the 3D pose structures into multiple 2D planes related to multiple viewpoints of the same scene. However, multiple-view camera setting is expensive and often difficult to implement in such scenarios.

Several efforts have been made for estimating the 3D view of human pose from a sequence of 2D images captured over time. In [2, 3], the motion information of the human over time is exploited and used for generating the 3D view of poses. Tekin et al. exploit the spatiotemporal information of the sequence of images to reduce depth ambiguity [17]. They apply two ConvNets to adjust the bounding boxes on the human body. Then a HOG descriptor is used to extract the human pose. 3D pose reconstruction methods based on a sequence of images are cheaper and easier to implement compared to a multiple-view camera setup. However, nonavailability of sequential views of a scene is a problem in this approach. Thus, single-image 3D reconstruction is gaining the attention of researchers.

2.2 Single-View 3D Human Pose Estimation

Fewer attempts have been made to estimate a 3D view of human pose from a single image [4, 14, 16]. Radwan et al. employed a 2D body part detector with an occlusion avoidance mechanism [14]. They created multiple views of the person synthetically by applying a twin Gaussian Process Regression (GPR) in a cascaded manner. In [16], a Bayesian approach is applied using a discriminative 2D body part detector model and a probabilistic generative model based on latent variables. Brauer et al. extracted the votes for candidate 2D joints to obtain a probability distribution for each candidate [4]. They compared the votes with the 3D model prior to the joint points to obtain the 3D view of the poses.

After the introduction of deep learning, several deep learning-based methods have been proposed for 3D reconstruction of human pose from a single image [6, 7, 20]. Encoder–decoder CNN architectures have shown to provide good results in generating 3D views of human poses from single images. However, the popular encoder–decoder architectures often fail to reconstruct 3D views of anthropometric regular body poses accurately in real-life scenarios. To overcome this drawback,

Kien et al. proposed a part-based model where individual body parts are represented as nodes in a graph. Poses are estimated based on the interdependency among the body parts [10]. Mehta et al. proposed an interesting CNN regressor architecture by regressing 2D to 3D joint points for pose estimation [11]. Wang et al. represented 3D human poses by a sparse combination of structural pose priors [19]. The 3D poses are reconstructed from the 2D poses by minimizing an L_1 norm between the 2D and estimated 3D poses, which makes the system independent of the accuracy of the process of estimating the 2D pose.

For estimating yoga poses, minute differences between poses must be captured, which is difficult in the state-of-the-art methods. However, Kanazawa et al. proposed an end-to-end framework for 3D pose estimation where minute differences of poses are captured by the landmark points provided by an autoencoder architecture [9]. Following Kanazawa et al., we extract the 3D landmark points extracted by the autoencoder and feed the landmark points as features of a classifier, to classify the poses related to the yoga asanas. As of now, [8] is the only attempt toward providing digital guidance to practice yoga asanas. However, the proposed method is the first attempt to classify yoga asanas, which we discuss next.

3 Proposed Method

The proposed method for the classification of yoga asanas from a single image of yoga performance consists of two major steps: estimation of 3D pose and classification of the yoga asana based on the 3D pose.

3.1 3D Pose Estimation

For pose estimation, we train an autoencoder to extract the 3D pose landmark points following [9]. The autoencoder architecture is shown in Fig. 1. This autoencoder reconstructs a full 3D mesh of human pose from a single view of an image, where the performer is centered. We consider a pool of 3D meshes of human bodies with various shapes and poses as unpaired.

As shown in Fig. 1, the human-centered (preprocessed) image is passed to the autoencoder. Here the encoder is used to reduce the resolution of the input image, so that only useful low-dimensional features of the image are extracted. These extracted features are passed to an iterative 3D regression module whose main objective is to infer the parameters of the 3D human shape and the camera. Hence, the 3D joint points are projected on a 2D space. The interesting part in this training process is to identify whether the inferred parameters belong to the human or not. This is done using a discriminator network that is shown in Fig. 1. The discriminator's main objective is to identify the 3D parameters from the unpaired dataset. The prior of geometry is used by models that only predict 3D joint locations.

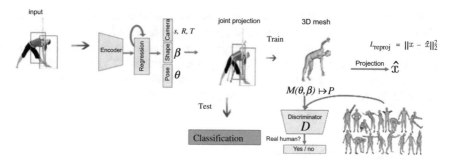

Fig. 1 Overall diagram of the proposed method

When ground truth 3D information is available, we can use it as an intermediate loss. To summarize, our overall objective is that if 3D information is not available, then $L = \lambda L_{reprojectionloss} + L_{des}$; otherwise $L = \lambda(L_{reprojectionloss} + L_{3Dloss}) + L_{des}$, where λ controls the relative importance of each objective, $L_{reprojectionloss}$ is defined in later sections, L_{des} is the loss due to discriminator, and L represents loss.

The 3D joint projection error is represented as $X(\theta, \beta)$, which is generated by the linear regression module. Here R is rotation due to camera $R \in \mathbb{R}^{3 \times P}$, where P represents the number of 3D joint points. T is translation due to camera $T \in \mathbb{R}^2$, and S is scalar due to camera $S \in \mathbb{R}^1$. Each iteration through the regression model infers parameters R, T, and S. The 2D joints are calculated from 3D joints using $S\eta(RX(\theta, \beta)) + T$, where η is the orthographic projection.

The loss near regression module is calculated as follows: If 2D joint is visible, then

$$L_{reprojectionloss} = \sum_i ||(X^i - X^{\wedge i}||; \qquad (1)$$

Otherwise, the projection loss is 0. Here $X^i \in \mathbb{R}^{2 \times K}$, $X^{\wedge i}$ is predicted, and X^i is the original joint point. Based on the loss, the weights are updated. Finally, using these 3D joints and the SMPL (Skinned Multi-Person Linear) model, a 3D pose of the human is reconstructed.

3.2 Classification of Yoga Asanas Based on Poses

The proposed framework for 3D pose estimation can perform well if the performer is located at the center of the image. Hence, proper image preprocessing is needed to make sure that the human performer is at the center of the image. We apply HOG features to detect and localize the human performer. Then this preprocessed image is passed to the autoencoder, which is able to reduce the resolution of the image without much loss of data. Then the low-dimensional feature vector is passed to a regression layer, which is able to predict the pose and camera properties. Using the SMPL model, the 3D landmark points are estimated from pose and shape parameters. The extracted 3D landmark points are used to classify the pose/asana performed by the person in the image using these predicted 3D joints as features. We use some standard machine learning classifiers like kNN, SVM, and neural networks. Next we describe the experimental setup for the proposed scheme.

4   Dataset and Experiments

As discussed in the Introduction, this study is the first attempt to classify yoga asanas from images. Hence, due to the nonavailability of datasets, we have created and annotated a dataset for this purpose. The images in the dataset are collected from the Internet. We annotate the collected data by providing class labels to the collected images. The collected images are challenging due to variation in poses between two performers of the same yoga asana. Also, viewpoint changes, illumination changes, scale changes, etc., make the dataset even harder. Figure 2 shows some sample images taken from the proposed dataset.

The proposed yoga pose dataset has 13 classes named as follows: 1. Ardha Ushtrasana, 2. Ardha Uttanasana, 3. Bhadrasana, 4. Bhujangasana, 5. Bridge posture, 6. Kapalabhati, 7. Padahastasana, 8. Sasakasana, 9. Savasana, 10. Tadasana, 11. Tree pose, 12. Trikonasana, and 13. Vakrasana.

The dataset contains 2129 images of all the 13 classes; 354 images are kept for testing and the remaining used for training purposes. We can observe from Fig. 2 that the poses related to Tadasana and Tree pose are similar. Also, Ardha Uttanasana and Bridge posture have almost the same appearance of human pose, which makes the dataset more challenging. Table 1 shows the number of images per class.

We have applied different classifiers to classify the yoga asana based on the landmark points. We apply the AlexNet model built with a block of eight layers: convolutional1, convolutional2, convolutional3, convolutional4, convolutional5, fully connected6, fully connected7, and soft max layer. Then the AlexNet model is trained and tested on the human pose/asana dataset directly. We also tried the 18-layer ResNet and 16-layer VGG models on the proposed dataset to classify the yoga poses. We also applied some handcrafted classifiers like kNN, SVM, etc. Next we discuss the results of the experiments performed on the proposed dataset.

5   Results

We have performed extensive experiments on the proposed dataset, and the results are given in this section. The accuracies of the proposed method when applied on the proposed dataset are shown in Table 2. From Table 2, we observe that the kNN classifier with $k = 6$ gives a good accuracy; however, the highest accuracy

Fig. 2 Sample images from the proposed dataset. (**a**) Ardha Ushtrasana, (**b**) Ardha Uttanasana, (**c**) Bhadrasana, (**d**) Bhujangasana, (**e**) Bridge posture, (**f**) Kapalabhati, (**g**) Padahastasana, (**h**) Sasakasana, (**i**) Savasana, (**j**) Tadasana, (**k**) Tree pose, (**l**) Trikonasana, and (**m**) Vakrasana

Table 1 Number of images per class in the proposed dataset

Sl. no	Class name	Number of images
1	Ardha Ushtrasana	168
2	Ardha Uttanasana	148
3	Bhadrasana	68
4	Bhujangasana	230
5	Bridge posture	226
6	Kapalabhati	138
7	Padahastasana	179
8	Sasakasana	94
9	Savasana	126
10	Tadasana	126
11	Tree pose	284
12	Trikonasana	241
13	Vakrasana	104

Table 2 Accuracies obtained by different classifiers on the 3D landmark points

Classifier	Testing accuracy
kNN ($k = 6$)	71.0%
SVM (RBF kernel)	59.0%
SVM (linear)	71.5%

Table 3 Confusion matrix for kNN

Class	1	2	3	4	5	6	7	8	9	10	11	12	13
1	24	2	0	0	1	0	0	2	0	1	2	1	0
2	2	19	0	1	1	0	0	0	0	0	1	0	0
3	0	0	8	2	0	3	0	0	0	1	0	0	1
4	0	0	0	32	0	1	0	0	0	2	1	0	2
5	0	0	0	1	24	0	0	1	2	0	1	0	0
6	1	0	0	0	0	22	0	0	0	0	2	0	1
7	1	5	0	0	0	0	22	0	0	2	3	0	0
8	3	2	0	0	2	1	4	5	0	0	1	0	0
9	0	0	0	1	3	0	0	0	15	0	1	0	0
10	0	1	0	0	0	0	0	0	0	13	8	0	0
11	3	4	0	0	1	1	0	0	0	3	30	0	0
12	2	2	1	0	1	0	0	0	1	0	2	28	0
13	0	0	1	3	0	0	0	0	0	0	1	0	12

is achieved by linear SVM. Table 3 shows the confusion matrix when the kNN classifier is applied on the landmark points. Table 4 depicts the true positive (TP), false positive (FP), true negative (TN), and false negative (FN) results along with the recall and precision measures for each class when kNN is applied. Table 5 shows the confusion matrix for linear SVM. Table 6 shows the recall and precision measures for linear SVM.

Table 7 shows the confusion matrix for the neural network (NN) classifier applied on the proposed dataset. Table 8 shows the recall and precision for NN classifier. The overall accuracy of the neural network classifier is around 74%.

Table 4 Evaluation results for kNN

Class	FP	FN	TN	TP	Precision	Recall
1	9	12	230	24	0.72	0.66
2	5	16	235	19	0.79	0.54
3	7	2	246	8	0.53	0.8
4	6	8	222	32	0.84	0.8
5	5	9	230	24	0.82	0.73
6	4	6	232	22	0.84	0.78
7	11	4	232	22	0.66	0.84
8	13	3	249	5	0.277	0.62
9	5	3	239	15	0.75	0.83
10	1	9	241	13	0.92	0.59
11	12	23	224	30	0.71	0.56
12	9	1	226	28	0.75	0.96
13	5	4	242	12	0.70	0.75

Table 5 Confusion matrix for linear SVM

Class	1	2	3	4	5	6	7	8	9	10	11	12	13
1	22	1	0	0	1	0	2	0	0	1	6	0	0
2	0	16	0	0	0	0	1	0	0	0	1	6	0
3	0	0	8	4	0	1	0	0	0	1	0	0	1
4	2	0	0	29	1	0	0	0	0	1	3	0	2
5	1	0	0	1	26	0	1	0	0	0	0	0	0
6	0	0	0	1	0	21	0	0	0	0	3	0	1
7	0	4	0	1	0	0	21	1	0	4	1	1	0
8	1	0	1	1	2	0	2	8	0	0	2	1	0
9	0	0	0	0	6	1	0	0	12	0	1	0	0
10	0	1	0	0	0	0	0	0	0	10	11	0	0
11	0	0	0	5	0	0	0	0	0	0	36	0	1
12	0	1	0	0	0	0	0	0	1	1	3	31	0
13	0	0	0	2	0	0	0	0	0	0	1	1	13

We have tested some popular convolutional neural networks and compared the results in Table 9. Because of the small size of the dataset, the AlexNet model (being a shallow network) provides a better result than other deeper networks such as VGG 16 and ResNet 18, which perform even worse than the handcrafted classifiers. Table 10 shows the confusion matrix for AlexNet. Table 11 shows the recall and precision measures for the AlexNet classifier. We can observe from the confusion matrices that Bridge posture is the easiest asana to recognize due to its different appearance compared to the other asanas, as depicted in Fig. 2. On the contrary, Sasakasana and Vakrasana are the most difficult asanas to recognize by a machine learning-based system, probably because of the less number of available images.

Table 6 Evaluation results for linear SVM

Class	FP	FN	TN	TP	Precision	Recall
1	11	4	231	22	0.67	0.84
2	8	7	237	16	0.67	0.69
3	7	1	245	8	0.53	0.89
4	9	15	224	29	0.76	0.66
5	3	10	227	26	0.89	0.72
6	5	2	232	21	0.81	0.91
7	12	6	232	21	0.63	0.78
8	10	1	245	8	0.44	0.89
9	8	1	241	12	0.6	0.92
10	12	8	243	10	0.45	0.56
11	6	32	217	36	0.86	0.52
12	6	3	222	31	0.84	0.91
13	4	5	240	13	0.76	0.72

Table 7 Confusion matrix for NN

Class	1	2	3	4	5	6	7	8	9	10	11	12	13
1	22	0	0	1	0	0	2	2	0	1	3	2	0
2	1	16	0	0	0	0	0	1	1	0	0	5	0
3	0	0	9	4	0	0	0	0	0	0	1	0	1
4	0	0	0	33	0	0	0	0	0	1	2	0	2
5	0	1	0	1	24	0	1	1	1	0	0	0	0
6	0	0	0	2	0	19	0	0	0	0	3	0	2
7	0	6	0	2	0	0	20	1	0	3	1	0	0
8	0	0	0	2	1	0	2	10	0	0	2	1	0
9	0	0	0	2	4	0	1	0	13	0	0	0	0
10	0	1	0	1	0	0	0	0	0	16	4	0	0
11	0	0	0	5	0	1	1	0	0	1	33	1	0
12	0	2	0	0	0	0	0	0	0	0	3	32	0
13	0	0	2	1	0	0	0	0	0	0	1	1	12

6 Observations/Conclusion

We have proposed a method for classifying yoga asanas from images of yoga performances. We have applied an autoencoder to extract the 3D landmark points of human pose during yoga performance. The 3D landmark points are then fed into the classifiers to obtain the results of classification of yoga asana. The landmark points have shown potential as feature descriptors for classifying the minute variations in

Table 8 Evaluation results for NN

Class	FP	FN	TN	TP	Precision	Recall
1	11	1	237	22	0.66	0.96
2	8	10	243	16	0.66	0.61
3	6	2	250	9	0.64	0.81
4	5	21	226	33	0.86	0.61
5	5	5	235	24	0.82	0.83
6	7	1	240	19	0.73	0.95
7	13	7	239	20	0.60	0.74
8	8	5	249	10	0.55	0.66
9	7	2	246	13	0.65	0.86
10	6	6	243	16	0.72	0.72
11	9	20	226	33	0.78	0.62
12	5	10	227	32	0.86	0.76
13	5	5	247	12	0.70	0.7

Table 9 Accuracies using popular deep networks

Net	Testing accuracy
AlexNet	83.05%
ResNet 18	60%
VGG 16	30%

Table 10 Confusion matrix for AlexNet

Class	1	2	3	4	5	6	7	8	9	10	11	12	13
1	27	0	0	0	1	1	2	0	0	0	0	1	1
2	0	21	0	0	0	0	0	0	0	0	1	2	0
3	0	0	8	1	1	4	0	0	1	0	0	0	0
4	0	1	0	36	0	1	0	0	0	0	0	0	0
5	0	0	0	0	28	0	0	0	0	0	0	0	0
6	0	0	1	1	0	21	0	0	0	0	2	0	1
7	1	4	0	0	0	0	27	0	0	0	0	0	0
8	1	0	0	0	2	0	3	8	3	0	0	0	1
9	0	0	0	0	2	0	0	0	18	0	0	0	0
10	0	3	0	0	0	0	0	0	0	17	2	0	0
11	0	0	0	1	0	0	2	0	0	2	37	0	0
12	0	0	0	0	1	0	0	0	0	0	0	36	0
13	0	0	0	2	1	1	0	1	2	0	0	0	10

human poses across various asanas. Extensive experiments have been carried out with some handcrafted and deep learning classifiers. The deep learning classifiers are generally performing worse (except AlexNet) compared to the handcrafted features. In the future, a bigger dataset can be generated and the above experiments can be carried out to observe the effect of a deeper network in classifying yoga asana images. Also, a spatiotemporal feature extractor can be deployed on videos of yoga performances, extending this work to video applications.

Table 11 Evaluation results for AlexNet

Class	FP	FN	TN	TP	Precision	Recall
1	6	2	267	27	0.81	0.93
2	3	8	273	21	0.87	0.72
3	7	1	286	8	0.53	0.88
4	2	5	258	36	0.94	0.88
5	0	8	266	28	1	0.77
6	5	7	273	21	0.80	0.75
7	5	7	267	27	0.84	0.79
8	10	1	286	8	0.44	0.88
9	2	6	276	18	0.90	0.75
10	5	2	277	17	0.77	0.89
11	5	5	257	37	0.88	0.88
12	1	3	258	36	0.97	0.92
13	7	3	284	10	0.58	0.76

Acknowledgments The authors would like to acknowledge the Science and Engineering Research Board (SERB), Govt. of India, for the financial support provided in the form of project number ECR/2016/000652 to conduct this project.

References

1. Amin, S., Andriluka, M., Rohrbach, M., Schiele, B.: Multiview pictorial structures for 3d human pose estimation. In: Proceedings of BMVC (2013)
2. Andriluka, M., Sigal, L.: Human context: modeling human-human interactions for monocular 3d pose estimation. In: Articulated Motion and Deformable Objects, pp. 260–272. Springer, Berlin (2012)
3. Andriluka, M., Roth, S., Schiele, B.: Monocular 3d pose estimation and tracking by detection. In: Proceedings of CVPR, pp. 623–630. IEEE, Piscataway (2010)
4. Brauer, J., Hubner, W., Arens, M.: Generative 2d and 3d human pose estimation with vote distributions. In: Advances in Visual Computing. Springer, Berlin (2012)
5. Burenius, M., Sullivan, J., Carlsson, S.: 3d pictorial structures for multiple view articulated pose estimation. In: Proceedings of CVPR, pp. 3618–3625. IEEE, Piscataway (2013)
6. Elhayek, A., de Aguiar, E., Jain, A., Tompson, J., Pishchulin, L., Andriluka, M., Bregler, C., Schiele, B., Theobalt, C.: Efficient convnet-based marker-less motion capture in general scenes with a low number of cameras. In: Proceedings of CVPR, pp. 3810–3818. IEEE, Piscataway (2015)
7. Elhayek, A., de Aguiar, E., Jain, A., Tompson, J., Pishchulin, L., Andriluka, M., Bregler, C., Schiele, B., Theobalt, C.: Marconi-convnet-based marker-less motion capture in outdoor and indoor scenes. IEEE Trans. Pattern Anal. Mach. Intell. **39**(3), 501–514 (2016)
8. Jain, H., Harit, G.: A framework to assess sun salutation videos. In: Proceedings of ICVGIP (2016)
9. Kanazawa, A., Black, M.J., Jacobs, D.W., Malik, J.: End-to-end recovery of human shape and pose. In: Computer Vision and Pattern Recognition (CVPR) (2018)
10. Kien, H.K., Hung, N.K., Chau, M.T., Duyen, N.T., Thanh, N.X.: Single view image Based— 3d human pose reconstruction. In: Proceedings of Knowledge and Systems Engineering. IEEE, Piscataway (2017)

11. Mehta, D., Sridhar, S., Sotnychenko, O., Rhodin, H., Shafiei, M., Seidel, H.P., Xu, W., Casas, D., Theobalt, C.: Vnect: Real-time 3d human pose estimation with a single RGB camera. ACM Trans. Graph. **36**, 1–14 (2017)
12. Pons-Moll, G., Baak, A., Helten, T., Muller, M., Seidel, H.P., Rosenhahn, B.: Multisensor-fusion for 3d full-body human motion capture. In: Proceedings of CVPR, pp. 663–670. IEEE, Piscataway (2010)
13. Pons-Moll, G., Baak, A., Gall, J., Leal-Taixe, L., Mueller, M., Seidel, H.P., Rosenhahn, B.: Outdoor human motion capture using inverse kinematics and von Mises-Fisher sampling. In: Proceedings of ICCV, pp. 1243–1250. IEEE, Piscataway (2011)
14. Radwan, I., Dhall, A., Goecke, R.: Monocular image 3d human pose estimation under self-occlusion. In: Proceedings of ICCV, pp. 1888–1895. IEEE, Piscataway (2013)
15. Sarafianos, N., Boteanub, B., Ionescub, B., Kakadiarisa, I.A.: 3d human pose estimation: a review of the literature and analysis of covariates. Comput. Vis. Image Underst. **152**, 1–20 (2016)
16. Simo-Serra, E., Quattoni, A., Torras, C., Moreno-Noguer, F.: A joint model for 2d and 3d pose estimation from a single image. In: Proceedings of CVPR, pp. 3634–3641. IEEE, Piscataway (2013)
17. Tekin, B., Rozantsev, A., Lepetit, V., Fua, P.: Direct prediction of 3d body poses from motion compensated sequences. In: Proceedings of CVPR, pp. 991–1000. IEEE, Piscataway (2016)
18. von Marcard, T., Pons-Moll, G., Rosenhahn, B.: Human pose estimation from video and IMUs. IEEE Trans. Pattern Anal. Mach. Intell. **38**(8), 1533–1547 (2016)
19. Wang, C., Wang, Y., Lin, Z., Yuille, A.: Robust 3d human pose estimation from single images or video sequences. IEEE Trans. Pattern Anal. Mach. Intell. (2018). https://doi.org/10.1109/TPAMI.2018.2828427
20. Zhou, X., Zhu, M., Leonardos, S., Derpanis, K., Daniilidis, K.: Sparseness meets deepness: 3d human pose estimation from monocular video. In: Proceedings of CVPR. IEEE, Piscataway (2016)

IHIRD: A Data Set for Indian Heritage Image Retrieval

Dipannita Podder, M. A. Shashaank, Jayanta Mukherjee, and Shamik Sural

Abstract Computational approaches are extensively applied to preserve heritage artifacts. Archival of heritage assets is one of its primary focuses, accounting for the ease of accessibility of digital information. To develop an efficient and reliable archival-and-retrieval system of heritage images, it is necessary to have an extensive data set of heritage artifacts, which consists of various kinds of monuments in their digital representation. In this chapter, we develop an image data set, specifically on Indian heritage monuments, called *Indian Heritage Image Retrieval Data set* (IHIRD), and test it on several retrieval methods. Images of various heritage monuments, like sculptures and paintings, are the elements of this data set. We experimentally evaluate various content-based image retrieval (CBIR) and semantically driven CBIR schemes using this data set and report their performances.

Keywords Image retrieval · Indian Heritage Image Data set · Content-based image retrieval · Ontology

1 Introduction

Since the majority of heritage monuments have been exhibited in outdoor galleries for hundreds of years, they suffer from unavoidable physical damage due to natural and human activities. To preserve the remnants of those artifacts that depict our past, continuous monitoring and maintenance is required. Digital archiving of heritage images is one of the most significant efforts toward this. Various systems have already been proposed to archive images related to cultural heritage. Particularly

D. Podder (✉) · M. A. Shashaank
Advanced Technology Development Center, Indian Institute of Technology, Kharagpur, Kharagpur, India

J. Mukherjee · S. Sural
Computer Science and Engineering, Indian Institute of Technology, Kharagpur, Kharagpur, India

© Springer Nature Switzerland AG 2021
J. Mukhopadhyay et al. (eds.), *Digital Techniques for Heritage Presentation and Preservation*, https://doi.org/10.1007/978-3-030-57907-4_4

in a country like India, the diverse cultural and geographical as well as dynamic historical events have influenced the creation of various artistic styles and forms, such as monuments, mural paintings, dance, music, etc. The study of these ancient artworks helps us understand the history of civilization. Under the initiative of the Government of India, a data bank of Indian art and culture, called Kalasampada,[1] has been developed. This project aims at disseminating different cultural resources. It also includes several walk-throughs of selected archeological monuments and sites like Brihadeshwara Temple (Thanjavur, Tamil Nadu), Humayun's Tomb (New Delhi), Khajuraho (Madhya Pradesh), etc. A classical dance retrieval system, called *Nrityakosha*, has been described in [21]. This system provides an annotation tool for digitized dance artifacts. Mallik et al. [22] archived the mural paintings of India. They matched the mural images semantically with the help of their narrative text segments along with features and patterns of the paintings. A domain ontology guides the semantic matching. A mobile vision app was developed at IIIT Hyderabad to retrieve information given the query image of a heritage object. However, it is currently applicable to only Golkonda Fort and the temples of Hampi [27]. This app also provides an image-based GPS (Pseudo-GPS) tool for helping visitors of those heritage sites. In [12], the abstract patterns in images of Indian monuments are discovered, and images of tombs, forts, mosques, etc., are categorized. The convolutional neural network is used to classify the images with the help of domain ontology.

Currently, several groups of researchers are working on digital preservation, restoration, and archiving of heritage images using different computational approaches. Experiments on such systems require a proper data set to validate and assess their performance. For this purpose, many of them use internal and local data sets, most of which are not publicly available. An image data set is presented in [10] for evaluating heritage image processing algorithms (such as texture classification, 3D reconstruction, content-based image retrieval, and image inpainting). This data set includes images of different temples in Bishnupur[2] (i.e., Rasmancha, Kalachand, Shyamrai, Madan Mohan, Jor Bangla, Radha Madhav, and Nandalal). Since all the temples of Bishnupur are made of terracotta, the texture and carving style of monuments are almost of similar rendering. The carving style, cultural aspects, and aesthetics of artworks of monuments pertaining to different locations and eras are known to vary widely. However, such diversity is not addressed in this data set.

In this chapter, we present a heritage image database for image retrieval systems, which consists of images of several monuments from different eras and geographically distributed locations. The locations of these monuments are dispersed in heritage sites of Karnataka, Andhra Pradesh, and West Bengal in India. The architectural styles in each of these temples are different because of the regional influence in evolution of culture. The data set captures the variations in architectural

---

[1]http://www.ignca.nic.in/dlrich.html.

[2]http://www.asikolkata.in/bankura.aspx.

Fig. 1 Examples of different architectural styles. (**a**) Chala style architecture (Jor Bangla temple). (**b**) Vijayanagara architecture (Gopura of Krishna temple). (**c**) Hoysala architecture (Chennakesava temple of Beluru)

styles due to their diverse mixtures (Fig. 1). In this data set, each class comprises similar looking images that are visually grouped. The existing state-of-the-art image retrieval data sets, UKB data set [26] and Holidays data set [14], mostly comprise images of the same class that belong to the same place, taken from different viewing angles, under different illumination. In this data set, we include images that belong to the same scene in one class. Also, the images that depict a mythological event with a similar carving style are considered a class. The concepts related to the images are also tagged in the metadata.

We perform content-based image retrieval (CBIR) on this data set with diverse architectural style and exhaustive metadata. A CBIR system has three important tasks, namely, feature extraction, indexing of the database, and computing similarity among representative feature vectors. Selection of an appropriate combination of feature extraction techniques and distance functions for computing similarity is of paramount importance. The local feature extraction techniques, such as Scale-Invariant Feature Transform (SIFT) [20], Affine Scale-Invariant Feature Transform (ASIFT) [25], Histogram of Oriented Gradients (HoG) [7], Speeded-Up Robust Features (SURF) [5], etc., are used in object-based image retrieval problems. The statistics of these generated descriptors are aggregated to represent an image in a compact feature vector of finite dimension. The Bag of Visual Words (BoVW) representation [31], Fisher Vector Encoding (FV) [28, 29], and Vector of Locally Aggregated Descriptor (VLAD) [1, 15, 17] are some of the widely used state-of-the-art techniques of feature representation. However, the size of residual vector of FV and VLAD is sufficiently large. These high-dimensional feature vectors are compressed into a manageable length using the product quantization method [16], hashing-based feature compression [18, 32], etc. The encoded feature vector of a query image is matched with the pre-estimated feature vectors of archived images. Euclidean distance, weighted Euclidean distance, Manhattan distance, etc., are used to estimate the difference between features of a query image from the images of the search space [9]. The work reported in [9] used an ANN classifier to compute similarity measures. The ANN classifier classifies the feature vectors into one or more classes. Recently, convolutional neural networks (CNNs) have been used in CBIR algorithms to encode the rich semantics of images into a compact global image descriptor [2, 34]. Although pre-trained networks are used in CBIR, transfer learning and domain adaptation are adopted by some CNN models on training sets [4]. Some CBIR algorithms, based on deep learning, encode input images of different sizes and aspect ratios [3, 33]. The methods proposed in [2, 11] address the lack of geometric invariance of CNN features. In [6], an image is decomposed into semantic regions before being processed by the CBIR algorithm by using deep feature factorization.

We propose a probabilistic approach to select the appropriate combination instead of using the popular image retrieval performance metrics, such as MAP, F-Score, etc. The Bag of Visual Words (BoVW) [31] and Vector of Locally Aggregated Descriptor (VLAD) [1] feature representation techniques are used to describe the content of an image. Experiments are performed to determine the best of these two image representations for heritage images. However, the CBIR analyzes the visual content but cannot understand the conceptual entity of a query image. For example, only the sculptures with a similar carving style can be retrieved for the query image *Ganesha*. The entity *Ganesha* cannot be understood by the CBIR system, which may lead to users' needs not being met. To fill this gap, we augmented domain ontology in the CBIR system and provided more relevant results to users.

This chapter is organized as follows. The heritage sites of the monuments from where digital images are captured are briefly described in Sect. 2. Creation of ground truth data is described in Sect. 3. In Sect. 4, we describe the methodology for implementing CBIR for this data set. The experimental results are discussed in Sect. 5. Finally, we conclude in Sect. 6.

2   Description of the Data Set

Our data set includes images from several heritage sites in West Bengal (Bishnupur and Murshidabad), Karnataka (Halebidu, Hampi, Beluru, Somanathapura, Shivamogga, Ikkeri, Hosagunda, Doddagaddavalli, and Kaidala), and Andhra Pradesh (Surabheswara Kona). These places are acknowledged as UNESCO World Heritage Sites. Various historical and mythological stories are depicted on the walls and pillars of the monuments of these places (Fig. 2). We capture the images using two

| (a) | (b) | (c) |

Fig. 2 Different kinds of depictions in the temples of Hampi. (**a**) Hazara Rama temple. (**b**) Vitthala temple. (**c**) Mahanavami Dibba

high-resolution digital SLR cameras of resolution 10M pixels and 18M pixels in natural daylight. The size of the image files in the data set ranges from 300 KB to 15 MB.

Among various heritage sites, Hampi and Bishnupur have many temples. Most of the temples are dedicated to different avatars of Vishnu, and these characters are carved in these locations. Various granite sculptures are found in the temples that follow the Vijayanagara architecture. This reveals long-established expertise in rock-cutting techniques. In contrast, the temples of Bishnupur are made of terracotta. In Hampi, pyramidal gateways, called Gopuras [24], exist at the entrances of these temples. Another signature of the Vijayanagara architectural pattern, brave Yali, is observed in the temples of Hampi. A brief summary of the monuments that are considered in our data set is given in Table 1.

Table 1 Brief description of some of the monuments included in our data set

Monument sites		Highlights
Hampi	Achyutaraya temple	Temple dedicated to Tiruvengalanatha, an avatar of Vishnu.
	Chandikeshwara temple	Vishnu's temple with richly carved pillars. Decorated by series of carvings of Yalis.
	Hazara Rama temple	Illustrates mythological events related to Ramayana. Many courtly and ceremonial structures are present.
	Krishna temple	Temple dedicated to Bala Krishna, near the main market of Hampi.
	Lakshmi Narasimha temple	Giant monoliths of Ugra-Narasimha statue.
	Mahanavami Dibba	Celebrated chamber. Consists of elements like procession of animals, joy of people, marching soldiers, etc.
	Sasivekalu and Kadlekalu Ganesha	Two giant monoliths of Ganesha.
	Viroopaksha temple	Dedicated to Shiva, where several deities are still being worshipped.
	Vishnu temple	Near the complex of Vitthala temple. One of the prominent structures.
	Vitthala temple	Houses the iconic stone chariot and musical pillars.
Keladi and Ikkeri	Rameshwara, Veerabhadra, and Aghoreshwara temples	Hoysala–Dravida architecture that was refined by Nayaka rulers.

(continued)

Table 1 (continued)

Monument sites		Highlights
Shravanabelagola	Bahubali Gomateshwara temple	One of the largest monolithic statues of Bahubali. Temple complex is a blend of Hindu and Jain cultures.
Beluru	Channakeshava temple	Fascinating sculptures and carvings of Hoysala–Chalukya styles. Dedicated to Channakeshava, an avatar of Vishnu.
Somanathapura	Chennakesava temple	Typical Hoysala architecture, without much damage. Dedicated to Channakeshava.
Chitradurga	Chitradurga fort	One of the few Indian forts that has never been conquered.
Halebidu	Hoysaleswara temple	Delicate carvings on walls depict scenes of mythology and art. Structures are made from soapstone in Hoysala architecture.
Doddagaddavalli	Lakshmi Devi temple	The deities are built in the architectural styles of Hoysala. Deities are still being worshipped.
Shivamogga	Shivappa Nayaka palace	Several temples are dispersed throughout the district. Many sculptures and monuments arranged in the city's museum.
Hosagunda	Uma Maheshwara temple	The architecture is built in Chalukya styles. Recently excavated. One of the dispersed temples in Shivamogga.
Bishnupur	Jor Bangla temple	Classic Chala style of architecture [23]. Richly ornamented with terracotta carvings.
	Lalji temple	Built in Ekaranta style with decorations on low-relief carvings [23].
	Rasamancha	An unusual elongated pyramidal structure made of bricks over altar of laterite stones.
	Madan Mohan temple	Chala style architecture. Carvings on the walls depict scenes from Ramayana, Mahabharata, and Puranas.
	Shyamarai temple	Richly decorated with carvings of terracotta that feature many aspects of Krishna leela.
Murshidabad	Palaces and religious complexes	A cluster of palaces, temples, mosques, and churches, which are a blend of various religions and administrations over the years.
Giddalur	Surabheswara Kona	Icons of various deities carved on granite stone.

3   Data Set Preparation

The heritage data set consists of images of different heritage objects. The images are taken from multiple viewing directions under different illumination. We have primarily considered the following two aspects for ground truth preparation: (1) grouping images of the same scenes and (2) grouping images that depict the same mythological object/story with similar carving styles. The ground truth is created with careful manual supervision considering these aspects. Some examples of the

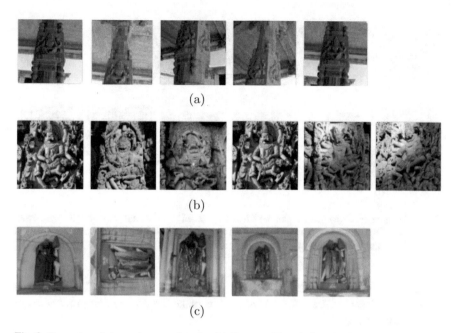

Fig. 3 Examples of classes in ground truths. (**a**) Concept: **Narasimha**. (**b**) Concept: **Narasimha**. (**c**) Concept: **Hanuman-Gandhamadana Parvat**

class consisting of similar images are shown in Fig. 3. Two differently carved *Narasimha* are shown in Fig. 3a and b. The first class consists of images of the same scene, which are taken from different viewing angles. In this image, the sculpture of the mythological character *Narasimha* is depicted. The images that are displayed in Fig. 3b do not belong to the same scene, but sculptures of *Narasimha* are present with similar carving style in these scenes. All of these images are captured from different parts of Hoysaleswara temple at Halebidu, Karnataka. Since the images are taken from the same temple, their carving style is quite similar.

From a pool of 2060 images, we group 1102 images into 237 different classes. Each class describes a theme that consists of several images that are taken from different viewing directions and at varying illumination. Some of the images in the data set are tilted/ rotated at the time of image capturing with respect to similar sets of other images. Every class has a specifically reserved query image in which the object of interest is clearly visible. The theme of each class is also mentioned in its respective ground truth. The proposed data set is available at http://www.facweb.iitkgp.ac.in/~jay/ihird/index.html. The flow of annotation of the data set is discussed below.

Step 1: Grouping Images of the Same Theme of a Specific Monument
In this step, all the visually similar images belonging to a specific monument are grouped together. At first, we select a monument, and then the visually similar images of an object or the images that capture the same scene and theme are grouped

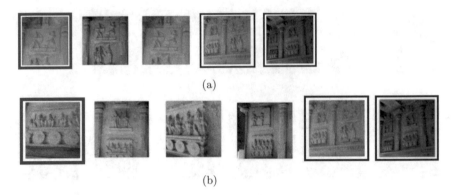

Fig. 4 The images of (**a**) *Class a* and (**b**) *Class b* are taken from Vitthala temple. The representative images of the classes are marked in blue, and the images that belong to both classes are marked in red. The red marked images share the same theme

together. Each group of similar images is referred to as a class. These selected images are discarded from the image pool to make the elimination process easier at each iteration.

Step 2: Combining Similar Images That Belong to Different Classes
In this data set, more than one object and mythological story is depicted on an image. In the previous step, we group the images according to the similarity of theme and remove them from the image pool. On account of this, the images that illustrate two or more themes are included in one of the candidate classes and are excluded from other candidates. In Fig. 4, an example is shown where two different classes are associated with similar images. The similar image pairs that fall into different classes are marked in the figure for reference. So, for every class k, we have displayed images of the other classes and select the images that share the similar themes of k. These selected images are also included in the class k.

Step 3: Include Unassigned Images in Respective Classes
As a consequence of the initial steps, similar images of a single image I may be grouped under different classes, and they are removed from the image pool. Also in the second step, only the images of different classes are considered. In this situation, the image I may be left isolated in the image pool. For example, in Fig. 5, such a case is shown. All visually similar images of such an isolated image (marked in red in Fig. 5) are already included in other classes. Hence, it has no similar image in the image pool. It is also observed that the carving style of some of the objects may resemble entirely different monuments. Such images are ignored due to the grouping by artifacts of monuments. For example, in Fig. 6, the left-most image does not belong to the same type of monuments as the others. Thus, it was ignored in a common group in the first phase in spite of being visually similar. In this latter phase, it is included in the common class. In this phase, such isolated unassigned images of the database are assigned to their appropriate classes. The isolated image

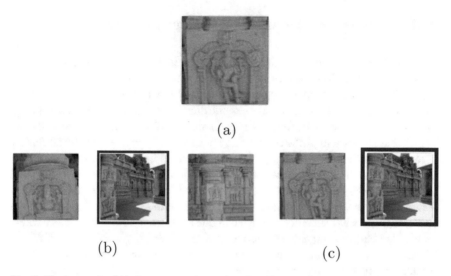

(a)

(b)   (c)

Fig. 5 The image should belong to two classes, but class *B* cannot be constructed in the first two steps, because the image is removed from the image pool after creation of class *A*. (**a**) The common image that should belong to class *A* and class *B*. (**b**) Class *A*. (**c**) Class *B*

Fig. 6 Same concept is depicted in the images where the carving style of objects (i.e., Ram, Lakshmana, Hanuman) is the same. But they belong to different monuments

and its visually similar images (which were previously included in other classes) are listed together to create a new class. If the class was formerly created, then those images are included in that respective class.

We briefly summarize three steps of annotation as follows (1) The visually similar images of any specific monument are grouped together to create several sets of similar images. Each set of similar images is referred to as a class. The images that are grouped together in each iteration are removed from the image pool. (2) The images that share two or more depictions are included in respective classes irrespective of monument. (3) The isolated images, similar images of which are already grouped into other classes, are included in those classes. Such images are assigned to their respective classes, if the classes containing similar images to that image are present; otherwise, new classes are created to accommodate them.

4 Development of Content-Based Image Retrieval System

A CBIR system has various components, such as feature extraction, indexing, and the search. The performance of the system depends on choosing the appropriate feature representation, indexing scheme, and distance functions for measuring similarity of images in the domain of application. In this section, the methodology for implementing the CBIR for a heritage database is discussed. An object is carved in different stones with different carving styles at heritage sites. The local feature descriptors are found to be appropriate to represent an image of these objects.

At first, the 64-dimensional scale and rotation-invariant Speeded-Up Robust Features (SURF) extraction technique [5] is used to detect and describe the local features of the image. These SURF descriptors of all the images in the database are clustered using a K-means clustering technique to generate visual vocabulary where each of the cluster centers is referred to as a visual word. We use the BOVW and VLAD feature representation techniques to encode the image content. The extracted feature vectors of each image are mapped to the nearest cluster center or visual word. The count of all the feature vectors that are assigned to each visual word is noted. This histogram representation of a feature vector of every image with respect to the visual words is referred to as the BoVW [31] representation. But the difference between the cluster center and its corresponding feature vectors is accumulated to derive the VLAD representation [1]. There are various distance functions used to compute similarity between a pair of feature vectors. For example, Euclidean distance, Weighted Euclidean distance, Manhattan distance, and Cross-correlation distance are used for the multi-dimensional feature vector, whereas Histogram Intersection, Histogram Euclidean distance, and Histogram quadratic distance are preferred for the histogram-based feature vector [9]. Since Manhattan distance and Euclidean distance are found to be appropriate for BoVW and VLAD feature representation [1], their approximate distances are also used in this study to explore their usefulness in CBIR. An appropriate combination of feature representation and distance function is essential for an effective CBIR system.

Usually, the performance of a retrieval system is measured by the ROC curve, top precision measure [35], etc. Choice of query images in experimental trials of retrieval affects the evaluation. Moreover, the evaluation process becomes computationally expensive and time consuming due to the exhaustive experimentation. In this chapter, a query-independent probabilistic approach is proposed to evaluate the performance of a CBIR system. Subsequently, using this evaluation a combination of feature representation and distance function for the heritage image data set has been chosen. This is discussed in Sect. 4.1. After choosing the appropriate feature vector and distance function, we index the image database using the state-of-the-art Locality Sensitive Hashing [8], which is discussed in Sect. 4.2. The domain ontology is incorporated with CBIR to reduce the semantic gap in search. This methodology is discussed in Sect. 4.3.

4.1 Selection of Feature Descriptor and Distance Function

Let us assume that there are N images in the database (D). The distances between $\binom{N}{2}$ image pairs are computed, and the image pairs are categorized as similar and dissimilar. The computed distances between image pairs are included in the similar set ω_s and the dissimilar set ω_{ds} depending on the category. Errors arise when the distances between the image pairs belonging to the similar class are assigned to the dissimilar class and vice versa. The main objective here is to select the combination of a feature vector representation and distance function for which the probability of error is the least. This is computed by observing the probability density functions (PDF) of similar and dissimilar distance values.

The class conditional probability distribution functions (PDFs) of ω_s and ω_{ds} are modeled with the Generalized Extreme Value (GEV) distribution [13]. The GEV distribution is extremely versatile to model data as it combines μ (location), σ (scale), and ξ (shape) of a distribution. An example of modeling data using the GEV distribution is shown in Fig. 7. These parameters are computed from the data using Probability Weighted Moment (PWM). It is claimed that PWM-based estimators perform better than a classical maximum likelihood estimation (MLE) for a small number of samples [19]. At first, we determine $P(x|\omega_s)$ and $P(x|\omega_{ds})$ from data using GEV distribution. The probability of error is given by the following equation:

$$
\begin{aligned}
P(E_\tau) &= P(x \in \omega_s | \omega_{ds}) + P(x \in \omega_{ds} | \omega_s) \\
&= P(\omega_{ds}) \int_{\omega_s} P(x|\omega_{ds})\,dx + P(\omega_s) \int_{\omega_{ds}} P(x|\omega_s)\,dx \\
&= P(\omega_{ds}) \int_{min(x)}^{\tau} P(x|\omega_{ds})\,dx + P(\omega_s) \int_{\tau}^{max(x)} P(x|\omega_s)\,dx
\end{aligned}
\tag{1}
$$

In this method, the point where $P(\omega_{ds})P(x|\omega_{ds}) \geq P(\omega_s)P(x|\omega_s)$ is considered as the decision boundary for the similar and dissimilar classes. It is marked

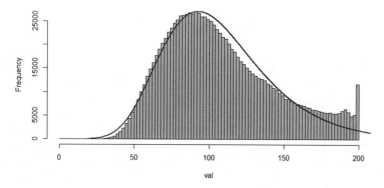

Fig. 7 Data modeling using GEV distribution

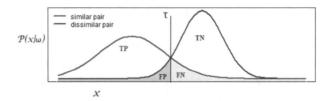

Fig. 8 Illustration of probability of error for class conditional probability density function

---

Algorithm 1 Algorithm of Calculating the Probability of Error

---

Require: N images in the database (D).
Ensure: Error
1: Compute distances for total $\binom{N}{2}$ image pairs
2: Create set with similar distance values ω_s and dissimilar distance values ω_{ds}
3: Estimate mean μ_s, μ_d standard deviation σ_s, σ_d and skewness ξ_s, ξ_d of similar and dissimilar distance values using Probability Weighted Moments
4: Model class conditional PDFs of similar and dissimilar distance values with GEV distribution

$$P\left(x|\omega_s\right) = f(x) = \exp\left(-\left[1 + \xi_s\left(\frac{x-\mu_s}{\sigma_s}\right)\right]^{-\frac{1}{\xi_s}}\right)$$

$$P\left(x|\omega_{ds}\right) = g(x) = \exp\left(-\left[1 + \xi_d\left(\frac{x-\mu_d}{\sigma}\right)\right]^{-\frac{1}{\xi_d}}\right)$$

5: Compute intersecting point of $f(x)$ and $g(x)$ as τ
6: $\tau = $ minimum value of x where $P(\omega_{ds})P\left(x|\omega_{ds}\right) \geq P(\omega_s)P\left(x|\omega_s\right)$
7: $p(E_\tau) = P(\omega_{ds})\int_{min(x)}^{\tau} P\left(x|\omega_{ds}\right)dx + P(\omega_s)\int_{\tau}^{max(x)} P\left(x|\omega_s\right)dx$

---

with a black line in Fig. 8 and mentioned as τ. Also, the PDF of similar and the PDF of dissimilar image pairs are shown with red and blue lines, respectively, and the area that represents $p(E_\tau)$ is marked in yellow. The main objective of this method is to reduce the $p(E_\tau)$, which leads to improvement of precision. The algorithm for calculating the probability of error is presented in Algorithm 1. The combination of feature representation technique and distance function with minimum $P(E_\tau)$ is chosen.

4.2 Indexing of the Image Database

Since the retrieval of similar images by comparing all the images in the database with a query image is computationally expensive, we adopt the state-of-the-art Locality Sensitive Hashing (LSH) [8] to index the image database. In this approach, the high-dimensional image vectors are projected onto a scalar line and the hash index of the image is prepared. The usefulness of this technique is in putting the similar high-dimensional vector into the same bucket. To generate a hash table, the multi-dimensional data points are projected onto a scalar line using the following equation:

$$h^{v,b}(\overrightarrow{x}) = \left\lfloor \frac{\overrightarrow{x} \cdot \overrightarrow{v} + b}{w} \right\rfloor. \tag{2}$$

In this equation, w is the width of each quantization bin, $\overrightarrow{x}$ is the high-dimensional data point, $\overrightarrow{v}$ is a randomly selected vector from a Gaussian distribution, and b is a random variable uniformly distributed between 0 and w. We construct multiple hash tables to increase the chance that the query image can be hashed in the same bucket of closer points. The hash index of a feature vector of an image from the database is stored. The feature vector of the query image is projected with the hash function, and the image is hashed onto the bucket of these hash tables. All the corresponding images of those buckets, on which the query image is hashed, are fetched. Finally, distance is computed between the query image and the images that are fetched from hash tables. The experiments are performed by varying the size of bucket width and number of hash tables to find the optimal parameters for the given data set, and the optimal parameters that are decided from experimentation are shown in Table 2. The steps of implemented CBIR with indexing are shown in Fig. 9.

Table 2 Parameters used for implementation of Locality Sensitive Hashing

Success probability	0.95
Number of projections	1
Width of hash table (bucket width)	5
Number of hash tables	10

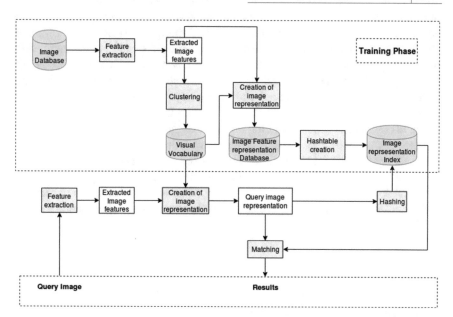

Fig. 9 Content-based image retrieval system with index structure

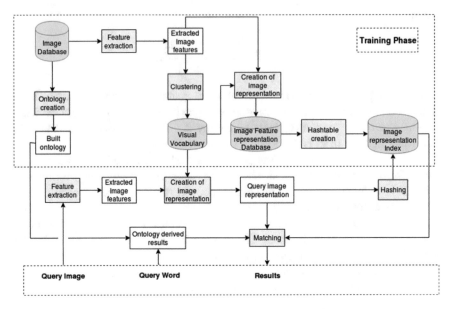

Fig. 10 Ontology-driven content-based image retrieval system with index structure

4.3   Ontology-Driven Content-Based Image Search

Since the machine-driven image features cannot interpret the concept of the query image, a semantic gap is created between query and retrieved images. We use the domain ontology to incorporate the concept of the query in the search. Various Hindu mythological stories and characters are depicted on the monuments' walls of the images that are included in the data set. We use the ontology of Hindu mythology [30][3] to include these concepts in the search. In the first phase of this retrieval, the ontology is explored with query keywords to find the semantically related instances. After that, the image database is searched with the semantic keywords by matching them with the metadata of the image. Image feature vector representation of the query image is generated with the pretrained visual vocabulary. Then, the system hashes the feature vector of the query image into the generated hash tables. The probable visually similar images are fetched from the hash tables. The final content matching is performed only with the contextually similar images among the fetched images. Figure 10 shows the workflow of the ontology-driven CBIR.

---

[3] As a typical case study.

5 Experimental Results

We performed several experiments to retrieve the most relevant images for a query. These experimental results are presented in this section. The mean average precision (MAP) [35] is used to evaluate the retrieval system. In this work, we find the number of relevant images that are retrieved at top-k position. The precision is measured as the ratio of relevant retrieved documents to all the retrieved images. However, it cannot check how many relevant documents are retrieved by the algorithm. This precision method underrates the performance when the number of relevant images is less and the value of k is high. We consider the ratio of the number of relevant retrieved images to the total number of relevant images in the database, if the number of relevant images in the database is less than the number of retrieved images. The precision is calculated by excluding the query image from the retrieved results, and the total number of retrieved results ranges from 1 to 10. The precision, P_k, is obtained as of the kth query image:

$$P_k = \frac{|I_t \cap I_v|}{min(|I_t|, |I_v|)},$$ (3)

where P_k is refers to precision up to kth retrieved result, and $\{I_t\}$ and $\{I_v\}$ are the set of retrieved results and relevant results of the query. The precision is calculated by excluding the query image from the retrieved results. The average precision (AP_i) for ith query is calculated with Eq. (4), where N_r is the number of retrieved images:

$$AP_i = \frac{\sum_{k=1}^{N_r} P_k}{N_r}.$$ (4)

The MAP for N_t query images is given by Eq. (5):

$$MAP = \frac{\sum_{i=1}^{N_t} AP_i}{N_t}.$$ (5)

An appropriate feature vector and a distance function are required for a good CBIR. We use the proposed probabilistic method for the selection along with the Mean Average Precision. In this experiment the size of vocabulary for VLAD vector representation is taken to be 64, 128, 256, and 512, whereas the size of vocabulary is taken to be 1000, 2000, 5000, and 10,000 for BoVW. The experimental results are shown in Tables 3 and 4. Pearson's correlation coefficient is calculated between probability of error and MAP, and we observe that the value of the correlation

Table 3 Results for VLAD feature representation of heritage data set

Vocabulary size	Performance metric	Distance metric				
		L1 norm	L2 norm	WtD	CWD	WtCWD
64	MAP	0.526	0.55	0.535	0.548	0.55
	Error rate	0.4608	0.4503	0.4745	0.4835	0.4586
128	MAP	0.5	0.561	0.509	0.557	0.562
	Error rate	0.4816	0.4345	0.4916	0.4986	0.4317
256	MAP	0.397	0.583	0.45	0.554	0.578
	Error rate	0.5312	0.3753	0.4998	0.5216	0.433
512	MAP	0.27	**0.608**	0.382	0.576	**0.601**
	Error rate	0.609	**0.354**	0.4892	0.4937	**0.4297**

Table 4 Results for BoVW feature representation of heritage data set

Vocabulary size	Performance metric	Distance metric				
		L1 norm	L2 norm	WtD	CWD	WtCWD
1000	MAP	0.434	0.299	0.26	0.326	0.311
	Error rate	0.7321	0.8696	0.8608	0.8625	0.8657
2000	MAP	0.455	0.273	0.187	0.329	0.293
	Error rate	0.7218	0.91	0.8866	0.9023	0.9066
5000	MAP	0.499	0.229	0.115	0.289	0.25
	Error rate	0.6881	0.9188	0.8813	0.9325	0.9238
10,000	MAP	0.524	0.164	0.077	0.27	0.201
	Error rate	0.636	0.9097	0.8743	0.9374	0.9188

coefficient is -0.848. High negative correlation validates the fact that obtained MAP is higher with the lower probability of error. However, it is also observed from the experimental results that VLAD works well with L_2-norm and $WtCWD$. This combination increases MAP while decreasing the probability of error. In Table 3, the best possible combinations are marked in bold for the heritage data set. We choose VLAD feature representation technique and L_2-norm for further experimentation.

As discussed in Sect. 4.2, the optimal bucket size and number of hash tables should be selected for better precision with lower computation time. The experimental results for finding the optimal parameters are shown in this section. Since the high-dimensional points are projected onto a scalar line with a randomly generated Gaussian vector, the results may vary. To address this issue, we performed 50 iterations and took the optimal parameter, previously mentioned in Table 2, to hash the feature vectors. We achieve good MAP in less time by pruning a sufficient number of dissimilar images with these parameters. All the iterations and the mean and standard deviation of the results are tabulated in Tables 5, 6, and 7. It is observed that MAP and average retrieval time both rise with increasing number of hash tables. In Table 8, the best retrieval performance among the 50 iterations is tabulated. Some

Table 5 Observed MAP value with respect to change of hash tables and bin width

# hash tables	Bin width			
	5	10	15	20
5	0.212 ± 0.020	0.275 ± 0.0215	0.322 ± 0.0231	0.334 ± 0.016
10	0.315 ± 0.021	0.364 ± 0.0128	0.462 ± 0.0155	0.501 ± 0.013
15	0.328 ± 0.0154	0.467 ± 0.017	0.504 ± 0.0104	0.526 ± 0.017

Table 6 Variation of search space with respect to change of hash tables and bin width

# hash tables	Bin width			
	5	10	15	20
5	521 ± 70.57	704 ± 79	917 ± 81.14	895 ± 48.71
10	846 ± 81.28	975 ± 53.71	1376 ± 49.57	1556 ± 55.71
15	876 ± 57.85	1424 ± 67	1536 ± 45.71	1768 ± 42.14

Table 7 Average retrieval time (in ms) for change in hash tables and bin width

# hash tables	Bin width			
	5	10	15	20
5	223.63 ± 4.21	206.75 ± 3.23	257.38 ± 8.52	227.85 ± 4.677
10	320.68 ± 10.5	320.68 ± 7.72	421.94 ± 10.74	472.57 ± 4.29
15	1991.56 ± 62.441	1772.15 ± 93.544	1717.3 ± 99.03	2021.1 ± 56.59

Table 8 Experimental results for finding an optimal parameter to implement the LSH

# hash tables	Examined parameters	Bin width			
		5	10	15	20
5	MAP	0.478	0.601	0.575	0.565
	Size of search space	1327	1982	1830	1737
	Avg. retrieval time (ms)	0.74	0.757	0.7616	0.748
10	MAP	0.608	0.534	0.601	0.608
	Size of search space	2055	1623	2003	2055
	Avg. retrieval time (ms)	0.803	0.934	0.976	1.063
15	MAP	0.608	0.596	0.594	0.607
	Size of search space	2057	1968	1943	2053
	Avg. retrieval time (ms)	2.71	2.66	2.61	2.83

Fig. 11 Retrieval results of heritage data set

results for heritage image retrieval are shown in Fig. 11. In this example, the left-most image is the query image and the relevant retrieved images are marked in blue.

Only the structural features of images are captured by the CBIR system. But the incorporation of the semantic meaning of the query can help in the search. A two-phase scheme is adapted to retrieve heritage images, which works with both the context and content of images and narrows down the semantic gap in the search space. Since various Hindu mythological stories and characters are depicted on the monuments' walls of the images that are included in the data set, we use the ontology of Hindu mythology [30] (see footnote 3) to include those concepts in the search. In the first phase of retrieval, the ontology is explored with the query keywords. If more than one keyword is given by the user, then for every keyword the related instances are retrieved and the common instance is considered as related data. The ontological similarity, i.e., the length of the shortest path between the queried individual and ontological instances, is computed to find the semantically related words [30]. In this work, the directly connected concepts are considered as semantically similar. The experimental result for choosing the ontological distance threshold is mentioned in Table 9. The system performs best for ontological distance 1. After that, the database is searched with the semantic keywords by matching them with the metadata/tag of the image and creating the new search space for CBIR. In Table 10, the comparison between ontology-driven

Table 9 Performance variation of ontology-driven CBIR

Ontological distance	MAP	Size of search space	Average retrieval time (ms)		
			Time to search in ontology	Image search time	Total search time
1	0.678	194	46.91	11.96	58.87
2	0.669	278	67.63	14.91	82.54
3	0.658	378	94.73	19.4	114.13
4	0.652	505	137.3	25.28	162.58
5	0.647	601	173	30.75	203.75
6	0.646	635	195.29	30.65	225.34
7	0.646	679	200.52	31.72	232.24
8	0.646	684	214	32.93	246.96
9	0.646	686	217.8	32.62	250.42
10	0.646	688	218.64	32.96	251.6

Table 10 Comparison between CBIR and ontology-driven CBIR systems

Search type	MAP	Size of search space	Average retrieval time (ms)
CBIR	0.601	1982	87.64
Ontology-driven CBIR	0.678	194	58.87

CBIR and best performing CBIR technique is presented. The total retrieval time in the ontology-driven CBIR system is calculated by summing up the time taken for ontology graph generation and image search from the pruned set. Some examples of the two retrieval schemes are shown in Fig. 12. Images of *Krishna* and *Rama and Demon with Bow in Chariot* are given as a query by mentioning the concepts. With the help of ontology (driven by concept), the proposed system retrieves images with better ranking and relevance. An ontological query extracts all the properties of existing classes, subclasses, and individuals and delivers the results accordingly. Within this pruned set of images, visually similar images are searched by CBIR algorithm and a similar image set is retrieved.

6   Conclusion

In this chapter, we present an image retrieval data set that consists of images of different heritage monuments in India. We group visually similar images into a class. The images of objects are grouped by their monument types and carving styles. We include images of various monuments from different places in India. A major cluster of the monuments that are included in the data set belongs to Vijayanagara, Hoysala, and Terracotta architecture styles. An appropriate combination of feature representation and distance metric is chosen to perform content-based retrieval of heritage images. A CBIR system is implemented using the selected combination. An attempt to fill the semantic gap between the content and context of query images is made by incorporating an ontology with CBIR to retrieve results satisfactorily in line with users' need.

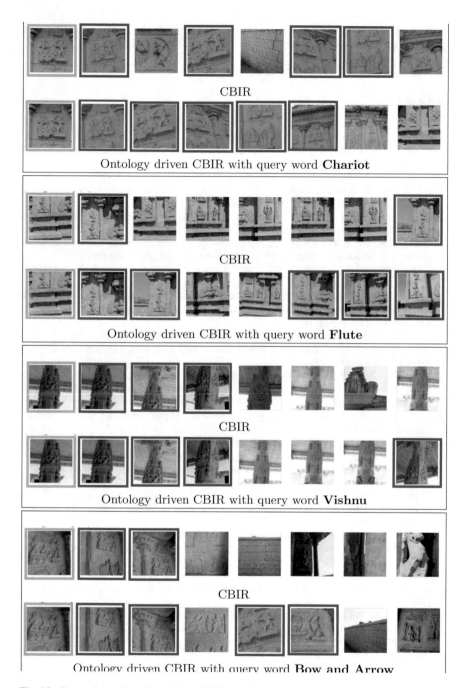

CBIR

Ontology driven CBIR with query word **Chariot**

CBIR

Ontology driven CBIR with query word **Flute**

CBIR

Ontology driven CBIR with query word **Vishnu**

CBIR

Ontology driven CBIR with query word **Bow and Arrow**

Fig. 12 Comparison of ontology-driven CBIR with CBIR

Acknowledgments This work was carried out under the sponsorship of the Department of Science and Technology, Govt. of India, through sanction number NRDMS/11/1586/2009.

References

1. Arandjelovic, R., Zisserman, A.: All about VLAD. In: Proceedings of the 2013 IEEE Conference on Computer Vision and Pattern Recognition, CVPR '13, pp. 1578–1585. IEEE Computer Society, Washington (2013)
2. Arandjelovic, R., Gronat, P., Torii, A., Pajdla, T., Sivic, J.: NetVLAD: CNN architecture for weakly supervised place recognition. In: Proceedings of the IEEE Conference on Computer Vision and Pattern Recognition, pp. 5297–5307 (2016)
3. Babenko, A., Lempitsky, V.: Aggregating deep convolutional features for image retrieval (2015). Preprint, arXiv:1510.07493
4. Babenko, A., Slesarev, A., Chigorin, A., Lempitsky, V.: Neural codes for image retrieval. In: European Conference on Computer Vision, pp. 584–599. Springer, Berlin (2014)
5. Bay, H., Ess, A., Tuytelaars, T., Van Gool, L.: Speeded-up robust features (SURF). Comput. Vis. Image Underst. **110**(3), 346–359 (2008)
6. Collins, E., Süsstrunk, S.: Deep feature factorization for content-based image retrieval and localization. In: 2019 IEEE International Conference on Image Processing (ICIP), pp. 874–878. IEEE, Piscataway (2019)
7. Dalal, N., Triggs, B.: Histograms of oriented gradients for human detection. In: 2005 IEEE Computer Society Conference on Computer Vision and Pattern Recognition (CVPR'05), vol. 1, pp. 886–893, June 2005
8. Datar, M., Immorlica, N., Indyk, P., Mirrokni, V.S.: Locality-sensitive hashing scheme based on p-stable distributions. In: Proceedings of the Twentieth Annual Symposium on Computational Geometry, pp. 253–262. ACM, New York (2004)
9. ElAlami, M.: A new matching strategy for content based image retrieval system. Appl. Soft Comput. **14**, 407–418 (2014)
10. Ghorai, M., Purkait, P., Santra, S., Samanta, S., Chanda, B.: Bishnupur heritage image dataset (BHID): a resource for various computer vision applications. In: Proceedings of the Tenth Indian Conference on Computer Vision, Graphics and Image Processing, pp. 80. ACM, New York (2016)
11. Gong, Y., Wang, L., Guo, R., Lazebnik, S.: Multi-scale orderless pooling of deep convolutional activation features. In: European Conference on Computer Vision, pp. 392–407. Springer, Berlin (2014)
12. Gupta, U., Chaudhury, S.: Deep transfer learning with ontology for image classification. In: 2015 Fifth National Conference on Computer Vision, Pattern Recognition, Image Processing and Graphics (NCVPRIPG), pp. 1–4 (2015)
13. Hosking, J.R., Wallis, J.R., Wood, E.F.: Estimation of the generalized extreme-value distribution by the method of probability-weighted moments. Technometrics **27**(3), 251–261 (1985)
14. Jegou, H., Douze, M., Schmid, C.: Hamming embedding and weak geometric consistency for large scale image search. In: Proceedings of the 10th European Conference on Computer Vision: Part I, ECCV '08, pp. 304–317. Springer, Berlin (2008)
15. Jégou, H., Douze, M., Schmid, C., Pérez, P.: Aggregating local descriptors into a compact image representation. In: 2010 IEEE Computer Society Conference on Computer Vision and Pattern Recognition, pp. 3304–3311, June 2010
16. Jegou, H., Douze, M., Schmid, C.: Product quantization for nearest neighbor search. IEEE Trans. Pattern Anal. Mach. Intell. **33**(1), 117–128 (2011)

17. Jégou, H., Perronnin, F., Douze, M., Sánchez, J., Pérez, P., Schmid, C.: Aggregating local image descriptors into compact codes. IEEE Trans. Pattern Anal. Mach. Intell. **34**(9), 1704–1716 (2012)
18. Jiang, K., Que, Q., Kulis, B.: Revisiting kernelized locality-sensitive hashing for improved large-scale image retrieval. In: 2015 IEEE Conference on Computer Vision and Pattern Recognition (CVPR), pp. 4933–4941, June 2015
19. Kang, S., Song, J.: Parameter and quantile estimation for the generalized Pareto distribution in peaks over threshold framework. J. Korean Stat. Soc. **46**(4), 487–501 (2017)
20. Lowe, D.G.: Distinctive image features from scale-invariant keypoints. Int. J. Comput. Vis. **60**(2), 91–110 (2004)
21. Mallik, A., Chaudhury, S., Ghosh, H.: Nrityakosha: preserving the intangible heritage of Indian classical dance. J. Comput. Cult. Herit. **4**(3), 11 (2011)
22. Mallik, A., Chaudhury, S., Madan, S., Dinesh, T., Chandru, U.V.: Archiving mural paintings using an ontology based approach. In: Asian Conference on Computer Vision, pp. 37–48 (2012)
23. Mangaonkar, P.: Temples of Bengal: material style and technological evolution. In: Chitrolekha International Magazine on Art and Design, pp. 3–17 (2012)
24. Michell, G.: Architecture and Art of Southern India: Vijayanagara and the Successor States 1350-1750, vol. 6. Cambridge University Press, Cambridge (1995)
25. Morel, J.-M., Yu, G.: Asift: a new framework for fully affine invariant image comparison. SIAM J. Imaging Sci. **2**(2), 438–469 (2009)
26. Nister, D., Stewenius, H.: Scalable recognition with a vocabulary tree. In: 2006 IEEE Computer Society Conference on Computer Vision and Pattern Recognition (CVPR'06), vol. 2, pp. 2161–2168 (2006)
27. Panda, J., Sharma, S., Jawahar, C.V.: Heritage app: annotating images on mobile phones. In: Proceedings of the Eighth Indian Conference on Computer Vision, Graphics and Image Processing, ICVGIP '12, pp. 3:1–3:8. ACM, New York (2012)
28. Perronnin, F., Liu, Y., Sánchez, J., Poirier, H.: Large-scale image retrieval with compressed fisher vectors. In: 2010 IEEE Computer Society Conference on Computer Vision and Pattern Recognition, pp. 3384–3391, June 2010
29. Perronnin, F., Sánchez, J., Mensink, T.: Improving the fisher kernel for large-scale image classification. In: Daniilidis, K., Maragos, P., Paragios, N. (eds.) Computer Vision – ECCV 2010, pp. 143–156. Springer, Berlin (2010)
30. Podder, D., Mukherjee, J., Aswatha, S.M., Mukherjee, J., Sural, S.: Ontology-driven content-based retrieval of heritage images. In: Heritage Preservation, pp. 143–160. Springer, Berlin (2018)
31. Sivic, J., Zisserman, A.: Video Google: efficient visual search of videos. In: Ponce, J., Hebert, M., Schmid, C., Zisserman, A. (eds.) Toward Category-Level Object Recognition. Lecture Notes in Computer Science, vol. 4170, pp. 127–144. Springer, Berlin (2006)
32. Tang, J., Li, Z., Wang, M., Zhao, R.: Neighborhood discriminant hashing for large-scale image retrieval. IEEE Trans. Image Process. **24**(9), 2827–2840 (2015)
33. Tolias, G., Sicre, R., Jégou, H.: Particular object retrieval with integral max-pooling of CNN activations (2015). Preprint, arXiv:1511.05879
34. Zheng, L., Yang, Y., Tian, Q.: Sift meets CNN: a decade survey of instance retrieval. IEEE Trans. Pattern Anal. Mach. Intell. **40**(5), 1224–1244 (2017)
35. Zuva, K., Zuva, T.: Evaluation of image retrieval systems. Int. J. Comput. Sci. Inf. Technol. **4**(3), 35–43 (2012)

Object Spotting in Historical Documents

Sugata Das and Sekhar Mandal

Abstract Spotting is finding the location of a particular object without explicitly knowing the entire content in a collection of objects. In this chapter, we consider two types of objects. We consider the word in a document image as an object. Another object is an artifact that is present in terracotta panel images. The proposed object spotting method is based on Wave Kernel Signature (WKS) under the foundation of quantum mechanics. The query image and the document/panel image are smoothened first, and then the Scale Invariant Feature Transform detector is used to obtain the keypoints in both the query image and the document/panel image. Each keypoint is described in terms of WKS. The WKS descriptors represent the average probability of measuring a quantum mechanical particle at a specific location based on quantum energy. In the case of word spotting, a two-step searching technique is introduced to find the region of interest in the document image under test. On the other hand, a single-step searching technique is used to spot figures present in the panel image corresponding to a particular query image. The proposed method is tested on three historical Bangla handwritten datasets and one historical English handwritten dataset, as well as a terracotta panel image dataset. The performance of the proposed method is evaluated using standard metrics.

Keywords Word spotting · Figure spotting · Scale Invariant Feature Transform · Wave Kernel Signature · Histogram of Oriented Gradient · Speeded Up Robust Features

1 Introduction

For a particular time period, any sort of artifact that conveyed some information about history was treated as a historical source. Generally, historical sources are classified into two groups: primary and secondary. A primary source is something

S. Das (✉) · S. Mandal
Indian Institute of Engineering Science and Technology, Shibpur, Howrah, West Bengal, India
e-mail: sekhar@cs.iiests.ac.in

© Springer Nature Switzerland AG 2021
J. Mukhopadhyay et al. (eds.), *Digital Techniques for Heritage Presentation and Preservation*, https://doi.org/10.1007/978-3-030-57907-4_5

that originates from the past. It serves as an original source of information about the topic. It might be a chronicle, a piece of poetry, a document, a painting, a sculpture, an architecture, an instrument, or any tool. A secondary source is built upon the primary sources, e.g., a current physics textbook.

Primary sources can be classified as written and nonwritten sources. Written sources are documents that are written independently in a language or medium. Nonwritten sources are artistic sources (such as architecture, sculpture, and painting), daily objects (such as apparels, tools, and instruments), and photography. In this chapter, we mainly focus on historical Bangla handwritten documents and cultural artifacts (terracotta ornaments).

All over the world, libraries and museums contain a huge number of ancient historical documents. These kinds of documents can be considered as a cultural heritage, as they convey both tangible and intangible cultural aspects. Generally, historical archives include handwritten documents of eminent scientists, writers, and artists, as well as letters or forms of well-known administrators that help reorganize the historical sequences of a particular time period. One of the organizations in India that archives such documents is the Asiatic Society, Kolkata [51], from where we collected the historical Bangla handwritten documents. It archives a large number of handwritten Bangla manuscripts that are related to Bengali mythology. For reliable storage and effective access, preservation of these documents in digital format is necessary [36, 52].

Cultural artifacts reveal details of the socioeconomic conditions, cultural and religious activities of the people, and political and administrative setup of the various rulers and dynasties of a bygone era. The "Jorbangla" (JB) temple and the "Madan Mohan" (MM) temple of Bishnupur in West Bengal (India) are such heritage sites. The "Jorbangla" (JB) temple was built by the Malla king Raghunatha Singha in 1655 AD, and another Malla king Durjan Singha built the "Madan Mohan" (MM) temple in 1694 AD. These temples are made of laterite stone and some of the finest examples of the classical temple architecture of Bengal. The "Jorbangla" (JB) is in the form of a pair of hut-shaped structures with sloping roofs (called "Bengalchala") joined together and surmounted by a "sikhara" or tower on the top. The "Madan Mohan" (MM) is with a single "sikhara" on a curved "Bengalchala" roof. The exterior and interior walls and the ceilings of both the temples depict exquisite and elaborate terracotta ornamentations. These terracotta panels narrate typical scenes from the epics such as Ramayana, Krishnalila, hunting or fighting scenes, and various other depictions of contemporary social life. So, detecting or spotting a character or a pose in the form of a subimage in an image or in a collection of images helps extract semantics and descriptions of such illustrative panels.

Spotting means finding the location of a particular object without explicitly knowing the entire content in a collection of objects. In our work, we consider two objects, one is a word and the other is a cultural artifact/figure. In the context of textual documents, it is known as word spotting. Word spotting is the task of finding the location of keywords in the document without transcribing the document or query word. It is an alternative method of indexing keywords where automatic transcription or annotation is not possible. Generally, historical manuscripts are very degraded in nature due to aging and weathering, faded stroke width, broken strokes, etc., and there is also the hurdle of unconstrained writing style. The performance of the traditional OCR is far from satisfactory for these types of documents. Hence, Manmatha et al. [31] first proposed the word spotting method as an alternative to indexing.

On the other hand, figure spotting is one of the important applications in the field of content-based image retrieval. In the present work, the query image is part of an image stored in the dataset, and it may occur in more than one image and in more than one place in the target image(s). The objective of figure spotting in our case is to spot an item where a query image is provided for searching similar objects from the terracotta panel image.

This chapter focuses mainly on object spotting. Here, object is used to mean either a word image or a figure. In the context of text image, when a query word image is spotted in the document image, it is termed word spotting, and when a query figure is spotted in the panel image, it is termed figure spotting. Here, we use the Wave Kernel Signature as a feature descriptor for object spotting, and a comparative study is done with the other feature descriptor for figure spotting.

2 Related Work

A brief overview of the existing works related to word spotting and figure spotting for historical document image is given below.

2.1 Word Spotting

In the last decade, several word spotting methods have been reported in the literature. All of them have the same objective (i.e., to find the query word within a particular document image). A brief overview of the existing works related to word spotting is given below.

Depending on the layout of the input document image, the word spotting method is divided into two types: *segmentation-based* method and *segmentation-free* method. In the case of segmentation-based word spotting, the input document image is segmented into a collection of lines/words first, and then the word spotting algorithm is applied to the segmented image. On the other hand, the word spotting algorithm is applied directly to an unsegmented document image in the case of the segmentation-free method.

The segmentation-based word spotting method follows a pipeline of binarization, de-noising, and text layout analysis toward line and/or word segmentation. Several researchers [19, 20, 31, 32, 41, 42, 50, 55] follow this pipeline to segment the document image into lines and words for the purpose of word spotting. After segmentation, different structural features or machine-driven features are retrieved from these lines or words toward word spotting.

Rath et al. [41] proposed a word matching algorithm for historical handwritten documents where a projection profile of the word image, word profile, and background-to-ink transition features are obtained for each of the segmented word images. Finally, matching of word images is done by the classical Dynamic Time Warping (DTW) algorithm. Syeda et al. [49] proposed an indexing technique for handwritten document images. Here, handwriting variations are managed by assembling the group of word segments from the interletter spacing. Geometrical hash table is used to find the probable location of similar-shape words in the document image of a query image.

In [50], a word spotting system based on line segmentation, continuous dynamic programming, and Slit Style Histogram of Gradient (SSHOG) feature is reported. DTW is used to find the similarity sequences. The drawback of this system is its high dimensionality, which increases the computational cost.

In [43], the authors proposed a local descriptor for word spotting in handwritten documents. This descriptor is highly similar to the SIFT [29] descriptor. A sliding window is moved over the word to describe the word as a sequence of descriptors. Classification performance is measured using two classifiers (HMM and DTW). Perronnin et al. [44] propose a model-based measure of similarity between vector sequences. Each sequence is mapped to a semicontinuous HMM (SC-HMM), and the similarity between SC-HMMs is computed. Here, each word is represented by a set of vectors, and the method is tested on handwritten documents. Bidirectional Long Short-Term Memory Neural Networks and CTC Token Passing algorithm are presented in [16] for keyword spotting in handwritten documents. This system assumes that all text lines are segmented. A sequence of feature vectors is extracted from each text line, which is the input to the neural network. The features are the same as mentioned in [14]. The abovementioned approaches need proper segmentation of lines, which is very difficult due to the long ascender and descender of a handwritten character.

Segmentation of lines (words) from a handwritten document is a difficult task due to unconstrained writing style (i.e., different intraspace between characters within a word and interspace between words, different spaces between lines, long ascender and descender). Hence, researchers [22, 27, 45, 46, 56, 57] are attracted toward the segmentation-free word spotting model for handwritten documents.

One such method [46] describes a patch-based framework where every patch is described by a bag-of-visual-words (BoW) [11] based on the scale invariant feature descriptor (SIFT) [29], and the patch is refined by the latent semantic indexing technique. Then a voting scheme is used to localize the zone where the query word appears in the document.

The technique proposed in [45] uses bag-of-features Hidden Markov Models (HMMs) for spotting printed Bangla words. The preprocessing like line or word segmentation is not required for this method. Lee et al. [25] proposed a word spotting method using SIFT. The keypoints extracted from the document are stored in the database. The extracted keypoints from the query word are matched with keypoints stored in the database. A clustering of the matching pairs provides the query word in the document.

An omni-lingual word retrieval system for ancient manuscripts is reported in [27]. The system accepts the ASCII string as a query (called a *Query-by-String*) and describes it precisely. Each document is modeled as a combination of an alphabet, a glyph book, and a grammar. The cohesive matching scheme is involved in finding the zone of interest.

A segmentation-free word spotting technique with Exemplar SVMs is reported in [3]. Here, Exemplar SVM is used to produce the query word in an unsupervised way. HOG features are used to describe documents, and a sliding window is moved from left to right to locate the most similar region to the query word.

Zhang et al. [56, 57] proposed a segmentation-free word spotting method based on Heat Kernel Signature (HKS). HKS is used for 3D shape matching as a state-of-the-art feature descriptor [35, 48]. Hust et al. [17] proposed a segmentation-free word spotting method that uses Fourier descriptor. Four different types of key points are detected to identify lines, corners, and blobs. The similarity between the query word and a particular word present in the document is measured using a more relaxed part-based matching technique.

In [47], another segmentation-free keyword spotting technique is proposed for historical documents. This method is based on the bag-of-visual-words model using SIFT descriptors in a patch-based framework. The method follows the *Query-by-Example* paradigm.

Depending on the representative model, word spotting methods can also be categorized as a *learning-free* or *learning-based* method. In the learning-free method, a similarity matching scheme is used to find the instances of the query word without using any training process. On the contrary, if a word spotting method needs to deploy the machine learning technique to train the representative model, then it is termed as learning-based method.

The methods proposed in [19, 20, 31, 41, 42, 45, 46, 50, 55–57] are learning-free word spotting methods. These methods extract necessary features from document images and do the spotting by similarity measure. Labeled data is not required for learning-free methods.

2.2 Figure Spotting

Cultural heritage resources can be broadly classified into two categories, namely, tangible and intangible heritage resources [53]. Buildings, historic places, monuments, and artifacts belong to tangible heritage resources that are considered notable of preservation for the future. On the other hand, performing arts, social practices, rituals, festive events, knowledge, and practices that we inherit from our ancestors fall into intangible heritage resources.

Over a decade, various researchers have developed various techniques for preserving these intangible and tangible heritage resources for their purposeful applications. Applications of intangible heritage preservation are presented in [1, 10, 30, 54].

Bacci et al. [7] provide a historical and archaeological analysis of the Basilica of Bethlehem. The archaeological analysis shows that without altering the basic weight-bearing structure how the major changes are done in the structure in its entirety. In [21], a method has been proposed for automatic reconstruction of 3D archaeological relief objects from line drawings. The construction of relief objects consists of two steps: base estimation and relief construction. For base estimation in a particular drawing, models having similar outline are searched within a database. The most similar model is deformed to get the best-match drawing. The deformation is done by solving a linear optimization problem. The outline of the 3D model that is most similar to the given drawing is chosen for relief construction. Aletras et al. [2] proposed a technique to find out similar items in a digital library. They used a combination of a corpus and knowledge-based approaches for similarity measure.

A monument recognition method is reported in [4]. This technique uses kNN classification and landmark recognition techniques to recognize a monument in an image. The proposed method classifies the images by kNN classifier based on a local feature-based image similarity definition. The local descriptors used by the method are SIFT, SURF, ORB, and BRISK.

A Naïve Bayes classifier model [40] based on edge histogram is used to group the Thai E-San Heritage images into two classes: (1) heritage images that involve human activities and (2) heritage images with nonhuman activities.

In [13], a method of image retrieval using repetitive patterns by SIFT is reported. The repetitive part of the image is represented by a lattice or line pattern. Mishra et al. [34] proposed a real-time system for retrieving heritage images. The database images and query images are described by 64D SURF descriptors. In addition to SURF, the color channels are also used to measure the similarity. Principal component analysis is done to make the system efficient. Next, multidimensional indexing of the precomputed image features is performed based on SR-tree.

In [23], a decision fusion framework is used to retrieve the images from artistic repositories. The framework introduces a compensatory operator based on fuzzy theory for combining different feature similarities to provide the user with a set of tools for modeling various conceptual queries.

A system for seamless cross-collection content and meta-data-based searching of museum image collections database is proposed in [26]. Here, the multiscale color coherence vector (MCCV) technique is used, which can provide an effective subimage retrieval. If the subimage and the target are at different resolutions, this method also works well.

Ardizzone et al. [5] have presented an image retrieval system for an artistic database on cultural heritage. They propose similarity function-based membership values of the fuzzy c-means theory. In [18], an image retrieval technique is presented for efficient search in cultural heritage images. Here, the proposed method extracts features by using LBP and clusters them as low-level patterns. Higher-level patterns are formed from the low-level patterns by pattern instantiation. The similarity between two patterns is identified as a function of the similarity between both the structure and the measure components of the patterns.

In [37], a computer vision application on mobile phones is demonstrated. One can take a picture at a heritage site and get the associated annotations on his/her mobile phone using the application. For this, a bag-of-visual-words (BoW) image retrieval system and an annotated database of images have been used.

Picard et al. [38] have proposed an automatic labeling and interactive search method for cultural heritage collections. In the labeling phase, a set of keywords is inferred automatically for each newly digitized artifact. The wordbook of all possible keywords can be very large. These keywords are to ease the work of specialists searching throughout the entire collection by querying very precise keywords.

The rest of this chapter is organized as follows. Section 3 describes the proposed method of object spotting, which includes detection of keypoints, description of keypoints using WKS, selection of candidate/essential keypoints, spotting the zone of interest, and zone ranking. Experimental results on different datasets and related comparison with existing techniques are presented in Sect. 4. The concluding notes are put in Sect. 5.

3 Proposed Method

The proposed object spotting method starts with detection of keypoints, followed by the generation of WKS at each keypoint both in the query image and in the document/panel image. Selection of candidate keypoints in the document/panel image is done by comparing the signatures of keypoints in both images. For the word spotting problem, an extra step is necessary for the refinement of candidate keypoint selection called essential keypoint selection. To do that, the query image is divided into four equal quadrants, and mean signatures are estimated for each quadrant and one for the whole query word. A sliding window having size equal to the bounding box of the query image is considered. The center of the window is placed at each candidate keypoint in the document image. The mean signatures of the window are estimated for each keypoint in the similar manner. To select an essential keypoint in the document, the mean signatures of a keypoint in the document are compared to the mean signatures of the query image. Finally, the zones of interest are selected from the document/panel images and ranked according to the similarity with the query image. The steps are elaborated in subsequent sections.

3.1 Keypoint Detection

Due to environmental changes with the passage of time as well as manhandling by many ignorant generations, the objects collected from the documents or temples are

of very degraded quality. So, before the keypoint detection, a mean filter is applied
to the query image and the document/panel image repeatedly (in our case, thrice)
for smoothing and noise reduction, and then the SIFT [29] detector is used to obtain
the keypoints in the query image as well as in the document/panel image. Figure 1
shows the keypoints obtained in a query image using the SIFT detector.

In the case of word spotting, the keypoints in the background region are not
considered for further processing as these keypoints do not give any meaningful
information about the text stroke. To remove these keypoints, the gray-level
histogram of the image is obtained, as shown in Fig. 2. The cubic interpolation
function is used to smoothen the histogram. It is evident from Fig. 2 that the
histogram is a bimodal one, and the upper boundary of its first hump is considered
as a threshold to remove the keypoints appearing in the background region. The
keypoints that are on text strokes are only considered for further processing.

3.2 Keypoint Descriptor

Each keypoint is described by WKS using a local patch. First, we discuss the
theoretical background of WKS briefly, and then the use of WKS is presented to
describe each keypoint. WKS exhibits the behavior of a quantum particle over the
shape surface as described by the Schrödinger equation on the underlying manifold.
It characterizes the shape of an object from a 3D triangular mesh structure in an
isometric-invariant manner due to the in-variance property of Laplace–Beltrami
operator in isometric deformation of an object. According to Aubry et al. [6], the

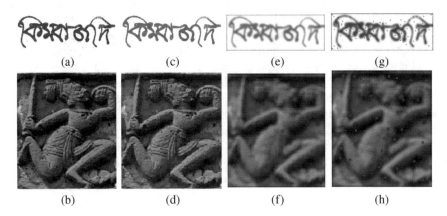

Fig. 1 An example of keypoint selection. First row from document image and second row from
the panel image. (**a**) and (**b**) Original image. (**c**) and (**d**) Gray-scale image. (**e**) and (**f**) Smoothened
image. (**g**) and (**h**) Keypoints (in red color)

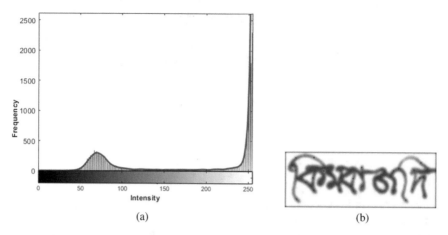

(a)   (b)

Fig. 2 (**a**) Vertical lines are the histogram of the gray-level image shown in Fig. 1c, and red line is the smoothened histogram. (**b**) Keypoints on the strokes

basic idea of WKS is to characterize a point $x \in X$ by the average probabilities of quantum particles of different energy levels to be measured in x. The behavior of a quantum particle on a surface is governed by the following Schrödinger equation:

$$\left(i\Delta_M + \frac{\partial}{\partial t} \right) \psi(x, t) = 0, \tag{1}$$

where Δ_M is the Laplace–Beltrami operator of M (M is 3D Riemannian manifold) and $\psi(x, t)$ is the complex wave function, $\psi(x, t) : M \times R_{>0} \rightarrow C$. Despite an apparent similarity of Eq. (1) to the heat equation, the multiplication of the Laplacian (Δ_M) by the complex unity (i) in the Schrödinger equation has a dramatic impact on the dynamics of the solution. Instead of representing diffusion, ψ now has an oscillatory behavior.

Let us assume that the quantum particle has an initial energy distribution around some nominal energy described by the probability density function $f(E)$ with expectation value E. The solution of the Schrödinger equation can then be expressed in the spectral domain [6] as

$$\psi_E(x, t) = \sum_{k=0}^{\infty} e^{iE_k t} f_E(E_k) \phi_k(x). \tag{2}$$

The probability to measure the particle at a point $x \in M$ at time t is given by $|\psi(x, t)|^2$. Integrating it over the time space gives WKS, which is the average probability that a particle is at x. Thus, the WKS is defined as

$$WKS(x, E) = \lim_{T \to \infty} \frac{1}{T} \int_0^T |\psi(x, t)|^2 \, dt. \tag{3}$$

Since the functions of $e^{-iE_k t}$ are orthogonal for the L^2 norm, the WKS can be rewritten as

$$WKS(x, E) = \sum_{k=0}^{\infty} f_E(E_k)^2 \phi_k(x)^2. \tag{4}$$

However, the beauty of this equation is that the time parameter has been replaced by energy. Now the energy is directly related to the eigenvalues of the Laplace–Beltrami operator and therefore to an intrinsic notion of scale in the shape. By choosing an appropriate distribution of f_E in (4), one can derive a descriptor that characterizes the properties of the shape at different scales. Aubry et al. [6] considered a family of log-normal energy distribution centered around some mean log energy $e = \log(E)$ with variance σ^2, which defines $f_E(E_k)$ as follows:

$$f_E(E_k) \propto \exp\left(-\frac{(e - \log(E_k))^2}{2\sigma^2}\right). \tag{5}$$

Finally, $WKS(x, e)$ can be written as

$$WKS(x, e) = C_e \sum_k e^{\left(\frac{-(e - \log E_k)^2}{2\sigma^2}\right)} \phi_k^2(x), \tag{6}$$

where

$$C_e = \left(\sum_k e^{\left(\frac{-(e - \log E_k)^2}{2\sigma^2}\right)}\right)^{-1}.$$

In the proposed system, WKS is extracted at each keypoint in both the query image and the document image. Approximation of Laplace–Beltrami eigenfunctions is described in Sect. 3.3.

The number of eigenvalues and eigenvectors of the Laplacian and the value of σ are determined empirically, which is discussed in the experimental section. Each keypoint is described by a vector of dimension l ($l = 100$), and we call this vector a signature of the keypoint. Figures 3 and 4 show some keypoints and their corresponding signatures.

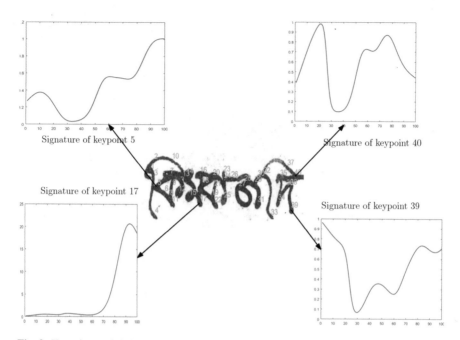

Fig. 3 Keypoints and their signatures from a query image from document image

The WKS is extracted within a patch whose center coincides with the keypoint (see Fig. 5). At each keypoint, WKS is determined within a square patch (P) of length S. For the word spotting, the size of the square patch P is determined automatically, whereas for the figure spotting, the size of the patch (23×23) is selected empirically.

In the word spotting, to determine the size of the patch we estimate the stroke width (sw) of the query image. The edge map of the query word is obtained using the Sobel operator. This edge detection may divide the image into a number of components. Each component is scanned row-wise (and column-wise), and the distance (w) between two consecutive white-to-black (WB) and black-to-white (BW) transitions is measured. The histogram of the w is obtained, and the value of the w for which the frequency is maximum is considered as width (sw) of the stroke of the query word. The length of the square patch is considered as $S = (2sw + 1)$.

Due to aging, most of the documents/panels have nonuniform intensity distribution, and some of the characters are faded compared to the background. To get the uniform intensity distribution within the patch, intensity normalization is done using the following equation:

$$I_n(x, y) = \frac{[I(x, y) - m]}{s}, \tag{7}$$

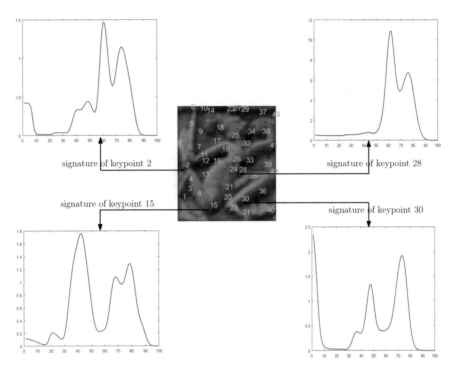

Fig. 4 Keypoints and their signatures from a query image from the panel image

Fig. 5 An example of patches, each of size 21×21

where $I(x, y)$ is the intensity of the pixel at location (x, y) and $I_n(x, y)$ is the normalized intensity at the same location. Here, m and s are the mean intensity of pixels and the standard deviation of the intensities, respectively, within the patch P.

Now, each image patch P is embedded into 3D Riemannian manifold M (see Fig. 6). For this transformation, we define the mapping $f : P \rightarrow M$. More explicitly, it can be written as

$$f : X \rightarrow (x, y, I(X)) \quad \forall X \in P, \tag{8}$$

where $I(X)$ is the pixel intensity at $X = (x, y)$.

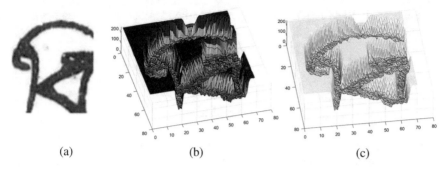

(a)   (b)   (c)

Fig. 6 An example of 2D image embedded into 3D manifold: (**a**) Patch of size 71×71 centered at 4th keypoint shown in Fig. 5. (**b**) 3D surface obtained from the image (**a**). (**c**) 3D triangular mesh of (**b**)

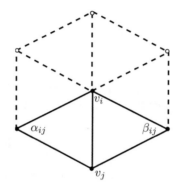

Fig. 7 An example of one-ring neighbors

3.3 Estimation of Laplace–Beltrami Operator

The Laplace–Beltrami eigenfunctions are obtained by the cotangent scheme described in [39] as follows.

Let $V = \{v_1, v_2 \ldots v_{n_v}\}$ be the vertices of the triangular mesh associated with the image patch embedded in 3D manifold. We approximate the discrete Laplacian as an $n_v \times n_v$ matrix $L_{n_v \times n_v} = Q^{-1}W$, where W is a sparse matrix computed as

$$W_{ij} = \begin{cases} \frac{\cot \alpha_{ij} + \cot \beta_{ij}}{2} & \text{if } v_i \text{ and } v_j \text{ are adjacent} \\ 0 & \text{otherwise,} \end{cases} \tag{9}$$

where α_{ij} and β_{ij} are two opposite face angles depicted in Fig. 7. Q is a diagonal matrix in which $Q_{ii} = Q_m$ is the area of all triangles T from the one-ring neighborhood of v_i. The algorithm proposed in [33] is used to calculate Q_m, which is given below.

For every triangle T in the one-ring neighborhood of the vertex v_i, compute

$$Q_m = \begin{cases} \frac{1}{8} \sum_{j \in N_i} (\cot \alpha_{ij} + \cot \beta_{ij}) \parallel v_i - v_j \parallel^2 \\ \qquad \text{if the angle of } T \text{ at } v_i \text{ is nonobtuse} \\ \sum_{j \in N_i} (\frac{area(T)}{2}) \text{ if the angle of } T \text{ at } v_i \text{ is obtuse} \\ \sum_{j \in N_i} (\frac{area(T)}{4}) \quad \text{otherwise,} \end{cases} \tag{10}$$

where N_i is the number of adjacent one-ring vertices of v_i.

Now the eigenvectors and the eigenvalues of discrete Laplace–Beltrami operator are calculated from the solution of generalized eigenvalue problem $W\Phi = \Lambda Q\Phi$, where Λ is a diagonal matrix consisting the eigenvalues $\{E_i\}$ and Φ contains the eigenvectors $\{\phi_i\}$. These eigenvalues $\{E_i\}$ and eigenvectors $\{\phi_i\}$ are used in Eq. (6).

3.4 Object Spotting

For a given query image, our task is to efficiently find the same or similar types of object(word/figure) in a particular document/panel image. In order to do this, our process is divided into the following steps:

- Selection of keypoints from the document/panel, which are similar to any one of the keypoints present in the query image.
- For the word spotting, some of the keypoints obtained as an output of the first step may belong to words that are not similar to the query word. Hence, a second level of keypoint selection is required to eliminate the redundant keypoints, and this is done in the second step.
- Next, zone scores are estimated to find out the zone of interest where the query word may be present.
- Finally, the spotted zones are ranked according to similarity index value.

The following sections elaborate the details of the word spotting process.

3.4.1 Candidate Keypoint Selection

If the signatures of a keypoint in the document/panel are similar to the signatures of any keypoint in the query image, then we consider the keypoint in the document/panel as a candidate keypoint.

Assume that for a given query image there are n keypoints, each keypoint is denoted by q_k, and the corresponding signature associated with the keypoint q_k is represented by $sig(q_k)$, $k \in \{1, 2, \ldots, n\}$. Let l be the dimension of each signature. For a particular document/panel image, let there be m keypoints, denoted as dc_j, and the signature of the keypoint dc_j denoted as $sig(dc_j)$, $j \in \{1, 2, \ldots, m\}$.

In order to find the similar keypoints in the document/panel image, we use the Euclidean distance metric to measure the similarity between the keypoints present in the query image and those in the document/panel image. The distance between the signature of kth keypoint in the query image and the signature of jth keypoint in the document/panel image is obtained using the following equation:

$$d(k, j) = \sqrt{\sum_{i=1}^{l}(sig(q_{ki}) - sig(dc_{ji}))^2}. \qquad (11)$$

The steps for finding similar keypoints in the document/panel image are as follows:

1. Calculate $d(k, j), \forall j \in 1, 2, \ldots m$.
2. Arrange these m distances in increasing order.
3. Take z as the threshold value of similarity distance measure.
4. Find those keypoints where $d(k, j) \leq z$, and consider these keypoints in the document similar to kth keypoint in the query word.

The above steps are repeated n times, as there are n number of keypoints in the query word. The threshold value z is estimated automatically.

A graphical representation of the sorted distances is shown in Fig. 8a and c, which is obtained in Step 2. It is evident from Fig. 8a and c that the slope of the curve changes rapidly at its two ends. So, if we estimate the slope of the curve at each endpoint, then we get two high peaks where the slope changes rapidly. A part of the plot of the slope is shown in Fig. 8b and d. The distance at which the first peak from the left end of the gradient curve appears is considered as the threshold value z to select candidate keypoints in the document/panel image. The result of candidate keypoint selection is shown in Figs. 9b and 10b.

3.4.2 Selection of Essential Keypoints (for Word Spotting)

There are some candidate keypoints that still appear in words that are not similar to the query word. Hence, we try to eliminate those keypoints from the document image before spotting the zone of interest. Let n be the number of keypoints in the query image. So, the size of the signature matrix (S) for a particular query word is $[l \times n]$. The mean signature vector μ of S is obtained. The centroid of the keypoints in the query word is calculated using the following formula:

$$(c_x, c_y) = \left(\frac{\sum_{k=1}^{n} q_x^k}{n}, \frac{\sum_{k=1}^{n} q_y^k}{n} \right), \qquad (12)$$

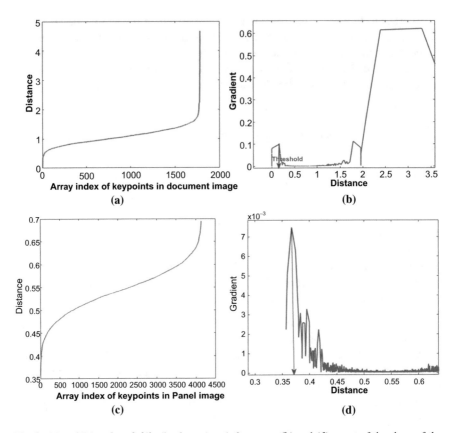

Fig. 8 (**a**) and (**c**) a plot of $d(k, j)$ where $j = 1, 2, \ldots, m$. (**b**) and (**d**) a part of the slope of the curve shown in (**a**) and (**c**), respectively

where (c_x, c_y) is the location of the centroid and (q_x^k, q_y^k) denotes the location of the kth keypoint.

Let $[M \times N]$ be the size of the query word, which is partitioned into four parts in such a way that the intersection of the horizontal partitioning line segment and the vertical partitioning line segment coincides with the centroid (c_x, c_y) (see Fig 11). The keypoints appearing in each part are considered, and their mean signature vector is obtained. Here, $\mu_1, \mu_2, \mu_3,$ and μ_4 denote the mean signature vector for the first, second, third, and fourth quadrants, respectively. Another mean signature μ is taken from whole word. Hence, a particular query word is described by five signature vectors, each having a dimension l.

The center of a window of size $[M \times N]$ is made to coincide with each candidate keypoint in the document. The window is also partitioned into four parts such that the intersection of the partitioning line segments coincides with (mp_x, mp_y). The coordinates (mp_x, mp_y) are obtained in the following way:

$$mp_x = L_x + c_x, \quad mp_y = L_y + c_y, \tag{13}$$

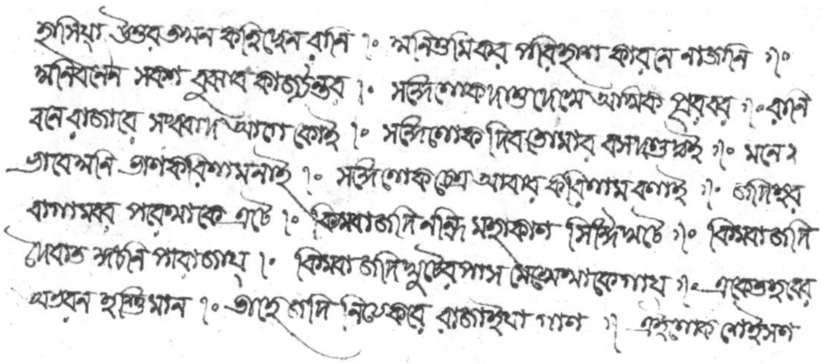

Fig. 9 An example of candidate selection in a document image: (**a**) All the keypoints in a document detected using SIFT. (**b**) Candidate keypoints appear in document for the query word as shown in Fig. 1c

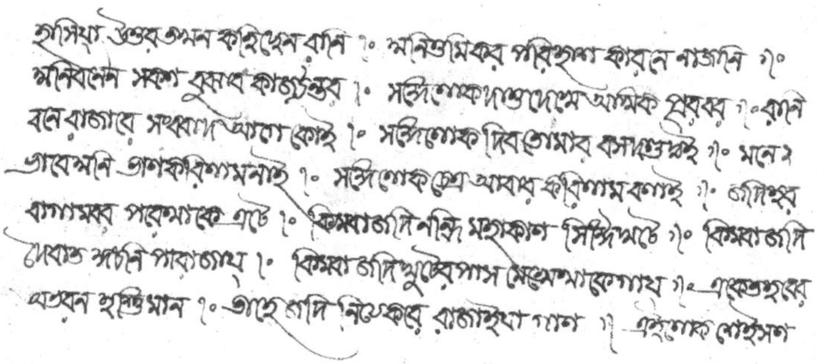

Fig. 10 An example of candidate keypoint selection in a panel image. (**a**) Keypoint detected using SIFT. (**b**) Candidate keypoints using WKS for the query image shown in Fig. 1d

where (L_x, L_y) are the coordinates of the top-left corner of the window. This ensures that the size of each quadrant of the window is equal to the size of the corresponding quadrant of the query word.

The same procedure is applied to describe a candidate keypoint in the document with the help of five mean signature vectors. The candidate keypoint descriptors

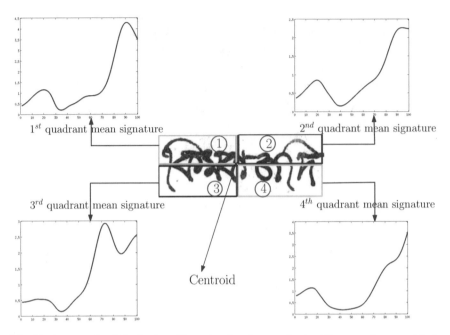

Fig. 11 An example of distribution of keypoints into four quadrants of the query image and their mean signatures

are denoted by m_c, m_{c1}, m_{c2}, m_{c3}, and m_{c4}. The descriptor m_c represents the mean signature vector for the whole window, m_{c1} denotes the mean signature vector for the first quadrant of the window, and so on for m_{c2}, m_{c3}, and m_{c4}.

The similarity between the zone enclosed within the aforesaid window and the query word is measured using Eq. (11). So, for each window whose center coincides with a particular candidate keypoint, we get five distances d, d_1, d_2, d_3, and d_4, where d is the distance between μ and m_c, d_1 is the distance between μ_1 and m_{c1}, and so on. The mean (md) of these distances and the location of the corresponding center are stored in a list L. This process is repeated for all the candidate keypoints present in a particular document. The list L is sorted in ascending order w.r.t. md. A graphical representation of the sorted values of md for a particular document (Fig. 9b) and a particular query word (Fig. 1c) is shown in Fig. 12.

The essential keypoints are those keypoints whose descriptors are more similar to the query word descriptors. In order to select a threshold value for similarity measure, the gradient of the curve shown in Fig. 12a is obtained, as shown in Fig. 12b. The distance at which the first peak occurs as shown in Fig. 12b is considered as threshold value for detecting essential key points, as it represents the minimum distance value between the query word and the local window of document candidate keypoints. The essential keypoints are shown in Fig. 13.

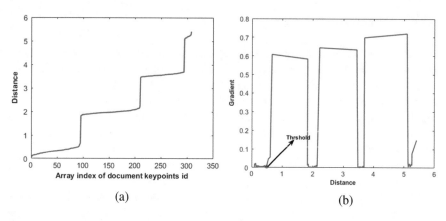

Fig. 12 (**a**) Graphical representation of the sorted values of *md*. (**b**) The gradient of the curve shown in (**a**)

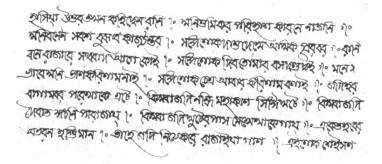

Fig. 13 Essential keypoints present in a particular document

3.4.3 Spotting Zones

The center of the aforesaid window of size $[M \times N]$ is placed at the essential keypoint (for word spotting) or candidate keypoint (for figure spotting) having the least distance value in the sorted list L. The number of keypoints (n_w) within the window is counted, and if $n_w \geq \lfloor k \times n \rfloor$, then the zone enclosed by the window is considered as a zone of interest. The keypoints present within the spotted zone are removed from L. This process is repeated until the list L is exhausted. The value of k is set empirically, and it may vary from dataset to dataset. The procedure for estimation of k is discussed in Sect. 4.4.

3.4.4 Ranking of Spotted Zone

A part of a word/figure in the document/panel may be similar to the query image, but this may not be actually the zone of interest. Hence, zone ranking is required. The number of keypoints within the spotted zone and the similarity distance metric are used to rank the spotted zones. The zones are ranked primarily according to the number of keypoints within each zone. If there is a tie, then the similarity distance metric is used to break the tie, and the zone corresponding to the least distance value will rank first.

The spotted zones are enclosed by colored bounding boxes, as shown in Figs. 14 and 15 for the query image shown in Fig. 1c and d, respectively.

In Fig. 14, the blue bounding box represents the spotted words, and the numbers above the box represent the ranking of the spotted region. In Fig. 15, the blue bounding box represents the correct spotted figures, whereas the red bounding box represents the incorrect spotted figure, and the numbers above the boxes represent the ranking value.

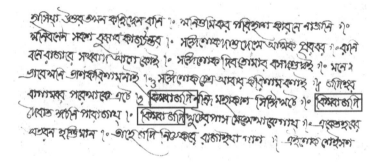

Fig. 14 Spotted words for the query word shown in Fig. 1c

Fig. 15 Spotted figures for the query image shown in Fig. 1d

4 Experimental Results

4.1 Datasets and Ground Truth for Word Spotting

The proposed method has been tested for word spotting on three historical Bangla handwritten datasets and one English handwritten George Washington (GW) dataset. The historical Bangla handwritten datasets are collected from the "Asiatic Society," Kolkata. Three Bangla datasets are "Hamsadiita-Vaishanava-Literature" written by Narashima Dasa, "Siva durga Vivah" by Divija Rajibalocana, and "Hamsadiita-Kavya" by Rupa Goswami. We call these datasets HN, SD, and HR, respectively. HN and SD datasets are written in Bengali in the years 1181 and 1259, respectively. These two datasets contain 18 pages and 10 pages, respectively. The HR dataset contains 28 pages.

All these datasets are scanned in 300 dpi. The number of words in HN, SD, and HR are 2124, 770, and 4256, respectively. The ground truth for all these datasets is created manually, and it contains transcriptions, top-left and right-bottom coordinates of the bounding box of each word. GW dataset [24] contains 20 pages and 4860 words. The ground truth for this dataset is available.

To measure the performance of the proposed method in word spotting, we use the protocol followed in [3, 47] where every word in a document is considered as query word and the corresponding spotted zones are ranked in each document of the dataset. If the bounding box of the spotted zone is overlapped with at least 50% of the bounding box of the word in the ground truth, then the spotted zone is considered as relevant. The mean average precision (mAP) and mean recall (mR) are used to measure the performance of the proposed method.

4.2 Datasets and Ground Truth for Figure Spotting

The proposed method is tested on two Indian heritage image datasets for figure spotting. This image database is available in [9]. We take 317 panel images of "Jorbangla" (JB) temple and 277 panel images of "Madan Mohan" (MM) temple, which are depicted on the interior and the exterior walls of the temples.

From these datasets, 61 figures from JB dataset and 52 figures from MM dataset are collected as query images, and each of the query images appears at least three times in a particular panel image. To create the ground truth, a 9-member team is formed from the Department of Architecture of our institute. All the query images and the datasets are given to each member, and they are asked to mark the most similar regions in each panel image corresponding to each query image. For a particular query image, if at least five people have marked the same regions in a panel image, then the marked regions in the panel image are considered as ground truth for that particular query image. With respect to the aforesaid query images, the JB test dataset contains 855 Ground-Truth Positive (GTP) figures and 2935 Ground-

Truth Negative (GTN) figures, whereas the MM test dataset has 747 GTP figures and 2564 GTN figures.

The performance of the proposed method in figure spotting is calculated by the same metric as word spotting. To compare the performance of the proposed method in figure spotting, we use three other classical features, namely, Scale Invariant Feature Transform (SIFT) [29], Speeded Up Robust Features (SURF) [8], and Histogram of Oriented Gradient (HOG) [12].

The proposed technique is implemented in MATLAB 7.12.0 (R2011 a) in a PC (Intel(R) Core(TM) i3-4005U 1.7GHz CPU running Ubuntu).

4.3 Determining the Value of σ

If there are n_e number of nonzero eigenvalues $(e_1, e_2, \ldots, e_{n_e})$ in ascending order, we calculate $e_{min} = \log(e_1)$ and $e_{max} = \log(e_{n_e})$. We define increment of eigenvalue, $\delta = (e_{max} - e_{min})/n_e$. σ is set to 7δ.

4.4 Selecting the Value of k

The parameter k plays a crucial role in spotting the zones, as mentioned in Sect. 3.4.3. It has, therefore, a significant impact on the performance of the proposed method.

The holdout cross-validation technique is used to select the value of k. Each dataset is divided into two sets, called the training set and the test set. From each dataset, we randomly select 70% of the total document pages as the training set, and the rest are taken as member of the test set. The value of k is selected using the training dataset. The selected value of k is used for the test dataset to measure the performance of the proposed method.

To select a proper value of k, we take 16 different values of k starting from 0.2 to 0.95 with a step size of 0.05 for word spotting and 18 different values of k starting from 0.05 to 0.9 with a step size of 0.05 for figure spotting.

We estimate the values of mean average precision and mean recall and their corresponding F1-scores for each training set for different values of k. Tables 1 and 2 show the estimated mAP, mR, and the F1-score for some values of k. We select the value of k for which the F1-score is maximized. It is evident from Tables 1 and 2 that the selected value of k is different for different datasets.

Table 1 The performance metrics for word spotting: mAP, mR, and F1-score for different values of k for training datasets

Database	Metric	k								
		0.200	0.300	0.400	0.500	0.550	0.600	0.700	0.800	0.900
SD	mAP	0.330	0.390	0.450	0.570	0.660	0.680	0.740	0.850	0.920
	mAR	0.950	0.947	0.943	0.940	0.932	0.830	0.730	0.640	0.540
	F1-score	0.489	0.552	0.609	0.709	**0.772**	0.747	0.734	0.730	0.680
HR	mAP	0.290	0.360	0.500	0.590	0.635	0.660	0.730	0.830	0.930
	mAR	0.937	0.933	0.930	0.928	0.925	0.870	0.750	0.650	0.510
	F1-score	0.442	0.519	0.650	0.721	**0.753**	0.750	0.739	0.729	0.658
HN	mAP	0.330	0.460	0.560	0.630	0.650	0.680	0.730	0.850	0.890
	mAR	0.931	0.927	0.923	0.917	0.869	0.790	0.720	0.611	0.540
	F1-score	0.487	0.614	0.697	**0.746**	0.743	0.730	0.724	0.710	0.672
GW	mAP	0.350	0.423	0.550	0.641	0.650	0.690	0.750	0.850	0.930
	mAR	0.961	0.957	0.955	0.953	0.893	0.790	0.690	0.610	0.470
	F1-score	0.513	0.586	0.698	**0.766**	0.752	0.736	0.718	0.710	0.624

F1-score value is highest for that corresponding k value

4.5   Results and Analysis

Now, the selected value of k is used for the test dataset to measure the performance of the proposed method in terms of mAP and mAR.

The performance metrics in figure spotting for the two Indian heritage image datasets and in word spotting for Bangla handwritten datasets are displayed in Tables 3 and 4, respectively.

The GW dataset is extensively accepted, and most researchers in the word spotting community have already used this dataset. Hence, for word spotting, we also compare the proposed method with the other methods using GW dataset. We summarize other methods and their performances in Table 5. It is evident from Table 5 that the proposed method performs better than the other methods except for the methods in [28, 50]. The methods in [28, 50] use fewer query words, which may be the reason for their better performance compared to the proposed method. However, our method is segmentation-free and does not require any learning mechanism, which are mandatory for the techniques proposed in [28, 50]. The results mentioned in Table 5 for the other methods are taken from the literature.

A set of outputs of the proposed method is also given from each of the datasets. The spotted regions in the images are shown by a colored bounding box, and the number above the bounding box signifies the rank of the spotted region. Figure 16 shows the query word and the corresponding spotted regions from the SD dataset.

Table 2 The performance metrics for figure spotting: mAP, mR, and F1-score for different values of *k* for training datasets

Database	Features	Metric	k 0.100	0.200	0.300	0.400	0.450	0.500	0.550	0.600	0.700	0.800	0.900
JB	SURF	mAP	0.375	0.467	0.559	0.661	0.715	0.754	0.784	0.817	0.851	0.891	0.919
		mAR	0.757	0.730	0.680	0.625	0.578	0.554	0.528	0.499	0.428	0.343	0.215
		F1-score	0.501	0.570	0.614	**0.642**	0.639	0.639	0.631	0.619	0.569	0.496	0.348
	SIFT	mAP	0.377	0.472	0.561	0.678	0.720	0.770	0.811	0.825	0.853	0.898	0.925
		mAR	0.786	0.758	0.709	0.643	0.608	0.571	0.538	0.512	0.449	0.349	0.227
		F1-score	0.509	0.582	0.626	**0.660**	0.659	0.656	0.647	0.632	0.588	0.502	0.364
	HOG	mAP	0.382	0.473	0.551	0.635	0.686	0.735	0.756	0.788	0.856	0.899	0.925
		mAR	0.804	0.772	0.736	0.699	0.657	0.636	0.609	0.572	0.449	0.346	0.222
		F1-score	0.517	0.587	0.630	0.665	0.671	**0.681**	0.675	0.663	0.589	0.500	0.359
	WKS	mAP	0.390	0.478	0.557	0.648	0.683	0.714	0.754	0.785	0.854	0.891	0.907
		mAR	0.828	0.799	0.754	0.715	0.693	0.657	0.625	0.588	0.451	0.351	0.230
		F1-score	0.530	0.598	0.641	0.679	**0.688**	0.685	0.683	0.672	0.591	0.504	0.367
MM	SURF	mAP	0.361	0.419	0.509	0.580	0.602	0.630	0.352	0.673	0.717	0.751	0.796
		mAR	0.758	0.709	0.632	0.559	0.510	0.477	0.444	0.419	0.353	0.299	0.239
		F1-score	0.489	0.526	0.564	**0.569**	0.552	0.543	0.529	0.516	0.473	0.428	0.367
	SIFT	mAP	0.362	0.417	0.512	0.517	0.612	0.638	0.673	0.709	0.780	0.843	0.883
		mAR	0.765	0.725	0.641	0.583	0.552	0.512	0.475	0.433	0.339	0.278	0.225
		F1-score	0.492	0.529	0.569	**0.581**	0.580	0.568	0.557	0.537	0.437	0.419	0.358
	HOG	mAP	0.365	0.430	0.517	0.580	0.622	0.661	0.668	0.735	0.804	0.841	0.887
		mAR	0.784	0.732	0.660	0.611	0.573	0.524	0.484	0.430	0.344	0.297	0.239
		F1-score	0.498	0.542	0.580	0.595	**0.596**	0.584	0.568	0.543	0.482	0.439	0.376
	WKS	mAP	0.362	0.448	0.530	0.588	0.628	0.675	0.720	0.754	0.823	0.867	0.896
		mAR	0.805	0.765	0.704	0.648	0.620	0.568	0.512	0.470	0.391	0.325	0.243
		F1-score	0.499	0.565	0.605	0.616	**0.624**	0.617	0.599	0.579	0.530	0.473	0.383

F1-score value is highest for that corresponding k value

Table 3 Performance
measure in figure spotting

Database	Features	mAP	mAR
JB	SURF	0.631	0.671
	SIFT	0.653	0.687
	HOG	0.611	0.753
	WKS	0.701	0.693
MM	SURF	0.560	0.581
	SIFT	0.584	0.513
	HOG	0.579	0.630
	WKS	0.623	0.681

Table 4 Performance
measure in word spotting

Database	mAP	mAR
SD	66.17	93.11
HN	62.26	90.73
HR	63.55	91.87

Table 5 Quantitative comparison of experimental results in word spotting using GW dataset

Method	Segmentation	Learning	Dataset	Performance in mAP (%)
Dynamic time warping (Rath and Manmatha [41])	Words	No	10 good quality images 2381 queries	40.90
Synthesized words (Liang et al. [28])	Words	Yes	20 pages, 38 queries	67.00
Semicontinuous HMMs (Rodriguez-Serrano and Perronnin [44])	Words	Yes	20 pages, all words set as query in training	53.10
Character HMMs (Fischer et al. [15])	Line	Yes	20 pages, all words appeared as queries in all four folds of training set	62.00
Slit Style HOG feature (Terasawa and Tanaka [50])	Line	No	20 pages, 15 queries	79.10
Heat Kernel Signature (Zhang and Tan [56])	No	No	20 pages, query length > 5	62.47
Exemplar SVM with re-ranking (Almazan et al. [3])	No	No	20 pages, all 4856 words as queries	59.13
Patch-based framework with Product Quantization and LSA (Rusinol et al. [47])	No	No	20 pages, all 4856 words as queries	61.35
Proposed method	No	No	20 pages, all 4856 words as queries	63.33

(a)

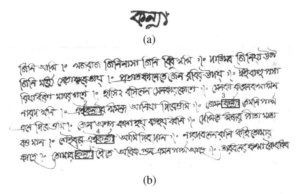

(b)

Fig. 16 (**a**) Example of a query word image. (**b**) Spotted regions enclosed by colored boxes in a document taken from the SD dataset

(a)

(b)

Fig. 17 (**a**) Example of a query word image. (**b**) Spotted regions enclosed by colored boxes in a document taken from the HN dataset

(a)

(b)

Fig. 18 (**a**) Example of a query word image. (**b**) Spotted regions enclosed by colored boxes in a document taken from the HR dataset

Some more results are shown in Figs. 17 and 18 from HN and HR datasets, respectively.

The proposed scheme does not use any domain knowledge of the script, and hence it is independent of the language used in the document. The proposed method is applied to the historical English handwritten GW dataset that is shown in Fig. 19.

(a)

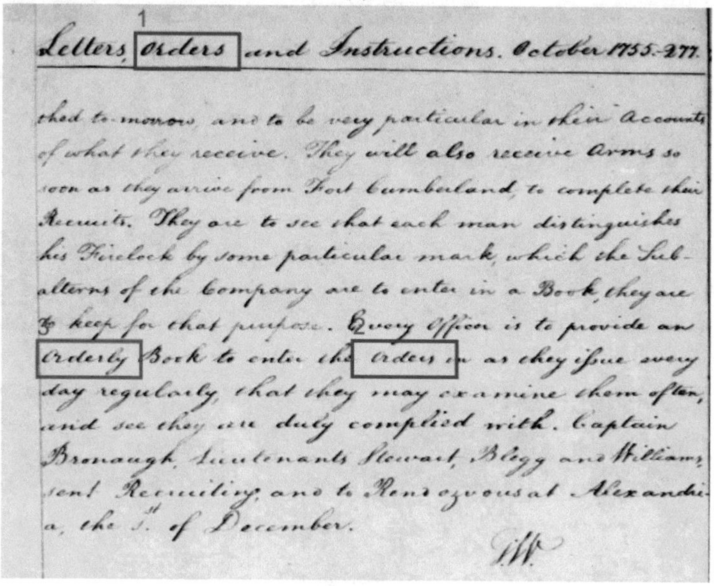

(b)

Fig. 19 (a) Example of a query word image. (b) Spotted regions enclosed by colored boxes in a document taken from a GW dataset

Another set of qualitative results are shown in Fig. 20 for figure spotting from MM datasets using different features. The blue rectangle represents the correct spotting zone, and the red rectangle denotes the incorrect spotting zone.

5 Conclusion

In this chapter, we have proposed an object spotting method for historical documents. Both the query image and document image are described by WKS descriptors. The Laplace–Beltrami operator in the WKS is isometric-invariant, and it is well suited for the shape analysis of nonrigid deformation of objects. For this reason, it is highly suitable for handwriting scenarios as well as for figure spotting scenarios where the same figure might have different poses or isometric deformations. The proposed method is script-independent, as we do not consider any domain knowledge for a particular language.

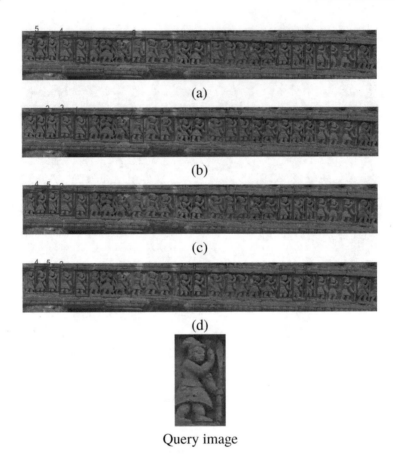

Query image

Fig. 20 An example of experimental results where the panel image is taken from the MM dataset. (**a**) Spotted zones using the SIFT feature. (**b**) Spotted zone using the SURF feature. (**c**) Spotted zone using the HOG feature. (**d**) Spotted zone using the WKS feature

References

1. Albanese, M., d'Acierno, A., Moscato, V., Persia, F., Picariello, A.: A multimedia semantic recommender system for cultural heritage applications. In: Proc. of 5th International Conference on Semantic Computing (ICSC), pp. 403–410. IEEE, Piscataway (2011)
2. Aletras, N., Stevenson, M., Clough, P.: Computing similarity between items in a digital library of cultural heritage. J. Comput. Cult. Herit. **5**(16), 1–19 (2012)
3. Almazán, J., Gordo, A., Fornés, A., Valvenya, E.: Segmentation-free word spotting with exemplar SVMs. Pattern Recognit. **47**, 3967–3978 (2014)
4. Amato, G., Falchi, F., Gennaro, C.: Fast image classification for monument recognition. J. Comput. Cult. Herit. **8**(18), 1–25 (2015)
5. Ardizzone, E., Chella, A., Pirrone, R., Gambino, O.: An image retrieval system for artistic database on cultural heritage. In: Proc. della Conferenza Italiana sui Sistemi Intelligenti (CISI), pp. 1–8. Citeseer (2004)

6. Aubry, M., Schlickewei, U., Cremers, D.: The wave kernel signature: a quantum mechanical approach to shape analysis. In: Proc. of International conference on Computer Vision, Workshop, pp. 1626–1623. IEEE, Piscataway (2011)
7. Bacci, M., Bianchi, G., Campana, S., Fichera, G.: Historical and archaeological analysis of the church of the nativity. J. Cult. Herit. **13**(4), e5–e26 (2012)
8. Bay, H., Ess, A., Tuytelaars, T., van Gool, L.: Speeded-up robust features (SURF). Comput. Vis. Image Underst. **110**(3), 346–359 (2008)
9. BHID: Bishnupur Heritage Image Database. http://www.isical.ac.in/~bsnpr. Accessed 7 Mar 2017
10. Chen, G.-F.: Intangible cultural heritage preservation: an exploratory study of digitization of the historical literature of Chinese Kunqu Opera Librettos. J. Comput. Cult. Herit. **7**(4), 1–16 (2014)
11. Csurka, G., Dance, C.R., Fan, L., Willamowski, J., Bray, C.: Visual categorization with bags of keypoints. In: Proc. of Workshop on Statistical Learning in Computer Vision, European Conference on Computer Vision, pp. 1–22 (2004)
12. Dalal, N., Triggs, B.: Histograms of oriented gradients for human detection. In: Proc. of Computer Vision and Pattern Recognition, pp. 886–893. IEEE, Piscataway (2005)
13. Doubek, P., Matas, J., Perdoch, M., Chum, O.: Image matching and retrieval by repetitive patterns. In: Proc. of 20th International Conference on Pattern Recognition (ICPR), pp. 3195–3198. IEEE, Piscataway (2010)
14. Fischer, A., Keller, A., Frinken, V., Bunke, H.: HMM-based word spotting in handwritten documents using subword models. In: Proc. of 20th International Conference on Pattern Recognition (ICPR), pp. 3416-3419. IEEE, Piscataway (2010)
15. Fischer, A., Keller, A., Frinken, V., Bunke, H.: Lexicon-free handwritten word spotting using character HMMs. Pattern Recognit. Lett. **33**(7), 934–942 (2012)
16. Frinken, V., Fischer, A., Manmatha, R., Bunke, H.: A novel word spotting method based on recurrent neural networks. IEEE Trans. Pattern Anal. Mach. Intell. **34**, 211–224 (2012)
17. Hast, A., Fornés, A.: A segmentation-free handwritten word spotting approach by relaxed feature matching. In: Proc. of 12th IAPR Workshop on Document Analysis Systems (DAS), pp. 150–155. IEEE, Piscataway (2016)
18. Iakovidis, D., Kotsifakos, E.E., Pelekis, N., Karanikas, H., Kopanakis, I., Mavroudakis, T., Theodoridis, Y.: Pattern-based retrieval of cultural heritage images. In: Proc. of the 11th Panhellenic Conference in Informatics (PCI) (2007)
19. Kesidis, A.L., Galiotou, E., Gatos, B., Pratikakis, I.: A word spotting framework for historical machine-printed documents. Int. J. Doc. Anal. Recognit. **14**, 131–144 (2011)
20. Khurshid, K., Faure, C., Vincen, N.: Word spotting in historical printed documents using shape and sequence comparisons. Pattern Recognit. **45**, 2598–2609 (2012)
21. Kolomenkin, M., Leifman, G., Shimshoni, I., Tal, A.: Reconstruction of relief objects from archeological line drawings. J. Comput. Cult. Herit. **6**(3), 1–19 (2013)
22. Konidaris, T., Kesidis, A.L., Gatos, B.: A segmentation-free word spotting method for historical printed documents. Pattern Anal. Appl. **19**(4), 963–976 (2016)
23. Kushki, A., Androutsos, P., Plataniotis, K.N., Venetsanopoulos, A.N.: Retrieval of images from artistic repositories using a decision fusion framework. IEEE Trans. Image Process. **13**(3), 277–292 (2004)
24. Lavrenko, V., Rath, T., Manmatha, R.: Holistic word recognition for handwritten historical documents. In: Proc. of First International Workshop in Document Image Analysis for Libraries, pp. 278–287. IEEE, Piscataway (2004)
25. Lee, D.R., Hong, W., Oh, I.S.: Segmentation-free word spotting using SIFT. In: Proc. of Southwest Symposium on Image Analysis and Interpretation, pp. 65–68. IEEE, Piscataway (2012)
26. Lewis, P.H., Martinez, K., Abas, F.S., Fauzi, M.F.A., Chan, S.C.Y., Addis, M.J., Boniface, M.J., Grimwood, P., Stevenson, A., Lahanier, C., Stevenson, J.: An integrated content and metadata based retrieval system for art. IEEE Trans. Image Process. **13**(3), 302–313 (2004)

27. Leydier, Y., Ouji, A., LeBourgeois, F., Emptoz, H.: Towards an omnilingual word retrieval system for ancient manuscripts. Pattern Recognit. **42**, 2089–2105 (2009)
28. Liang, Y., Fairhurst, M.C., Guest, R.M.: A synthesised word approach to word retrieval in handwritten documents. Pattern Recognit. **45**(12), 4225–4236 (2012)
29. Lowe, D.: Distinctive image features from scale-invariant keypoints. Int. J. Comput. Vis. **60**, 90–110 (2004)
30. Mallik, A., Chaudhury, S., H Ghosh. Nrityakosha: preserving the intangible heritage of Indian classical dance. J. Comput. Cult. Herit. **4**(11), 1–25 (2011)
31. Manmatha, R., Han, C., Riseman, E.: Word spotting: a new approach to indexing handwriting. In: Proceedings of IEEE Computer Vision and Pattern Recognition, pp. 631–637 (1996)
32. Marti, U.V., Bunke, H.: Using a statistical language model to improve the performance of an HMM-based cursive handwriting recognition systems. Int. J. Pattern Recognit. Artif. Intell. **15**, 65–90 (2001)
33. Meyer, M., Desbrun, M., Schröder, P., Bar, A.H.: Discrete differential geometry operators for triangulated 2-manifolds. In: Proc. of Visualization Mathematics. Springer, Berlin, pp. 35–57 (2002)
34. Mishra, S., Mukherjee, J., Mondal, P., Aswatha, S.M., Mukherjee, J.: Real-time retrieval system for heritage images. In: Proc. of Emerging Research in Electronics, Computer Science and Technology, pp. 245–253. Springer, Berlin (2014)
35. Moreno-Noguer, F.: Deformation and illumination invariant feature point descriptor. In: Proc. of Computer Vision and Pattern Recognition (CVPR), pp. 1593–1600. IEEE, Piscataway (2011)
36. Nagy, G.: Twenty years of document image analysis in PAMI. IEEE Trans. Pattern Anal. Mach. Intell. **22**(1), 38–62 (2000)
37. Panda, J., Sharma, S., Jawahar, C.V.: Heritage App: annotating images on mobile phones. In: Proc. of the Eighth Indian Conference on Computer Vision, Graphics and Image Processing (ICVGIP), number 3. ACM, New York (2012)
38. Picard, D., Gosselin, P.H., Gaspard, M.C.: Challenges in content-based image indexing of cultural heritage collections. IEEE Signal Processing Mag. **32**(4), 95–102 (2015)
39. Pinkall, U., Polthier, K.: Computing discrete minimal surfaces and their conjugates. Exp. Math. **2**, 15–36 (1993)
40. Polpinij, J., Sibunruang, C.: Thai heritage images classification by Naive Bayes image classifier. In: Proc. of 6th International Conference on Digital Content, Multimedia Technology and Its Applications (IDC), pp. 221–224. IEEE, Piscataway (2010)
41. Rath, T.M., Manmatha, R.: Word image matching using dynamic time warping. In: Proc. of Computer Vision and Pattern Recognition (CVPR), vol. 2, pp. 521–527. IEEE, Piscataway (2003)
42. Rath, T., Manmatha, R.: Word spotting for historical documents. Int. J. Doc. Anal. Recognit. **9**, 139–152 (2007)
43. Rodríguez, J., Perronnin, F.: Local gradient histogram features for word spotting in unconstrained handwritten documents. In: Proc. of International Conference on Frontiers in Handwriting Recognition (ICFHR) (2008)
44. Rodriguez-Serrano, J., Perronnin, F.: A Model-based sequence similarity with application to handwritten word spotting. IEEE Trans. Pattern Anal. Mach. Intell. **34**, 2108–2120 (2012)
45. Rothacker, L., Fink, G.A., Banerjee, P., Bhattacharya, U., Chaudhuri, B.B.: Bag-of-features HMMs for segmentation-free Bangla word spotting. In: Proc. of the 4th International Workshop on Multilingual OCR, vol. 5. ACM, New York (2013)
46. Rusiñol, M., Aldavert, D., Toledo, R., Lladós, J.: browsing heterogeneous document collections by a segmentation-free word spotting method. In: Proc. of International Conference on Document Analysis and Recognition (ICDAR), vol. 22, pp. 63–67. IEEE, Piscataway (2011)
47. Rusiñol, M., Aldavert, D., Toledo, R., Lladós, J.: Efficient segmentation-free keyword spotting in historical document collections. Pattern Recognit. **48**(2), 545–555 (2015)

48. Sun, J., Ovsjanikov, M., Guibas, L.: A concise and provably informative multiscale signature based on heat diffusion. Comput. Graph. Forum **28**, 1383–1392 (2009)
49. Syeda-Mahmood, T.: Indexing of handwritten document images. In: Proc. of Workshop on Document Image Analysis, pp. 66–73. IEEE, Piscataway (1997)
50. Teraswa, K., Tanake, Y.: Slit style HOG feature for document image word spotting. In: Proc. International Conference of Document Analysis and Recognition (ICDAR), pp. 116–120. IEEE, Piscataway (2009)
51. The Asiatic Society, Kolkata. https://asiaticsocietycal.com
52. Trier, I.D., Jain, A.K., Taxt, T.: Feature extraction methods for character recognition—a survey. Pattern Recognit. **29**(4), 641–662 (1996)
53. Vecco, M.: A definition of cultural heritage: from the tangible to the intangible. J. Cult. Herit. **11**(3), 321–324 (2010)
54. Vrochidis, S., Doulaverakis, C., Gounaris, A., Nidelkou, E., Makris, L., Kompatsiaris, I.: A hybrid ontology and visual-based retrieval model for cultural heritage multimedia collections. Int. J. Metadata Semant. Ontol. **3**(3), 167–182 (2008)
55. Zagoris, K., Pratikakis, I., Gatos, B.: Segmentation-based historical handwritten word spotting using document-specific local features. In: Proc. of International Conference on Frontiers in Handwritten Recognition (ICFHR), pp. 9–14 (2014)
56. Zhang, X., Tan, C.L.: Segmentation-free keyword spotting for handwritten documents based on heat kernel signature. In: Proc. of International Conference of Document Analysis and Recognition (ICDAR), pp. 827–831. IEEE, Piscataway (2013)
57. Zhang, X., Pal, U., Tan, C.L.: Segmentation-free keyword spotting for Bangla handwritten documents. In: Proc. of International Conference on Frontiers in Handwritten Recognition (ICFHR), pp. 381–386 (2014)

Part II
Restoration and Reconstruction of Digital Heritage Artifacts

Text Extraction and Restoration of Old Handwritten Documents

Mayank Wadhwani, Debapriya Kundu, Deepayan Chakraborty, and Bhabatosh Chanda

Abstract Image restoration is a crucial computer vision task. This chapter describes two novel methods for the restoration of old, degraded handwritten documents using a deep neural network. In addition, a small-scale dataset consisting of images of 26 heritage letters is introduced. The ground truth data to train the desired network is generated semi-automatically, involving a pragmatic combination of colour transformation, Gaussian mixture model-based segmentation and correction by using mathematical morphological operators. In the first approach, a deep neural network has been used for text extraction from the document image. The background is then reconstructed based on a Gaussian mixture model. Note that a Gaussian mixture model requires setting parameters manually; to alleviate this problem, we propose a second approach where both the background reconstruction and the foreground extraction (i.e. extracting text with its original colour) are achieved using a deep neural network. Experiments demonstrate that the proposed systems perform well on handwritten document images with severe degradation, even when trained with a small dataset. Hence, the proposed methods are ideally suited for digital heritage preservation repositories where the number of samples is low. It is worth mentioning that these methods can be extended easily for printed degraded documents as well.

Keywords Binarization · Image restoration · Deep learning · Auto-encoder · Digital heritage

M. Wadhwani
Indian Institute of Technology, Patna, Patna, India
e-mail: wadhwani.cs16@iitp.ac.in

D. Kundu (✉) · D. Chakraborty · B. Chanda
Indian Statistical Institute, Kolkata, India
e-mail: chanda@isical.ac.in

© Springer Nature Switzerland AG 2021
J. Mukhopadhyay et al. (eds.), *Digital Techniques for Heritage Presentation and Preservation*, https://doi.org/10.1007/978-3-030-57907-4_6

1   Introduction

Documents are an essential part of human civilization as they describe the evolution of civilization and keep a record of our past. The development and advancement of technology has boosted the digital documentation of tangible and intangible heritage artefacts. Though society is moving towards a paperless world, the importance of handwritten documents has retained its place because of the traditional culture it carries. These documents may also offer valuable insight into the nature of the writer. Compared to electronic or printed text, handwritten text carries additional information about the personality and mood of the writer. Hence, it is essential to preserve handwritten documents and extract precious information that was being conveyed during the time of writing.

Over time, documents undergo various kinds of degradation like ageing of pages, ink blotting, fading of ink colour, granular noise, and wear and tear of the writing medium (e.g. paper, palm leaves). Librarians and archivists have long been concerned with the problem of deterioration of writing media like papers, palm leaves, skins and others. Considering the need for safekeeping of heritage documents in electronic form and extracting information from them, this research primarily focuses on the digital restoration of handwritten paper documents that suffered from various kinds of degradation so that further processing of documents for character recognition and semantic interpretation can be facilitated.

One of the most familiar yet significant challenges in old historical document restoration is the back-impression (i.e. written impression propagated to the opposite side of the medium), especially with documents written using ink. This back-impression appears as noise in the document when the primary side is taken into consideration for subsequent processing and interpretation. Another problem encountered while processing such documents is the random variation in the colour intensity of ink used to write the text, i.e. the variation in the tones of the ink that was used. The problem is further complicated when the faded intensity of ink becomes close to that of back-impression. Another challenge is the folding marks that are visible on the document image due to improper storing of the document over a long period of time. Degradation also includes certain ink blots and granular noisy spots on the document.

This work addresses the problem of restoration of the useful content of handwritten documents and reconstruction of the 'most likely' appearance of the original documents. Figure 1 illustrates our objective. In other words, the objective of this work is focused specifically on denoising and restoration of appearance of a (primarily) handwritten document to its original form (i.e. before undergoing any degradation). We propose two different methods for image restoration. The first method employs a deep convolutional neural network (CNN) for text binarization and also a Gaussian mixture model (GMM) for extracting the background colour of the document image. Then the extracted text and the estimated background are combined to generate the final restored image. So this approach consists of three distinct steps and requires some human intervention. However, in the second

Fig. 1 Demonstration of the objective of this work. (**a**) Original degraded image and (**b**) restored image

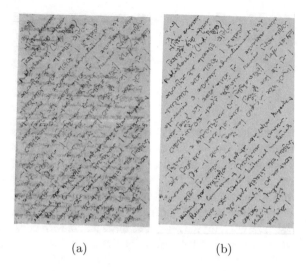

(a)   (b)

approach, a network is designed and employed to generate a restored document, given a degraded old document as input. The network consists of two parallel paths: one path extracts the foreground and the other the background separately with its proper colour. Finally, they are combined suitably in the network to achieve the final goal.

This work makes the following three main contributions:

1. We have built a heritage handwritten document dataset containing images of 26 Bengali letters of correspondence along with ground truths. The ground truth generation involves a semi-automatic method, which is discussed in Sect. 3.1. Along with the dataset, the ground truth generation approach can also be considered a contribution of this work. Details of our dataset are given in Sect. 1.1.
2. In the first approach for image restoration, we have developed a fully convolutional auto-encoder to extract the foreground text from the degraded document image. This is followed by a Gaussian mixture model (GMM)-based method for background reconstruction. Finally, the extracted text and the estimated background are combined to generate the restored document image. Note that GMM requires parameters to be set manually, which involves significant human intervention. This problem is bypassed in the second approach.
3. In the second approach, we have replaced the GMM part of the first method with a deep neural network and the text is extracted with its restored colour. So we call this foreground extraction rather than text extraction as in the first approach.

Experimental results show that both these methods are able to restore old handwritten documents well, even with very severe degradation. We also compared our results with the results of the winning methods of ICDAR 2017 [11] and ICFHR 2018 [12] on DIBCO datasets for text extraction (i.e. binarization) and obtained comparable results. For some of the images, our method gives better output compared to others.

1.1 Dataset

The heritage documents in which we are interested are neither large in number nor made readily accessible. Our dataset contains images of 26 letters between Professor Prasanta Chandra Mahalanobis and others (more than 50 years old, some of the period of World War II). These are from the 'P. C. Mahalanobis Memorial Museum and Archives' of the Indian Statistical Institute, Kolkata. These letters are written on very thin types of paper and are affected by various kinds of degradation. Our database contains the images of these letters with their corresponding ground truths. In our work, we have arbitrarily chosen 10 images for training and 16 images for testing (this is a subjective choice). The ground truth generation process is explained in Sect. 3.1. Heritage letters are not very easily available, and the number of such letters in reality is also very small. This explains the importance of this dataset. The dataset will be published online soon.

The rest of this chapter is organized as follows. Section 2 presents a brief survey of related works. Our proposed method, including training data generation and network training, is presented in Sect. 3. Experimental results are given in Sect. 4. Finally, in Sect. 5 we conclude the chapter and suggest some future directions of the work.

2 Literature Review

For the last couple of decades, numerous efforts have been made for the digital preservation of old handwritten manuscripts under various heritage projects [3], including the Indian initiative [7]. Restoration of manuscripts and handwritten documents has an important role in the preservation of cultural heritage. Various approaches and techniques have been tried by researchers to find an effective and widely applicable solution to the problem. Some of these methods involve restoration of single-sided low-quality document images (RSLDI) [8] and local linear level set method [13]. However, these methods may not be used directly in the presence of back-impressions. Back-impression due to ink bleed-through increases the difficulty in reading documents. An image restoration based on the bleed-through approach has been proposed in [5], whereas an attempt using a self-organizing map has been made in [16]. Garain et al. [6] have presented an approach to image binarization, which shows adaptability to uneven illumination and non-uniformity in background and foreground colours. Relatively more recent work has employed learning and labelling using the Markov model [1]. The concept of considering the distribution of pixel values of a document image as a mixture of Gaussian distributions and estimating related parameters using the expectation–maximization algorithm [4] is well studied. The distribution, in this approach, is decomposed into sub-distributions [9] representing various regions of the document image. Image restoration from the perspective of image segmentation has also been attempted [15], where the authors use K-means clustering. Note that all these methods utilize the properties of old handwritten documents or manuscripts, which are conceived based on careful observation and experience of the developer of the algorithms. So these are all model-driven approaches based on domain knowledge.

Recently, with the increasing success and popularity of deep learning techniques, there have been attempts to model this problem in a supervised framework. Many deep learning-based methods participated in the competition on binarization of old documents organized at ICDAR 2017 [11]. Method-1 in DIBCO2017 [11] used an ensemble of five deep FCNs (fully convolutional networks) that operated over multiple image scales, whereas Method-7, 17 in [11] modelled the problem using a convolutional auto-encoder. Method-10 used a U-net and Method-12 developed a DSN model with a multi-scale structure to learn text-like features from document images themselves to classify text and background from degraded document images. A recurrent neural network has also been explored in this domain by Method-13.

In our first method, the text or foreground extraction is done using a fully convolutional auto-encoder, and the background reconstruction using GMM. In our second method, a fully convolutional auto-encoder is employed for the background reconstruction. The foreground extraction in both methods is done with a neural network of similar architecture, with the only difference being in the number of input and output channels of the network. This implies that the performance of both methods in image binarization should be the same. We have compared the performance of the text extraction network of the first method and that of the winning methods of ICDAR 2017 and ICFHR 2018, both qualitatively and quantitatively, in Sect. 4.

3 Proposed Method

The proposed methods are developed by adopting two different approaches. Both methods exploit the convolutional neural networks, more specifically an auto-encoder, to achieve the goal. It is known that the training of such networks requires a large amount of data with ground truth. However, it is also known that ground truths of heritage documents are not available. So, our first task is to generate the ground truth of the class of heritage documents that we are interested in to build up the training data. In this context, we first describe our proposed Method-1 for restoring old handwritten documents. The first method consists of three distinct steps as detailed next.

3.1 Training Data Generation

This chapter proposes deep learning-based methods for image restoration. Supervised learning-based methods require ground truth for training. In this section, we explain different steps for ground truth generation to build up our proposed dataset. The first method carries out text binarization in the first step, and then it estimates the background of the restored image in an unsupervised way using the GMM technique in the second step. Finally, in the third step, extracted text and estimated background are combined to generate the restored image. The second method, on the other hand, trains in parallel two different neural networks with similar architecture to generate (1) the text with its restored colour (document image foreground) and (2) the expected background. Finally, the outputs of these two networks are suitably combined to form the restored image. Hence, in the second method we require three different ground truths for each degraded image in our dataset. Thus the ground truths are categorized as follows:

– Binarized text image—the foreground text mask of the document image (*required for the first method*).
– Expected foreground image—extracted foreground (text) of the document image with its restored colour (*required for the second method*).
– Estimated background image—restored background of the document image (*required for the second method*).
– Restored document image—reconstructed handwritten document image obtained by combining restored text and restored background (*required for the second method*).

3.1.1 Binarized Text Image Generation

Pre-processing The first step, like most other image processing algorithms, is a pre-processing step where we convert the input colour image to a greyscale one to simplify subsequent processing. We also improve the contrast of the resultant greyscale image to facilitate text–background separation. For the pre-processing of the data, there are two alternative approaches to convert colour images to greyscale image based on the quality of input image.

– If the background or colour of the writing medium (in this case, paper) is bright, the intensity at a pixel is computed as

$$I(x, y) = 0.30 * R(x, y) + 0.59 * G(x, y) + 0.1 * B(x, y), \qquad (1)$$

where R, G and B are red, green and blue components of colour at that pixel.
– Otherwise, the intensity at a pixel is computed as

$$I(x, y) = \max\{R(x, y), G(x, y), B(x, y)\}. \qquad (2)$$

Note that in both cases, the colour intensity of the ink is lower than that of the medium.

Text Extraction It is observed that the least distinguishable difference between the intensities (i.e. contrast) of two adjacent regions depends on the intensity of the neighbourhood. This is explained and quantified in Weber's law [2]. However, this perceptual criterion is not reflected in widely used metrics like Euclidean distance or Mahalanobis distance employed in common clustering and classification algorithms. So to facilitate text extraction we enhance the greyscale image by an appropriate non-linear transformation as

$$v = \mathcal{T}(I), \tag{3}$$

such that the perceptual difference is reflected in difference in grey values. As the image contains different types of signals (e.g. written text and background colour) and also noise, both structured (e.g. back-impression) and random, the probability density function or histogram of v may be expressed as a mixture of several, say, K number of, Gaussian distributions given by

$$p(v) = \sum_{i=0}^{K-1} P_i G_{\mu_i, \sigma_i}(v), \tag{4}$$

where μ_i and σ_i represent the mean and standard deviation of the i-th distribution, and P_i is its a priori probability. There are standard methods available to solve Eq. (4) to estimate P_i, μ_i and σ_i. For example, expectation–maximization is one such popular method. However, to obtain optimum result, this method requires the exact value of K, which unfortunately in most cases is not known. Since $p(v)$ is uni-variate and manual analysis is tractable, we may opt to determine the number of classes and the corresponding threshold boundary through observation and updating. Based on our domain knowledge, we take the value of K less than or equal to 4.

In this work, K GMM suggests that $K-1$ thresholds $\{t_1, t_2, \ldots, t_{K-1}\}$ decompose the image into k different types of regions. One of these is the text region that may be obtained by separating out the pixels either with value $v \leq t_1$ or $t_1 \leq v \leq t_2$ depending on the value of P_1 and P_2. In other words, the text is extracted by using adaptive grey-level thresholding based on analysis of local statistics. Note that Otsu's method [10] could not be applied because of the presence of more than two classes even within a local neighbourhood. It is known that the opening operation can efficiently remove black grain noise and protrusion in objects. Similarly, the closing operation can remove white grain noise (holes) and intrusions in objects. Spurious random (salt-and-pepper) noise as well as some structural defects in strokes/curves of handwriting produced due to thresholding are rectified using carefully chosen mathematical morphological operators (e.g. opening and closing). This post-processing method aims to achieve near perfect text extraction from the given image. Finally, the text image is blurred with a Gaussian kernel to

Fig. 2 Ground truth text binarization. (**a**) Original greyscale image and (**b**) output of text extraction process

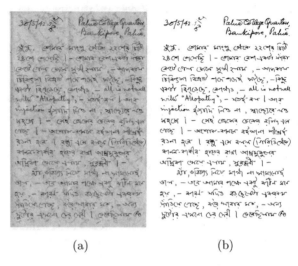

(a)   (b)

reduce the noise or structural defect, if any, still present. So the process in this step is semi-automatic and involves human intervention. The result of this step is shown in Fig. 2. The output is considered ground truth and will be used, along with the input image, to train the text extraction network of the first method.

3.1.2 Restored Foreground Image Generation

Foreground image generation includes text extraction followed by restoration of foreground (i.e. text) colour. Text extraction has already been discussed. After extraction of the texts, the original colours are restored using simple logical operation with the binarized text image and input image as operands.

In order to achieve colour restoration, the extracted binarized text image (say, background pixel is '0' and foreground '1') is AND-ed (or multiplied) by the input colour image to extract the colours present at the locations of the text. The performed operation can be expressed using Eq. (5). Here χ and χ' are the degraded image and its handwritten part, respectively, and T is the extracted (binarized) text image:

$$\chi'(x, y) = \gamma T(x, y) \times \chi(x, y). \tag{5}$$

Careful observation of heritage handwritten documents reveals, first, that in most of the cases the darker tone of the writing ink fades out (becomes lighter) over time. Second, the original ink tone usually varies due to pen pressure and writing speed. However, the fading effect is assumed to be uniform over the entire document. So in Eq. (5) a space-invariant parameter γ, where $0 < \gamma < 1$, is used to darken the tone of the colour in the restored foreground image. The result of this step is

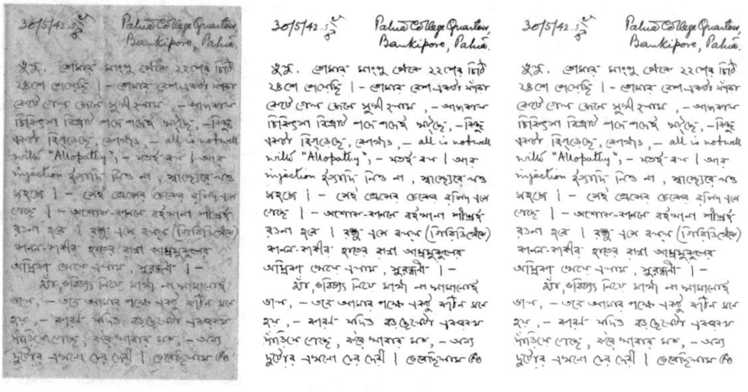

| | | |
| (a) | (b) | (c) |

Fig. 3 Result of ground truth foreground image generation. (**a**) Document image, (**b**) extracted text image and (**c**) output of foreground colour restoration process

shown in Fig. 3. Note that the restored foreground image will be used as ground truth in the second method. Third, uniform colour could have been assigned to all text (foreground) pixels, but it is not done to maintain a kind of real-life appearance.

3.1.3 Restored Background Image Generation

Since the background (the paper colour and texture on which the text was written) is one of the most essential components and dominating parts of the image, it is very important to have the original background reconstructed as a part of restoration of the original image. For this, we consider the degraded document image pixel values as a mixture of Gaussian distributions. This is formulated using Gaussian mixture modelling (GMM), where the observations are equal to the number of pixels present in the image, each with three colour channel measurements R, G and B.

$$p(\mathbf{c}) = \sum_{i=0}^{K-1} P_i G_{\mu_i, \Sigma_i}(\mathbf{v}), \qquad (6)$$

where μ_i and Σ_i represent the mean vector and co-variance matrix of the i-th distribution, and P_i is its a priori probability. $\mathbf{c}$ is a colour vector at pixel (x, y), i.e $\mathbf{c} = (R, G, B)^T$. Each Gaussian distribution represents one class, such as text colour, background colour, back-impression colour or noise. Using the expectation–maximization algorithm, the parameters μ_i, Σ_i and P_i are predicted. Consequently, the probability of each pixel belonging to each of the clusters is also computed. Then, the pixel is assigned to the cluster predicted with the highest probability. Note that the algorithm needs to know the number of clusters, which is the same as that obtained in Sect. 3.1.1. Thus, we use $K = 4$ and four mean colours of four clusters of a degraded image as shown in Fig. 4.

We then convert these (R, G, B) values of mean vector $\boldsymbol{\mu}_i$ to greyscale values using Eq. (1). The one with the lowest intensity (i.e. towards black) is generally taken to be foreground or text, while the cluster with the highest P_i corresponds to the background (assuming background pixels to be most frequent, which is true in almost all cases). The cluster(s) with a mean in between these two extremes generally corresponds to noise in the document, including the back-impression. In many cases, white pixels appear due to excess scanning area beyond the document region. Figure 4 shows four mean colours of four clusters corresponding to the image of a degraded document, where the colours refer to (clockwise: from top left) excess white portion due to scanning, background, text and back-impression, including grain noise. According to these findings, we form a matrix of the same size as the input image filled with random numbers generated following multivariate Gaussian distribution with mean vector $\boldsymbol{\mu}_i$ and co-variance matrix $\boldsymbol{\Sigma}_i$ corresponding to the background colour. Finally, a Gaussian blurring is applied to the generated matrix to smoothen the drastic variations in neighbouring pixels. Thus we reconstruct the background of the given degraded document image. Figure 5 shows the reconstructed background. Figure 5a shows the random number matrix generated following multivariate Gaussian distribution with mean vector and co-variance matrix corresponding to background colour, and Fig. 5b shows a Gaussian blurred version of Fig. 5a, which is, finally, used as a background of the restored document image. This image is used as ground truth of the background image in the second method.

Fig. 4 Predicted mean colour of various parts (or components) of an image predicted using Gaussian mixture model. The colours refer to (clockwise: from top left) excess white portion due to scanning, background, text and back-impression

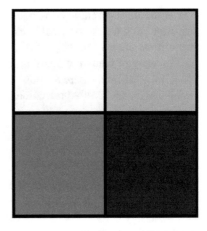

Fig. 5 Result of background reconstruction. (**a**) Random number matrix generated following multivariate Gaussian distribution of background colour and (**b**) Gaussian blurred version of (**a**) used as ground truth background of the document

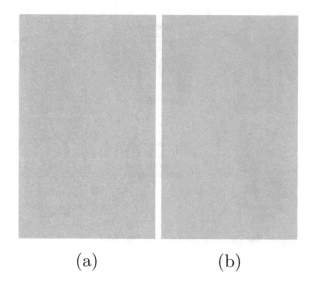

(a)   (b)

3.2 Proposed Method-1

A handwritten document such as a letter or manuscript primarily contains text and background, and the background should be smooth enough with uniform colour and brightness. In the previous sections, we have shown how the different components of a document image are restored using a semi-automatic method and then combined to complete the restoration. However, binarization is the most critical task, so in this method we employ a CNN that can extract the text portion with quite good accuracy from a greyscale input image. The proposed Method-1 consists of the following four steps:

1. Pre-processing: We follow the process described in Sect. 3.1.1. This step is applied on both training and test images.
2. Binarization or text extraction: This is done using a convolutional neural network (CNN), more specifically, an auto-encoder.
3. Restored foreground image generation: The same process as described already in Sect. 3.1.2 is followed here and is applied to all images in the dataset.
4. Restored background image generation: Here also the same process described in Sect. 3.1.3 is followed. This step is applied to all images.
5. Final document image restoration: The degraded document image is finally restored by combining the restored foreground image (from step 3) and restored background image (from step 4). More specifically, the foreground portion is overlaid on the background image.

The complete system is illustrated in Fig. 6. Steps 1, 3 and 4 are already described and discussed, so we skip them here. Also note that training samples for step 2 are already generated as described in Sect. 3.1.1. Below we discuss steps 2 and 5 in detail.

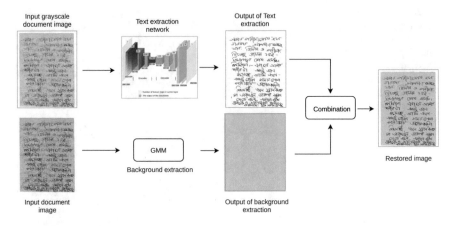

Fig. 6 Block diagram of proposed Method-1

3.2.1 CNN for Text Extraction

For text extraction, in this method, a fully convolutional auto-encoder is trained with patches of size 256×256 as input. We have taken overlapping patches from the input greyscale document image. The output is the corresponding greyscale text image patches, which should ideally be binary but in reality are a greyscale image. Corresponding ground truth to be compared with is already generated as described in Sect. 3.1.1.

The proposed network is shown in Fig. 7, which consists of four convolutional layers (encoder) and six convolutional transpose layers (decoder), having a stride of two for all layers except the last two layers where strides are one. Padding is enabled only for the last three layers. We have used $tanh$ function as the non-linear activation function for each layer except the final layer, where sigmoid function is taken as activation function to get the output within $(0,1)$, i.e. the defined greyscale range. Since our goal is to obtain a binary image of the handwritten document and extract the text part, to train the network we have used structural dissimilarity (DSSIM) as the objective function with patch size 23×23. The Structural Dissimilarity Index Metric (DSSIM) is related to the Structural Similarity Index Metric (SSIM) [17] by the following equation:

$$\mathrm{DSSIM}(W_p, W_g) = \frac{1 - \mathrm{SSIM}(W_p, W_g)}{2}, \tag{7}$$

where W_p and W_g are windows or patch of the predicted and corresponding ground truth data, respectively, of common size. Note that SSIM is defined as

$$\mathrm{SSIM}(W_p, W_g) = \frac{(2\mu_p\mu_g + C_1)(2\sigma_{p,g} + C_2)}{(\mu_p^2 + \mu_g^2 + C_1)(\sigma_p^2 + \sigma_g^2 + C_2)}, \tag{8}$$

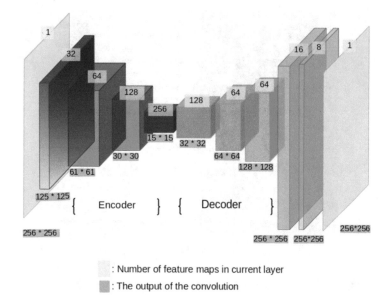

Fig. 7 Proposed neural network architecture for text extraction in Method-1

where μ and σ have their usual meaning, and C_1 and C_2 are constants greater than zero (introduced to avoid being divided by zero). The first reason for choosing this loss function is that the structure of the handwritten part is more important than its colour or intensity. Second, SSIM is a measure of image quality independent of brightness and contrast, which vary significantly in heritage documents. Figure 8b shows the output of our proposed network given in Fig. 8a as input.

The output of our text extraction network is a grey-level image $T_b(x, y)$. This image is 'toggle filtered' so that ink blotting is rectified followed by simple thresholding for binarization. Toggle filter is a decision-based mathematical morphological operator that sharpens the blurred edge [14]. Then we follow steps 3 and 4 for foreground colour restoration and background colour restoration. These two restored images are denoted by $T_c(x, y)$ and $B(x, y)$, respectively. The final restored image is then generated by combining $T_c(x, y)$ and $B(x, y)$. These steps are elaborated next.

3.2.2 Post-processing and Document Image Reconstruction

This is the final step for document restoration; from step 3, we have the intensity of each foreground pixel, which is then overlaid on the background image reconstructed in the previous sections. This results in the final restored image $R(x, y)$.

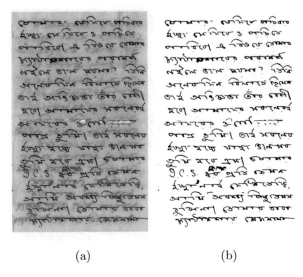

(a)   (b)

Fig. 8 Result of text extraction network of Method-1. (**a**) Input and (**b**) output

Steps 3 and 4 may be summarized as follows:

$$T'(x, y) = \text{toggle\_filter}\, [T_b(x, y)],$$

$$T_c(x, y) = \text{extract\_colour\_of}\, T_b(x, y) \text{ from } I(x, y)),$$

$$R(x, y) = T_c(x, y) \text{ overlay\_on } B(x, y).$$

Examples of restored image are shown in Figs. 9 and 10. These restored images are the final output of this method, i.e. Method-1. As observed, the restored image contains minimal noise. It is worth noting that the back-impression is completely removed here. The network architecture is generic for all document images as it is first converted to a greyscale image to obtain the output. Hence, it is independent of background colour. This restored document is used as ground truth for the second method.

3.3 Proposed Method-2

Although the first method achieves very good results, the main problem with that method is that it requires human interventions to some extent. Many parameters have to be set manually by trial and error. This is a tedious approach and leads to a user-specific solution. On the other hand, in the proposed Method-2, we exploit a complete learning-based system as demonstrated in Fig. 11, where human intervention is not at all required.

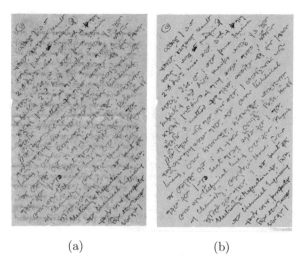

(a) (b)

Fig. 9 Demonstration of result of Method-1. (**a**) Original degraded document image and (**b**) restored image

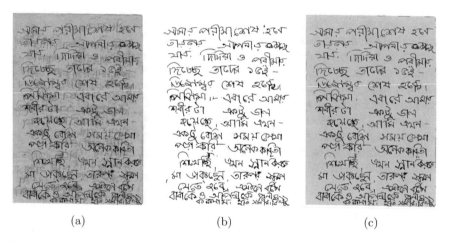

(a) (b) (c)

Fig. 10 Illustration of a result of Method-1. (**a**) Original degraded image, (**b**) output of text extraction network and (**c**) restored document image

This method builds a complete (end-to-end) network that has three distinct parts: (1) foreground extraction network for restoring the foreground pixel values, (2) background extraction network for restoring the background pixel values and (3) a simple model for reconstructing the final restored document image combining the output of the first two. Note that the required ground truths or training samples for these individual parts have already been generated in Sects. 3.1.2, 3.1.3 and 3.2.2, respectively. Descriptions and training of the networks are presented in the following subsections.

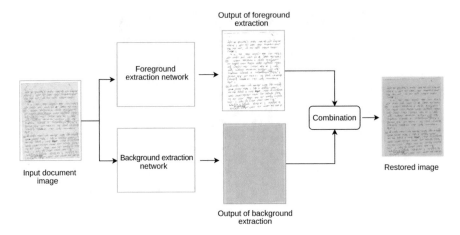

Fig. 11 Block diagram of proposed Method-2

3.3.1 CNN for Foreground Restoration

For foreground extraction, a fully convolutional auto-encoder model is trained. This network has similar architecture to the network shown in Fig. 7. The only difference is that the network has three channels in the input and output layers to deal with colour image. Input to this network is a patch of size 256×256 extracted from the normalized degraded colour document image with stride 50, and the output is the resultant patch containing only the restored handwritten part corresponding to the input patch. This network is trained using the ground truth generated in Sect. 3.1.2. This means the output of the network is compared with a corresponding patch of size 256×256 taken from the restored foreground image using Eq. (8). An output of foreground restoration is shown in Fig. 13b.

3.3.2 CNN for Background Restoration

This step is in parallel with the foreground restoration step. In this step, the same network as the foreground extraction network is trained for restoration of the background. We call this network a *background extraction network*. The output of this network is the patch containing the restored background of the corresponding given input patch. As discussed earlier, the background image suffers comparatively more impacts from degradation. Moreover, construction of the restored background image from the original image involves a large amount of pixel modification. For this reason, a comparatively higher number of training samples are needed to train the network. We have included horizontally and vertically flipped patches (see Fig. 12) extracted from the data samples also as training data. This network is also trained using DSSIM as objective function. Finally, the patches are combined

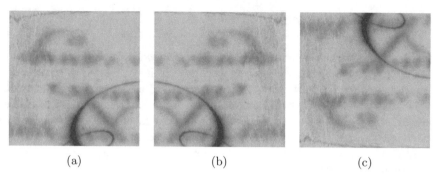

Fig. 12 Combinations of extracted patches considered for training. (**a**) Original patch, (**b**, **c**) horizontal and vertical flips of (**a**), respectively

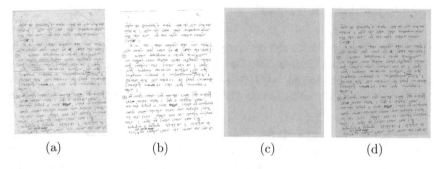

Fig. 13 Demonstration of result of Method-2. (**a**) Input degraded image, (**b**) output of foreground extraction network, (**c**) output of background extraction network and (**d**) reconstructed image obtained by combining (**b**) and (**c**)

properly and overlapping areas are averaged for reconstruction of the original background image. Figure 13c shows the output of this network for Fig. 13a as input.

3.4 Final Image Restoration

This is the final step where the two separate images (predicted foreground image and predicted background image) are merged to reconstruct a noise-free restored image. In order to perform the merging operation, we have picked up the colour pixels from the foreground image (χ') and assigned their pixel values to their corresponding location in the background image (β). Figure 13d shows the reconstructed image by merging Fig. 13b and c.

4 Experimental Results

In this section, we present both old document restoration and text extraction results of the proposed methods. We also compare our results with those of some well-known existing methods. However, this comparison is done only for the binarization or text extraction part, as the related results on image restoration are not available in the literature. In this work, we have chosen the auto-encoder network to solve the given problem. An auto-encoder is found to be very successful in data compression. Here also we wanted to preserve the core information, i.e. pure text and uniform background as the case may be, for document image restoration.

4.1 Implementation Details

Parameter Tuning There are certain parameters that need to be set manually through experimental observations. These parameters have a significant impact on the output. These parameters may be classified into two groups: (1) for training data generation and (2) for tuning the network. The major parameters in the first group are listed below:

1. **Number of Gaussian distributions in the mixture model:** The value of this parameter is decided by observing the image (or domain knowledge) and exploring the number of distinct peaks present in the colour histogram of the image. We have taken the value of this parameter as 4; the reason for this choice has already been explained in the previous section.
2. **Threshold:** This is a very important parameter required for binarization and text extraction from the greyscale version of the original degraded image. This is set manually by analysing the grey-level histogram of the image. This may be fine-tuned interactively based on the experimental results.

Similarly, the network-related parameters (in the second group) are as follows:

1. **Size of the patches:** The input patch size has an essential role in training as the patches containing local structure information (i.e. text) as well as global uniformity (i.e. background colour). A correct patch size helps us estimate distinctiveness between background and foreground and also identify noise— both structured and random. We have taken a patch size of 256×256 for both methods.
2. **Stride value:** We know that training a deep learning network requires a lot of data. On the other hand, the number of old handwritten document images is usually low. So we pick up patches from the images with overlap. First, during testing, non-overlap patches would create a blocking, so patch overlapping is necessary. Second, patch overlapping also leads to multiple estimates for each pixel, which eventually reduces the chance of error. The decision of stride value of this overlap has an important role to play as it helps us generate more patches

but with as little repetition as possible. A high stride value might miss the data variation, and a low stride value might increase the processing time and, in some cases, introduce blurring. For both approaches, we have set the stride value to 50.

3. **Number of layers:** Our proposed network (Fig. 7) contains 10 layers (excluding the input and output layers) with 4 convolution (encoder) and 6 convolution transpose layers (decoder). The numbers of filters in the convolution layers are 32, 64, 128 and 256, and those in the convolution transpose layers are 128, 64, 64, 16 and 8. The number of filters is chosen experimentally to produce acceptable results. The count of feature maps from left to right in the encoder part of the network is increasing and that in the decoder part is decreasing. The reason behind the increasing number of filters in the encoder part of the network is that as the network goes deeper, the receptive field size increases because the field of view of each kernel increases. Hence, feature maps of lower layers are primitive (e.g. basic shapes) and those in the deeper layers have high-level abstract features (e.g. complex shapes). This increase in abstraction is compensated by increasing the number of filters. The same concept (in the opposite direction) applies to the decoder part.

4. **Kernel size:** We took a varied set of kernel sizes for the network (Fig. 7). For the 4 layers in the encoder, the size of kernels is 8×8, 5×5, 3×3 and 2×2, respectively. And that for the decoder is 4×4, 2×2, 2×2, 1×1 and 2×2, respectively. The choice of having varying filter sizes is again experimental.

The first method requires all the parameters, while the second method requires only the parameters of the second group that are related to the network.

4.2 Results and Discussion

Results of Method-1 In Fig. 10 we have shown the result of Method-1 on one of the test images of our dataset. Figure 10a and c shows the original degraded image and the final restored image, respectively, while Fig. 10b shows the binarization result, or in other words, the output of the text extraction network. This is explicitly shown because text (foreground) extraction is the most challenging part of the whole process. So we have tested our method for text extraction on the DIBCO 2017 and H-DIBCO 2018 datasets. Both datasets consist of a large number of scanned images of old handwritten documents. We have compared the performance of our network both qualitatively and quantitatively with the recent methods available in the literature [11, 12] on the same datasets. The quantitative results are given in Table 1. The evaluation measures considered here are provided in [11] and [12]. Figures 14 and 15, however, show the qualitative comparison. For the results given in Fig. 14, we have trained our network from scratch on the DIBCO datasets of handwritten document images until 2016 available online, and for Fig. 15 training images are taken until 2017. It is also worth mentioning that since both of our methods use similar networks for text extraction, the image binarization performance will be the

Table 1 Values of evaluation measures of our proposed Method-1

(a) H-DIBCO 2018

Image number	FM	F_{ps}	PSNR	DRD
1	69.1938	73.0768	14.198	18.3311
2	64.8763	66.941	13.6041	19.5092
3	88.0551	93.638	14.2126	5.0711
4	62.4174	68.3201	16.0204	10.1883
5	60.0214	67.2715	13.5482	17.8569
6	91.9032	93.6577	17.9624	5.0096
7	86.6083	88.7234	20.0078	4.5071
8	84.8795	85.2728	14.4265	5.0316
9	84.9888	87.74	16.0626	8.8349
10	39.7524	52.7832	9.1852	23.1918
Average	73.26962	77.7425	14.9228	11.75316

(b) DIBCO 2017

Image number	FM	F_{ps}	PSNR	DRD
1	83.4926	83.4767	15.0561	4.6414
2	91.8133	95.7625	17.9206	2.5105
3	89.5671	89.4139	17.7092	4.436
4	86.3604	86.4057	17.6669	4.436
5	87.8957	88.5468	20.2084	3.9519
6	92.3053	93.4956	14.623	2.9862
7	91.3631	91.9622	14.3459	3.6802
8	90.5776	95.8514	18.5194	2.8965
9	87.8546	92.3609	16.0869	3.3333
10	89.9863	93.2925	15.5133	3.1154
Average	89.1216	91.05682	16.76497	3.59874

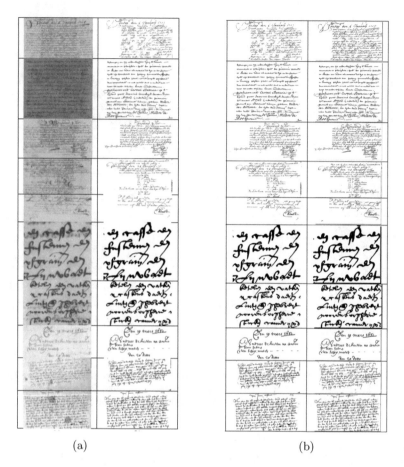

(a)   (b)

Fig. 14 (**a**) (Left to right) The H-DIBCO 2017 testing dataset, its corresponding ground truth, (**b**) results of the winner algorithm, results of our method (Image courtesy of [11] for the dataset images, ground truth and the winner results)

same for both methods, i.e. Method-1 and Method-2. Since our network gives grey-level output images, for hard binarization we apply a moving average technique on the grey-level histogram and then select a threshold for binarization by simple histogram analysis.

Results of Method-2 According to our discussion in Sect. 3, this method is divided into two processes, namely foreground extraction and background extraction using CNN. In Fig. 13a we have shown the degraded sample from the ISI-Letter dataset. This image is passed through the foreground extraction network and background extraction network separately. Figure 13b and c shows their respective outputs. The resultant restored image obtained by combining the aforementioned two images is

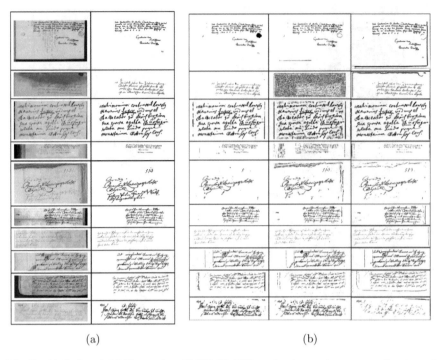

(a) (b)

Fig. 15 (**a**) (Left to right) The result on H-DIBCO 2018 testing dataset, its corresponding ground truth, (**b**) binarization results on H-DIBCO 2018 testing dataset from (left to right) the winner algorithm, the algorithm that ranked in the second position, our method (Image courtesy of [12] for the first four columns)

shown in Fig. 13d. In Fig. 16b we have shown a failure case, where Fig. 16a is given as input and it is revealed that the method could not handle a large ink blob (noise).

5 Conclusion

This chapter presents two methods for old handwritten document image restoration. Method-1 involves mainly two steps: text extraction using a fully convolutional auto-encoder and background generation using Gaussian mixture modelling. Finally, these two outputs are combined to generate the final restored image. Although this method gives convincing output, it requires significant manual intervention due to setting parameters at various stages. This issue has been addressed in Method-2, where both background and foreground are restored in parallel using two neural networks with similar architecture. Finally, restored foreground and background images are combined to reconstruct the (expected) original document image. Both our methods give quite appealing results for old handwritten document images even with severe degradation. The proposed methods can also be easily

Fig. 16 Failure case of Method-2. (**a**) Degraded image and (**b**) restored image

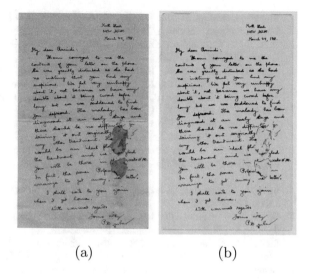

(a)   (b)

extended for printed old documents with a little tuning. This chapter also proposes a small-scale handwritten document image dataset containing 26 old handwritten letters. We plan to extend this work to handle varied types of letters and other documents in future.

Acknowledgement The work is partially supported by the Ministry of Human Resource Development under IMPRINT scheme Project no. 5326 titled 'Information Access from Document Images of Indian languages'.

References

1. Banerjee, J., Namboodiri, A.M., Jawahar, C.: Contextual restoration of severely degraded document images. In: IEEE Conference on Computer Vision and Pattern Recognition, 2009, CVPR 2009, pp. 517–524. IEEE, Piscataway (2009)
2. Chanda, B., Majumder, D.D.: Digital Image Processing and Analysis, 2nd edn. PHI Learning, New Delhi (2010)
3. Chanda, B., Chaudhuri, S., Chaudhury, S. (eds.): Heritage Preservation: A Computational Approach. Springer, Berlin (2018)
4. Dempster, A.P., Laird, N.M., Rubin, D.B.: Maximum likelihood from incomplete data via the EM algorithm. J. R. Stat. Soc. Series B Methodol. **39**, 1–38 (1977)
5. Dubois, E., Pathak, A.: Reduction of bleed-through in scanned manuscript documents. In: Proceedings of PICS, vol. 1, pp. 177–180 (2001)
6. Garain, U., Paquet, T., Heutte, L.: On foreground—background separation in low quality document images. Int. J. Doc. Anal. Recognit. **8**(1), 47 (2006)
7. Mallik, A., Chaudhury, S., Chandru, V., Srinivasan, S. (eds.): Digital Hampi: Preserving Indian Cultural Heritage. Springer, Berlin (2017)
8. Moghaddam, R.F., Cheriet, M.: RSLDI: restoration of single-sided low-quality document images. Pattern Recognit. **42**(12), 3355–3364 (2009)

9. Mohamed, O.M.M., Jaïdane-Saïdane, M.: Generalized Gaussian mixture model. In: 2009 17th European Signal Processing Conference, pp. 2273–2277. IEEE, Piscataway (2009)
10. Otsu, N.: A threshold selection method from gray-level histograms. IEEE Trans. Syst. Man Cybern. **9**(1), 62–66 (1979)
11. Pratikakis, I., Zagoris, K., Barlas, G., Gatos, B.: ICDAR 2017 competition on document image binarization (DIBCO 2017). In: 2017 14th IAPR International Conference on Document Analysis and Recognition (ICDAR), pp. 1395–1403. IEEE, Piscataway (2017)
12. Pratikakis, I., Zagoris, K., Barlas, G., Gatos, B.: ICFHR 2018 competition on document image binarization (H-DIBCO 2018). In: 2018 16th International Conference on Frontiers in Handwriting Recognition. IEEE, Piscataway (2018)
13. Rivest-Hénault, D., Moghaddam, R.F., Cheriet, M.: A local linear level set method for the binarization of degraded historical document images. Int. J. Doc. Anal. Recognit. **15**(2), 101–124 (2012)
14. Serra, J., Vincent, L.: An overview of morphological filtering. Circuits Syst. Signal Process. **11**(1), 47–108 (1992)
15. Setitra, I., Meziane, A.: Old manuscripts restoration using segmentation. Int. J. Electr. Energy **2**, 107–111 (2014)
16. Smigiel, E., Belaid, A., Hamza, H.: Self-organizing maps and ancient documents. In: International Workshop on Document Analysis Systems, pp. 125–134. Springer, Berlin (2004)
17. Wang, Z., Bovik, A.C., Sheikh, H.R., Simoncelli, E.P.: Image quality assessment: from error visibility to structural similarity. IEEE Trans. Image Process. **13**(4), 600–612 (2004)

Categorization and Selection of Crowdsourced Images Towards 3D Reconstruction of Heritage Sites

Ramesh Ashok Tabib, T. Santoshkumar, Varad Pradhu, Ujwala Patil, and Uma Mudenagudi

Abstract In this chapter, we propose a framework for the categorization and selection of crowdsourced images towards the 3D reconstruction of heritage sites. The categorization of crowdsourced heritage site images faces challenges due to high dimensionality and less inter-class variance. The categorization of low variant data using clustering techniques demands robust feature space representation. We propose IVAE (Inception-based Variational Autoencoder) to extract deep features from images towards latent space representation and clustering. The 3D reconstruction of heritage sites using categorized crowdsourced images is challenging due to the presence of redundant images affecting the computational complexity. Robust image selection plays a significant role, as it has a greater impact on the final 3D model. However, the image selection based on a single parameter is not sufficient for large-scale 3D reconstruction. We measure the similarity between the images using multiple parameters and generate a combined confidence score towards discarding images with redundant information. We demonstrate the results of the proposed framework using crowdsourced heritage data and show considerable improvement in the quality of reconstruction.

Keywords Crowdsourcing · Deep features · Categorization · Clustering · 3D reconstruction · Image selection · Dempster–Shafer Combination Rule (DSCR)

1 Introduction

In this chapter, we propose a framework for the categorization and selection of crowdsourced images towards the 3D reconstruction of heritage sites. Crowdsourced data is a collection of information harvesting society's wisdom, skill, creativity, reach and scale to solve a specific problem. Towards the 3D reconstruc-

R. A. Tabib (✉) · T. Santoshkumar · V. Pradhu · U. Patil · U. Mudenagudi
KLE Technological University, Hubballi, Karnataka, India
e-mail: ramesh_t@kletech.ac.in

© Springer Nature Switzerland AG 2021
J. Mukhopadhyay et al. (eds.), *Digital Techniques for Heritage Presentation and Preservation*, https://doi.org/10.1007/978-3-030-57907-4_7

tion of heritage sites, we plan to use the reach and scale of society to build the framework. Through crowdsourcing, we can assimilate dispersed data, typically at low cost compared to the traditional methods of data collection [4, 9, 23]. It is challenging to use this collected data for 3D reconstruction due to the extrinsic properties of data such as irrelevancy, noise and redundancy. This kind of data will not contribute to effective 3D reconstruction. Therefore, it is necessary to categorize and select suitable images for effective 3D reconstruction [10, 14]. We model a framework involving categorization, image selection and 3D reconstruction to address this problem.

Different categorization frameworks are available in the literature, ranging from the annotated data to unsupervised approaches. The authors in [1, 18] used Scale Invariant Feature Transform (SIFT) and Speeded Up Robust Features (SURF) to extract handcrafted features, and further these features are used for clustering. SIFT and SURF features emphasize the local information of an image and neglect global information. This may negatively affect the process of clustering and make the categorization of high-dimensional data challenging. The authors in [17, 19] discuss methods to represent data in the latent space towards generating a lower-dimensional representation and use the same towards clustering. This demands a non-linear mapping function 'f' ($z = f(X)$) to map image (X) to lower-dimensional space (z) with minimal loss in information. To address this, the authors in [19] use the self-supervised learning (autoencoders) [17] framework to learn a mapping function. The autoencoder network learns the visual representation of an image that facilitates the encoder to act as a perfect feature extractor and converts the image into an encoded form. The encoded data is decoded using a learnt decoder to reconstruct the input image. This model is trained to minimize reconstruction loss towards learning a better latent space representation. The trained autoencoder model is used for learning the representation of image in the latent space. During learning latent space representation, the autoencoder model undergoes a dilemma of compression and conceptualization, which misleads the clustering process. To address this, the authors in [7, 13] discuss the Variational Autoencoder (VAE) to train the model towards conceptualization but not for compression. Their objective is to obtain reconstruction information that infers through conceptualization, thereby overcoming data compression.

VAE approximates the probability distribution of input data to the latent space, such that the reconstructed image has the same probability distribution as that of the input image. VAE uses the Kullback–Leibler (KL) divergence loss function to find the difference between the actual probability distribution and the estimated probability distribution of the latent space. Minimizing this difference improves the performance of the model. The major challenge with VAE is that the reconstructed image has blur or other artefacts [3]. To address this, we propose an Inception-based Variational Autoencoder (IVAE) model for learning mapping function to represent the image in latent space. The formed latent space is clustered to get categorized images. Typically, all categorized images are considered for 3D reconstruction and may have redundant and irrelevant images that may affect quality of 3D reconstruction. Thus, we need to select the images before passing them to the reconstruction pipeline.

Several pipelines have been proposed for the selection of images for 3D reconstruction using large-scale data. The authors in [22] propose a technique for image selection using structure from motion (SFM) to compute the position and orientation of each camera to decide the contribution of each image towards 3D reconstruction. Based on the contribution of each image and the effect of its contribution to 3D reconstruction, a decision is made to select the image. The limitation in this approach is that the time taken is more than in a traditional approach since each image is checked for its contribution to the final 3D reconstruction. The authors in [8] propose an image-pair selection by creating a bag of visual words based on vector similarity and set similarity. The creation of a bag of visual words for large-scale 3D reconstruction demands larger memory resources. The tool used in the paper [6] is named Imaging Network Designer (IND), which clusters and selects vantage images in a dense imaging network. Thus, a suitable hardware arrangement is required.

Many methods have been proposed towards the selection of images for 3D reconstruction based on key-frame selection. The authors in [15] discuss the key-frame selection algorithm, where the number of feature points may decrease significantly as the baseline between the current frame and the last key-frame increases. The authors in [5] propose an image selection by the removal of redundant images, where images are sorted in the increasing order of the image size, so that the smaller images are eliminated. Each image is removed to check if the coverage constraint holds well after the removal. If the coverage constraint is satisfied, then the image is permanently eliminated. To address this, we propose to select the images based on a confidence score for reconstruction. We propose the following categorization and image selection steps for effective 3D reconstruction:

- We propose categorization using Inception-based Variational Autoencoder (IVAE).

  - We model IVAE for deep feature extraction.
  - We propose a variant of VAE loss function and model IVAE.
  - We compare the results of the proposed framework with different feature extraction methods and show its effect on clustering.

- We propose a model for image selection using a confidence factor.

  - We propose to generate the confidence factor by combining parametric scores using Dempster–Shafer Combination Rule (DSCR).
  - We use Structural Similarity Index (SSIM) and Fast Library for Approximate Nearest Neighbour (FLANN) as parametric scores to compute the confidence factor.

- We demonstrate the results of the proposed framework using crowdsourced heritage data and compare the results of the proposed framework with state-of-the-art methods.

In Sect. 2, we discuss the proposed framework for the categorization and selection of crowdsourced data. In Sect. 3, we discuss the results of the proposed framework and conclude in Sect. 4.

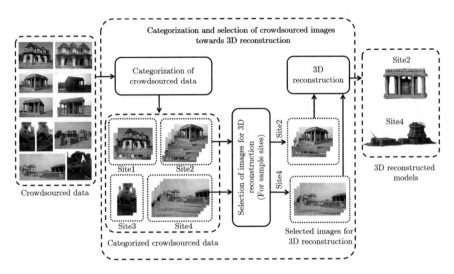

Fig. 1 Categorization and selection of crowdsourced images towards 3D reconstruction. Site2 and Site4 are demonstrated as sample sites

2 Categorization and Selection of Crowdsourced Images

In this section, we discuss the proposed framework for the categorization and selection of images for 3D reconstruction as shown in Fig. 1. Crowdsourced heritage data is categorized and redundant images are removed using image selection framework. We propose to categorize crowdsourced data (Site1, Site2, Site3 and Site4, as shown in Fig. 1) using the IVAE model. Redundant and inappropriate images from categorized heritage sites are removed using the image selection framework. Selected images are used for the 3D reconstruction of heritage sites.

2.1 Categorization of Crowdsourced Data

The framework for categorization of crowdsourced data is shown in Fig. 2. Towards the extraction of robust features from the image, we propose a deep learning-based feature extraction Inception-based Variational Autoencoder (IVAE), a variant of VAE. The VAE fails to capture a diverse representation of images. It introduces a blur in the reconstruction images. To enable the model to capture diverse representation of images, we extend the VAE architecture with inclusion of inception block in the encoder part. In IVAE, X is the given data, z is the latent space variable, $P(X)$ is the probability distribution of data, $P(z)$ is the probability distribution of the latent space variable and $P(X|z)$ is the distribution of generating data given a latent space variable. In the case of IVAE, the objective is to infer $P(z)$ from $P(z|X)$, which is the probability distribution that projects the data into latent space. Since

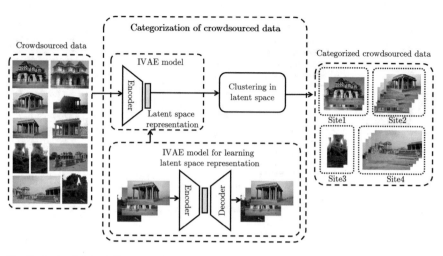

Fig. 2 Categorization of images using deep features for 3D reconstruction. Crowdsourced data is categorized into Site1, Site2, Site3 and Site4 as shown and can extend to many categories

the distribution $P(z|X)$ is unknown, we approximate it using simpler estimation function Q. In the process of training the IVAE, the encoder tries to learn the simpler distribution $Q(z|X)$ to minimize its difference with actual distribution $P(z|X)$. KL divergence gives the measure of a difference between two probability distributions and assists to map the probability distribution Q to the probability distribution P by using the difference between cross-entropy and entropy. Hence, the IVAE objective function includes KL divergence term facilitating better latent space representation:

$$D_{KL}(P|Q) = \sum_i P(i) \log \left(\frac{P(i)}{Q(i)} \right). \tag{1}$$

Due to the low inter-class variance in the heritage dataset, the latent space formed by the model fails to categorize the heritage data appropriately. To make the latent space more variant, we enable the model to learn versatile patterns. Since the learning pattern in the RGB space finds challenges as compared to the YCbCr space, we propose a modified loss function that includes mean square error (MSE) between Y (luminous) channel of an input image and the reconstructed image, respectively. It is observed that the IVAE model converges faster using Y channel. The IVAE objective function includes the proposed loss function facilitating better reconstruction image:

$$L_{\text{custom}} = L_{\text{Ychannel}} + L_{\text{KLDivergence}}. \tag{2}$$

The encoder part of the trained IVAE acts as a feature extractor and is used towards representation of the input image in the latent space. We perform clustering on the latent space to categorize the data. We use K-means for clustering, and the

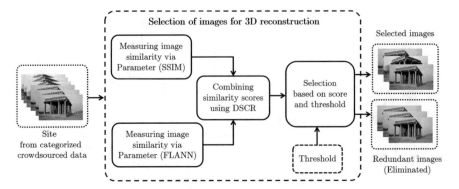

Fig. 3 Selection of images for 3D reconstruction. Site2 is demonstrated as a sample site for the selection framework

number of classes (k) is unknown. Thus, we estimate k using the Elbow method. The generated clusters undergo manual annotation.

2.2 Selection of Images for 3D Reconstruction

The framework for the selection of images is shown in Fig. 3. The similarity between images is measured using the confidence score generated using two parametric scores. We combine the two parametric scores using DSCR [20] to obtain the confidence score. We use the confidence score to decide whether the image is suitable for 3D reconstruction or not.

2.2.1 Parameters for Image Similarity

In large-scale 3D reconstruction, measuring the similarity via a single parameter is not sufficient as shown in Fig. 4. Different parameters give different similarity scores based on which selecting images becomes challenging. Thus, there is a need to combine the parametric scores to obtain a single confidence score towards image selection.

We use FLANN (Fast Library for Approximate Nearest Neighbours) [11] based matching as the first parameter (P_1). FLANN is a library for performing fast approximate nearest neighbour searches in high-dimensional spaces. We use the Structural Similarity Index (SSIM) [12, 21] as the second parameter (P_2). SSIM measures the perceptual difference between two similar images and is based on visible structures of the images. The SSIM index is calculated on various pairs of a window taken from both the images. Then the measure of SSIM between two

#	Query Image	FLANN parameter	SSIM parameter
Sample 1			
Sample 2			

Fig. 4 Selection of images using FLANN and SSIM. Different images are selected by using FLANN and SSIM individually. Quality of the 3D reconstruction is sensitive to the selection of input images

windows x of $image_1$ and y of $image_2$ of common size N×N is

$$SSIM(x, y) = \frac{(2\mu_x\mu_y + c_1)(2\sigma_{xy} + c_2)}{(\mu_x^2 + \mu_y^2 + c_1)(\sigma_x^2 + \sigma_y^2 + c_2)},$$ (3)

where μ_x is the average of x, μ_y is the average of y, σ_x^2 is the variance of x, σ_y^2 is the variance of y, $c_1 = (k_1 L)^2$ and $c_2 = (k_2 L)^2$ are the two variables to stabilize the division with weak denominator and L is the dynamic range of the pixel values (typically it is $2^b - 1$). Here $k_1 = 0.01$ and $k_2 = 0.03$ by default, and they are kept constant throughout our experimentation and b is the number of bits per pixel.

Let N be the total number of images in the dataset for 3D reconstruction. We perform one versus all similarity check. Let $image_i$ be the current query image. $image_i$ is compared with all the other $(N - 1)$ images in the dataset to compute the parametric scores P_1 and P_2. The FLANN-based parametric score P_1 is obtained by the number of valid ORB [16] matches between the image pair divided by the total number of features detected for one image (in our case, the total number of features to be detected for one image is fixed to 500). The SSIM-based parametric score P_2 is obtained by the SSIM score between the image pairs. The obtained parametric scores are combined using DSCR.

2.2.2 Confidence Score Using DSCR

We combine the two parametric scores using the Dempster–Shafer Combination Rule (DSCR) to obtain the confidence score. We decide if the given query image is suitable for 3D reconstruction based on the decision threshold set upon the confidence score to maximize the probability of images being similar. Let P_1 and P_2 be the parametric scores to be combined. DSCR combines two hypotheses

Table 1 Combination table

$\cap$	m_1^{belief}	$m_1^{disbelief}$	$m_1^{ambiguity}$
m_2^{belief}	ψ_1	ϕ	ψ_1
$m_2^{disbelief}$	ϕ	ψ_2	ψ_2
$m_2^{ambiguity}$	ψ_1	ψ_2	Ω

consisting of three parameters, mass of belief, mass of disbelief and mass of uncertainty rather than two parametric scores. We construct hypotheses hyp_1 and hyp_2 as a set of the mass of belief ($m(b)$), disbelief ($m(d)$) and uncertainty ($m(u)$), respectively. We set the mass of belief ($m_1(b)$) for hyp_1 as P_1 and the mass of belief ($m_2(b)$) for hyp_2 as P_2. We assume the mass of disbelief ($m_1(d)$) for hyp_1 and hyp_2 to be 0 and the mass of uncertainty ($m_1(u)$ and $m_2(u)$) for hyp_1 and hyp_2 as $(1-P_1)$ and $(1-P_2)$, respectively. We combine hyp_1 and hyp_2 using a combination table as shown in Table 1.

In Table 1, the product of the mass of belief of one hypothesis and the mass of disbelief of the other hypothesis gives rise to conflict and is represented by ϕ. The product of the mass of belief ($m_1(b)$) and the mass of belief ($m_2(b)$), or the product of the mass of belief ($m(b)$) and the mass of uncertainty ($m(u)$) represents joint belief and is represented by ψ_1. Similarly, ψ_2 represents the joint disbelief. The combined belief of two pieces of evidence is considered as the confidence score and is given by

$$Confidence\ score = \frac{\sum \psi_1}{1 - \sum \phi}. \tag{4}$$

The decision for selecting images suitable for 3D reconstruction is based on the threshold τ set upon the confidence score. The advantage of using DSCR for combining the two parametric scores is that it emphasizes the fact that if P_1 is the probability of the image being suitable for 3D reconstruction then $(1 - P_1)$ need not be the probability of the image not being suitable for 3D reconstruction and is also considered as uncertainty. The value of decision threshold τ is set to 0.5 heuristically, based on observations from experiments on various heritage sites.

3 Results and Discussions

In this section, we discuss the results obtained after the categorization and selection of images. The proposed methodology has been implemented on a workstation with 380GB RAM and 32GB NVIDIA Quadro GV100 graphics processor. We demonstrate our results on heritage datasets of Hampi and Koppal.

3.1   Categorization of Images

In this section, we present the results of categorization of images. In Fig. 5, we show that the reconstructed image using the IVAE model is better than the one using the VAE model and we infer that the IVAE model learns better representation in the latent space towards clustering as compared to the VAE model. The inception block in the IVAE model helps to learn local and global features of the data. We perform K-means clustering in the latent space generated by various models such as AE, VAE and the proposed IVAE. The clustering accuracy for various methods and datasets is shown in Table 2. In Table 2, pre-trained VGG16 shows better accuracy, as it is trained as a classifier using huge labelled data. The proposed method is modeled using unlabelled data and finds challenges to represent data in the latent space for clustering. The results in Table 2 and Fig. 5 show that the IVAE representation outperforms other methods. The categorized image clusters are considered by image selection algorithm towards estimation of irrelevant and redundant images.

(a)   (b)   (c)

Fig. 5 Compression of reconstruction using the VAE and IVAE models. Reconstruction using the IVAE model outperforms. (**a**) Original image. (**b**) Reconstructed image using the VAE model. (**c**) Reconstructed image using the IVAE model. Reconstruction using the IVAE model outperforms the reconstruction using the VAE model

Table 2 Clustering accuracy obtained using K-means clustering algorithm for various datasets using different feature extraction methods

Method	MNIST	PatternNet	Heritage data
PCA	62.3	48.5	47.1
VGG16	81.6	89.4	67.3
AE	69.2	53.4	48.7
VAE	71.1	62.7	68.0
IVAE (proposed method)	75.2	81.6	**78.6**

The bold text is to state that our accuracy is better than all in case of heritage dataset

3.2 Selection of Images

In this section, we demonstrate the results of image selection on heritage datasets considering categorized images. We compare our results with state-of-the-art [2, 10] methods using the number of images retained after the image selection process and the quality of the point cloud generated. We experiment with two heritage sites of Karnataka: (1) Sasivekalu Ganapati of Hampi and (2) Mahadeva Temple of Koppal.

Table 3 shows the comparison of results with and without the proposed framework. In our framework, the results obtained from image selection are considered for reconstruction using OpenMVG-OpenMVS. The results are compared by considering the entire dataset without image selection in the OpenMVG-OpenMVS pipeline.

The Sasivekalu Ganapati of Hampi dataset consists of 129 images, of which 49 images were redundant according to our framework. The model obtained by our framework is comparable with the state of the art. The reconstructed model of Sasivekalu Ganapati of Hampi is shown in Fig. 6.

Figure 6b and d represents the enlarged view of Ganesha from the model shown in Fig. 6a and c, respectively. Figure 6b contains many orange regions representing no reconstruction in region, when compared to Fig. 6d. The face of Ganesha in Fig. 6d is reconstructed well when compared to that in Fig. 6b. Thus, we show improvement in 3D reconstruction using image selection algorithm with reduction in time.

Since our objective is to work on large-scale 3D reconstruction, we experiment on large datasets like the Mahadeva Temple of Koppal consisting of 301 images, with redundant images. With our framework, 226 images are selected and a better 3D model was obtained. Without selection of images, the 3D model is distorted and misaligned. Extended part of reconstruction is observed due to inappropriate selection of images. Figure 7 shows the dense point cloud with and without our approach. Figure 7b shows the dense point cloud on Mahadeva Temple of Koppal without our framework. Figure 7c shows the dense point cloud on Mahadeva Temple of Koppal with our framework.

Table 3 Comparison of results with and without selection of images (heritage dataset)

Dataset	Number of images in dataset	Number of redundant images	Number of images retained using our approach	Percentage of time taken when compared to all images reconstruction
Sasivekalu Ganapati of Hampi	129	49	80	42.4242% (decrease)
Mahadeva Temple of Koppal	301	75	226	47.9644% (decrease)

(a)

(b)

(c)

(d)

Fig. 6 (**a**) 3D Reconstruction of Sasivekalu Ganapati using MVG-MVS pipeline with 129 images. (**b**) ROI: Ganapati Idol, reconstruction is not effective, and more holes are observed due to inappropriate selection of image pairs. (**c**) 3D reconstruction of Sasivekalu Ganapati using the MVG-MVS pipeline with selected 80 images. (**d**) ROI: Ganapati Idol, reconstruction is effective, and less holes are observed due to appropriate selection of image pairs

4   Conclusions

In this chapter, we have proposed a framework for the categorization and selection of crowdsourced images towards the 3D reconstruction of heritage sites. We have proposed a model to cluster the data using deep features generated by a mapping function. We have modeled the Inception-based Variational Autoencoder (IVAE) for extracting deep features from crowdsourced data. Towards refining deep features, we have proposed a variant of Variational Autoencoder (VAE) loss function and model IVAE. The extracted features are represented in the latent space and clustered

(a)

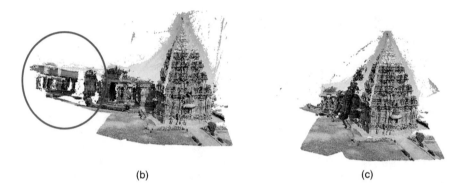

(b)   (c)

Fig. 7 (**a**) Original image. (**b**) 3D reconstruction of heritage site: Mahadeva Temple, Koppal, using the MVG-MVS pipeline with 301 images. Extended part of 3D reconstruction is observed due to inappropriate selection of images. (**c**) 3D reconstruction of heritage site: Mahadeva Temple, Koppal, using the MVG-MVS pipeline with 226 images

using K-means clustering algorithm. We have proposed to choose appropriate pairs for 3D reconstruction from categorized images based on a confidence score. We have computed the confidence score by combining FLANN and SSIM using DSCR to measure the similarity between images. We have modeled 3D reconstruction as a combination of unique images. We have shown better 3D reconstruction using the proposed framework.

References

1. Bay, H., Tuytelaars, T., Van Gool, L.: Surf: Speeded up robust features. In: Leonardis, A., Bischof, H., Pinz, A. (eds.) Computer Vision – ECCV 2006, pp. 404–417. Springer, Berlin (2006)

2. Cernea, D.: OpenMVS: open multiple view stereovision (2015). https://github.com/cdcseacave/openMVS
3. Dai, D., Tang, J., Yu, Z., Wong, H.S., You, J., Cao, W., Hu, Y., Chen, C.: An inception convolutional autoencoder model for Chinese healthcare question clustering. IEEE Trans. Cybern. 1–13 (06 2019). https://doi.org/10.1109/TCYB.2019.2916580
4. Estellés-Arolas, E., de Guevara, F.G.L.: Towards an integrated crowdsourcing definition. J. Inf. Sci. **38**(2), 189–200 (2012). https://doi.org/10.1177/0165551512437638
5. Furukawa, Y., Curless, B., Seitz, S.M., Szeliski, R.: Towards internet-scale multi-view stereo. In: 2010 IEEE Computer Society Conference on Computer Vision and Pattern Recognition, June, pp. 1434–1441 (2010). https://doi.org/10.1109/CVPR.2010.5539802
6. Hosseininaveh, A., Yazdan, R., Karami, A., Moradi, M., Ghorbani, F.: Clustering and selecting vantage images in a low-cost system for 3d reconstruction of texture-less objects. Measurement **99** (2016). https://doi.org/10.1016/j.measurement.2016.12.026
7. Jiang, Z., Zheng, Y., Tan, H., Tang, B., Zhou, H.: Variational deep embedding: a generative approach to clustering. ArXiv abs/1611.05148 (2016)
8. Kato, T., Shimizu, I., Pajdla, T.: Selecting image pairs for SFM on large scale dataset by introducing a novel set similarity. In: 2017 6th ICT International Student Project Conference (ICT-ISPC), May, pp. 1–4 (2017). https://doi.org/10.1109/ICT-ISPC.2017.8075347
9. Kittur, A., Smus, B., Khamkar, S., Kraut, R.E.: Crowdforge: Crowdsourcing Complex Work, pp. 43–52 (2011). https://doi.org/10.1145/2047196.2047202
10. Moulon, P., Monasse, P., Perrot, R., Marlet, R.: OpenMVG: Open multiple view geometry. In: International Workshop on Reproducible Research in Pattern Recognition, pp. 60–74. Springer, Cham (2016)
11. Muja, M., Lowe, D.G.: Fast approximate nearest neighbors with automatic algorithm configuration. In: VISAPP International Conference on Computer Vision Theory and Applications, vol. 1, pp. 331–340 (2009)
12. Patil, U., Mudengudi, U., Ganesh, K., Patil, R.: Image fusion framework. In: Das, V.V., Stephen, J., Chaba, Y. (eds.) Computer Networks and Information Technologies. Springer, Berlin (2011)
13. Pu, Y., Gan, Z., Henao, R., Yuan, X., Li, C., Stevens, A., Carin, L.: Variational autoencoder for deep learning of images, labels and captions. In: Lee, D.D., Sugiyama, M., Luxburg, U.V., Guyon, I., Garnett, R. (eds.) Advances in Neural Information Processing Systems 29, pp. 2352–2360. Curran Associates, Red Hook (2016)
14. Rao, Y., Fan, B., Wang, Q., Pu, J., Luo, X., Jin, R.: Extreme feature regions detection and accurate quality assessment for point-cloud 3d reconstruction. IEEE Access (2019). https://doi.org/10.1109/ACCESS.2019.2898731
15. Repko, J., Pollefeys, M.: 3d models from extended uncalibrated video sequences: Addressing key-frame selection and projective drift, pp. 150–157 (2005). https://doi.org/10.1109/3DIM.2005.4
16. Rublee, E., Rabaud, V., Konolige, K., Bradski, G.: Orb: An efficient alternative to sift or surf. In: 2011 International Conference on Computer Vision, November, pp. 2564–2571 (2011). https://doi.org/10.1109/ICCV.2011.6126544
17. Sainath, T.N., Kingsbury, B., Ramabhadran, B.: Auto-encoder bottleneck features using deep belief networks, pp. 4153–4156 (2012). https://doi.org/10.1109/ICASSP.2012.6288833
18. Satare, R.N., Khot, S.R.: Image matching with sift feature. In: 2018 2nd International Conference on Inventive Systems and Control (ICISC), pp. 384–387 (2018)
19. Song, C., Liu, F., Huang, Y., Wang, L., Tan, T.: Auto-encoder based data clustering. In: Ruiz-Shulcloper, J., Sanniti di Baja, G. (eds.) Progress in Pattern Recognition, Image Analysis, Computer Vision, and Applications, pp. 117–124. Springer, Berlin (2013)
20. Tabib, R.A., Patil, U., Ganihar, S.A., Trivedi, N., Mudenagudi, U.: Decision fusion for robust horizon estimation using Dempster-Shafer combination rule. In: 2013 Fourth National Conference on Computer Vision, Pattern Recognition, Image Processing and Graphics (NCVPRIPG), December, pp. 1–4 (2013). https://doi.org/10.1109/NCVPRIPG.2013.6776247

21. Z. Wang, Bovik, A.C., Sheikh, H.R., Simoncelli, E.P.: Image quality assessment: from error visibility to structural similarity. IEEE Trans. Image Process. **13**, 600–612 (2004). https://doi.org/10.1109/TIP.2003.819861

22. Yang, C., Zhou, F., Bai, X.: 3d reconstruction through measure based image selection. In: 2013 Ninth International Conference on Computational Intelligence and Security, December, pp. 377–381 (2013). https://doi.org/10.1109/CIS.2013.86

23. Zheng, F., Tao, R., Maier, H., See, L., Savic, D., Zhang, T., Chen, Q., Herman Assumpção, T., Pan, Y., Heidari, B., Rieckermann, J., Minsker, B., Bi, W., Cai, X., Solomatine, D., Popescu, I.: Crowdsourcing methods for data collection in geophysics: State of the art, issues, and future directions. Rev. Geophys. (2018). https://doi.org/10.1029/2018RG000616

Deep Learning-Based Filtering of Images for 3D Reconstruction of Heritage Sites

Ramesh Ashok Tabib, Sujaykumar Kulkarni, Abhay Kagalkar,
Vaishnavi Hurakadli, Abhijeet Ganapule, Rohan Raju Dhanakshirur,
and Uma Mudenagudi

Abstract In this chapter, we propose a deep learning-based pipeline for filtering of internet-sourced images towards 3D reconstruction of heritage sites. The 3D reconstruction of heritage sites facilitates creation of virtual walk-through, digital museum and augmented reality. Using internet-sourced images for 3D reconstruction of heritage sites is challenging, as these images may contain blur, text, occlusion, shadow and many other noises. We propose to include pruning and selection of images in the pipeline to select a suitable set of images for 3D reconstruction. We propose a method for pruning of images using learning-based classification models to eliminate the contribution of unwanted images in 3D reconstruction. We also propose a method to select a suitable set of images using a combination of mean-shift and hierarchical clustering algorithms. We demonstrate the proposed pipeline by generating various 3D models of cultural heritage sites.

Keywords Deep learning · 3D reconstruction · Pruning · Filtering · Classification

1 Introduction

In this chapter, we propose a deep learning-based filtering pipeline to address the issues in 3D reconstruction of heritage sites using internet-sourced images. With time and climatic changes, the texture, shape and colour of monuments fade or lose information. Monuments are ruined due to attacks (during war) and natural calamities. In order to preserve our cultural heritage and pass it on to the next generation, there is a need to store all information in digital format. One of the effective ways of storing information on heritage sites is through 3D models. 3D reconstruction using images collected from the internet is challenging due to

R. A. Tabib · S. Kulkarni · A. Kagalkar · V. Hurakadli · A. Ganapule · R. R. Dhanakshirur (✉) ·
U. Mudenagudi
KLE Technological University, Hubballi, Karnataka, India
e-mail: ramesh_t@kletech.ac.in

© Springer Nature Switzerland AG 2021
J. Mukhopadhyay et al. (eds.), *Digital Techniques for Heritage Presentation and Preservation*, https://doi.org/10.1007/978-3-030-57907-4_8

varying captured conditions and with different sensors. Most of the image-based reconstructions for the generation of a detailed and informative 3D model rely on the images chosen [1]. The input images to the reconstruction algorithm may contain artefacts like occlusion and shadow. These artefacts influence 3D reconstruction and result in distortion of shape and texture in reconstructed 3D models.

Most of the works in the literature on 3D reconstruction carry out pre-processing of input data towards better reconstruction [2–4]. The authors in [2] propose enhancement of images before 3D reconstruction and use the tone-mapping approach with Contrast Limited Adaptive Histogram Equalization (CLAHE). This results in amplification of local contrast adaptively and prevents amplification of local noise. The authors in [3] propose colour balancing, denoising of image and enhancement of raw images using adaptive median filters before 3D reconstruction. The authors in [4] use Semi-Global Matching (SGM) as an image matching technique, which is applied to Unmanned Aerial Vehicle (UAV) images to generate dense point cloud. These methods find challenges when applied to images with text, blur, occlusion and shadow. The following are proposed to address these challenges:

- We propose a deep-learning pipeline for filtering internet-sourced images towards better 3D reconstruction.
- We propose to prune internet-sourced images to eliminate unwanted images towards better 3D reconstruction.
- We propose to select a suitable set of images for a given query image by combining mean-shift and hierarchical clustering algorithms towards 3D reconstruction.
- We demonstrate our results using internet-sourced images and compare with existing reconstruction methods.

In Sect. 2, we discuss the proposed pipeline for filtering of images towards 3D reconstruction. In Sect. 3, we demonstrate the results of the proposed pipeline and its effect on 3D reconstruction and conclude in Sect. 4.

2   Filtering of Images Towards 3D Reconstruction

In this section, we discuss the proposed learning-based pipeline for filtering of internet-sourced images towards 3D reconstruction. The proposed pipeline includes pruning, selection of images and 3D reconstruction modules as shown in Fig. 1. Internet-sourced images with blur, shadow, text and occlusion are eliminated during the pruning process. A subset of filtered images is further selected for 3D reconstruction.

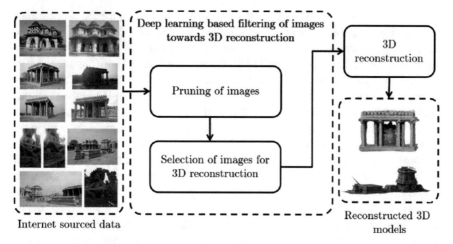

Fig. 1 Pipeline for filtering of images towards 3D reconstruction

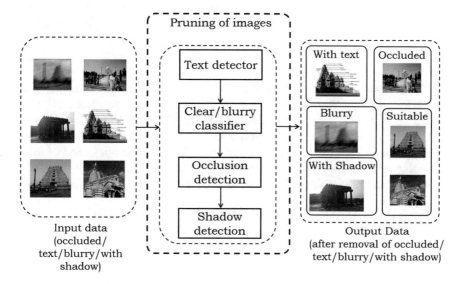

Fig. 2 Pruning of images

2.1 Pruning of Images

Internet-sourced images with text, blur, occlusion and shadow are input to pruning module as shown in Fig. 2. Internet-sourced images with text are filtered using a text detection algorithm (Tesseract Optical Character Recognition [OCR]) [5].

Blur detection in images using traditional methods is computationally expensive [6]. In order to reduce the complexity of blur detection, we use a binary classifier to classify the input images into blur and non-blur images. This classification includes feature extraction using stacked autoencoders [7, 8] and using the features as input for the binary classifier. The encoder consists of $64 \times 64 \times 3$ nodes as input, two intermediate stacked layers with 1024 and 512 nodes and 64 nodes as output. The input data is encoded to 64 nodes. These 64 nodes are decoded with the intermediate stacked layer of 512 and 1024 nodes to output $64 \times 64 \times 3$ nodes. The decoder reconstructs the input image. Initially, the stacked autoencoder is trained to extract the features, and then the decoder is replaced with a binary classification layer for classifying blur and non-blur images. The non-blur images are given as input to the occlusion detection module.

Most of the internet-sourced images with respect to cultural heritage comprise occluded objects in front of the monuments, which might affect the 3D reconstruction. Thus, we propose to detect occluded portions in order to eliminate these images. You Only Look Once (YOLO) [9] is used to generate bounding boxes on each object over input images. Our proposed algorithm computes the area of the bounding box, and depending on the effect of the area, the percentage of occlusion is calculated. If the percentage is greater than the particular threshold (heuristically we set the threshold to 20%), the algorithm discards the images. If there are overlapping multiple bounding boxes, we find the union of all multiple bounding boxes given as

$$\cup_{i=1}^{N} A = \{x \in U : \ni i \in \{1, 2, 3 \dots N\}, x \in A_i\}. \tag{1}$$

In Fig. 3, we observe that the threshold does not affect the 3D model if occlusion is less than 20%. In Fig. 3a and b, we show that the occlusion percentage is small, and by experiment it is observed that there is no significant effect on 3D models. In Fig. 3c and d, we see that the occlusion percentage is greater than 20% and covers the major part of the monument area, and by experiment it is observed that there is significant effect on 3D models. If the occlusion percentage is greater than 20%, then the 3D model contains hole in the occlusion area resulting in an incomplete 3D model (see Fig. 8).

The images with shadow usually affect the texture of reconstructed 3D models, which is an open problem to be solved. Some of the shadow detection algorithms in the literature are detailed in [10, 11]. However, these techniques do not provide desirable 3D models. Thus, we propose to use a convolutional autoencoder [12] as shown in Fig. 4 to eliminate the shadow images by classifying the images into shadow and non-shadow images. The convolutional autoencoder has $64 \times 64 \times 3$ size

(a)   (b)   (c)   (d)

Fig. 3 (**a, b**) Images retained and (**c, d**) images discarded on set threshold. (**a**) 7% occlusion. (**b**) 10% occlusion. (**c**) 28% occlusion. (**d**) 36% occlusion

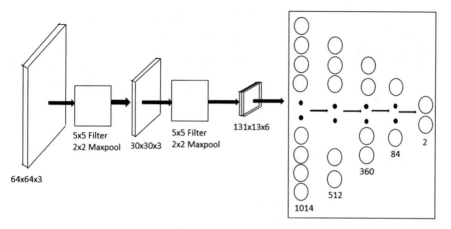

Fig. 4 Classification of shadow and non-shadow images

input layer, which is convolved by a 5 × 5 kernel with three channels. The convolved output is max-pooled with kernel size 2 × 2 and stride 2. This max-pooled output of size 30 × 30 × 3 is convolved by a 5 × 5 kernel with six channels. The convolved output is max-pooled with kernel size 2 × 2 and stride 2. This max-pooled output of size 13 × 13 × 6 is flattened and provided as input to the fully connected network with three hidden layers of size 512, 360 and 84 nodes, respectively. The last layer, i.e. fully connected output, is fed to the binary classifier to classify the images into shadow and non-shadow classes.

2.2 Selection of Images for 3D Reconstruction

The filtered images are processed to choose appropriate images as shown in Fig. 5 for 3D reconstruction. The autoencoder is trained to extract features that are mapped to the latent space. We use stacked autoencoder in Sect. 2.1 to represent data as latent points towards clustering. The two types of clustering algorithms considered are Meanshift [1] and Hierarchical [13]. We use content-based image retrieval (CBIR) [14] technique with considered clustering algorithms and compare the clusters with the input query image. The query image is obtained from curator or user. The intersection of obtained image clusters from mean-shift and hierarchical algorithms is considered for 3D reconstruction as shown in Fig. 5.

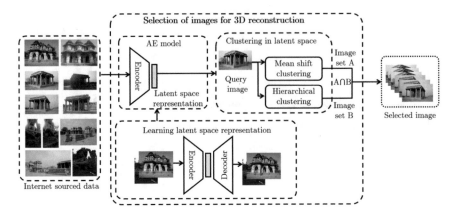

Fig. 5 Selection of images for 3D reconstruction

3 Results and Discussions

The implementation is carried out in the Intel Xeon i5 processor, 64 GB RAM, Nvidia Quadro K5000 graphic processor. In this section, we demonstrate the results of our pipeline and compare the results with existing 3D reconstruction techniques. We used openMVG and openMVS[15] pipeline for 3D reconstruction.

We used 300,000 internet-sourced images as dataset, which comprises 60 heritage sites in India. Approximately 150,000 were discarded by our pipeline. We used 50,000 synthetically generated blurred and real blurred images for training stacked autoencoder. We obtained 95.432% test accuracy and 97.213% cross-validation accuracy from Stacked Autoencoder used for blur and non-blur classification (Table 1). We used standard shadow detection dataset [10] for training convolutional autoencoder, and we obtained 96.156% cross-validation accuracy and 94.591% testing accuracy from convolutional autoencoder used for shadow and non-shadow classification. We used openMVG and openMVS pipeline for 3D reconstruction. We performed subjective analysis for the obtained results with 100 volunteers and the ratings (rating between 1 and 5, 1 being the least and 5 being the highest) are recorded, as shown in Table 2.

Table 1 Results of the stacked autoencoder and convolutional autoencoder

Algorithm	Learning rate	No. of epochs	Time	Accuracy
Stacked autoencoder	0.001	1200	120 h	Cross-validation: 97.213%
				Testing: 95.432%
Convolutional autoencoder	0.0001	1500	216 h	Cross-validation: 96.156%
				Testing: 94.591%

Table 2 Subjective quality analysis for the obtained results with 100 volunteers and the corresponding ratings (rating between 1 and 5, 1 being the least and 5 being the highest)

Heritage site	Figure reference	Overall rating	Deviation	Spread
Pattadakal	Fig. 6a	3.23	0.83	1.9
	Fig. 6b	3.79	0.18	1.5
	Fig. 7a	3.16	0.23	1.4
	Fig. 7b	4.01	0.14	1
	Fig. 8a	2.38	0.15	0.7
	Fig. 8b	3.47	0.19	0.9
Hampi	Fig. 9a	1.46	0.21	1.35
	Fig. 9b	2.69	0.18	0.65
Pattadakal	Fig. 10a	2.68	0.20	1.4
	Fig. 10b	3.9	0.37	2.2
Sasivekal Ganpati	Fig. 10c	3.9	0.17	0.75
	Fig. 10d	4.2	0.2	1
Stone Chariot	Fig. 10e	3.4	0.16	0.8
	Fig. 10f	3.9	0.16	0.9

(a)   (b)

Fig. 6 (**a**) 3D model of Pattadakal obtained from images containing text. (**b**) 3D model of Pattadakal obtained after discarding images with text

In Figs. 6, 7, 8 and 9, we show the results of the individual stages of the proposed pipeline with the 3D reconstruction of the Pattadakal temple situated in Badami (Tq), Karnataka, India, and Stone Chariot, Hampi, Bellary, Karnataka, India. Figure 6a shows the 3D model reconstructed using 100 sample images of Pattadakal from the dataset among which 36 images contain text. Figure 6b corresponds to the 3D model reconstructed using 64 images after eliminating images with text. Figure 7a shows the 3D model reconstructed from 200 sample images of Pattadakal from the dataset among which 42 images contain blur. Figure 7b shows the 3D model reconstructed with 158 images after eliminating images with blur. Similarly, Figs. 8a and 9a correspond to the 3D models reconstructed using 200 and 150 images among which 14 and 27 images are occluded and contain shadow, respectively. Figures 8b and 9b represent the 3D models reconstructed using 186 and

(a)   (b)

Fig. 7 (**a**) 3D model of Pattadakal obtained from blurred images. (**b**) 3D model of Pattadakal obtained after the removal of blurred images

(a)   (b)

Fig. 8 (**a**) 3D model of Pattadakal obtained from images containing occlusion. (**b**) 3D model of Pattadakal obtained after discarding images containing occlusion

(a)   (b)

Fig. 9 (**a**) 3D model of Hampi obtained from images containing shadow. (**b**) 3D model of Hampi obtained after removing images containing shadow

123 images after eliminating occluded and shadow images, respectively. Figure 10 shows a comparison of 3D models reconstructed with and without the proposed filtering pipeline.

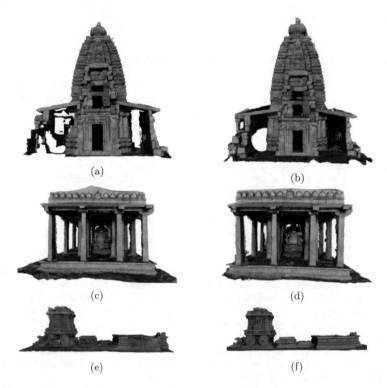

Fig. 10 (**a, c, e**) 3D models obtained without applying filtering pipeline and (**b, d, f**) 3D models obtained after applying filtering pipeline

4 Conclusions

In this chapter, we have proposed a deep learning-based filtering pipeline for processing internet-sourced images of heritage sites for better 3D reconstruction. 3D reconstruction of heritage sites, using images collected from the internet, is challenging since images may contain blur, text, occlusion and shadow artefacts with reported pre-processing methods. To improve the results for the internet-sourced images, we have proposed a pipeline with pruning and selection modules in order to select a suitable set of images for 3D reconstruction. We have also proposed a method to select the suitable set of images using a combination of mean-shift and hierarchical clustering algorithms. We have demonstrated the results of the proposed pipeline by generating various 3D models of cultural heritage sites and have performed subjective qualitative analysis on the obtained results.

References

1. Xiao, C., Liu, M.: Efficient mean-shift clustering using Gaussian KDTree. Comput. Graph. Forum **29**, 2065–2073 (2010)
2. Aldeeb, N., Hellwich, O.: Reconstructing textureless objects – image enhancement for 3D reconstruction of weakly-textured surfaces. In: Proceedings of the 13th International Joint Conference on Computer Vision, Imaging and Computer Graphics Theory and Applications – Volume 5: VISAPP, ISBN 978-989-758-290-5, pp. 572–580 (2018). https://doi.org/10.5220/0006628805720580
3. Ballabeni, A., Apollonio, F., Gaiani, M., Remondino, F.: Advances in image pre-processing to improve automated 3d reconstruction. In: ISPRS – International Archives of the Photogrammetry, Remote Sensing and Spatial Information Sciences (2015). XL-5/W4.315-323. https://doi.org/10.5194/isprsarchives-XL-5-W4-315-2015
4. Alidoost, Fatemeh & Arefi, Hossein. (2015). An image-based technique for 3D building reconstruction using multi-view UAV images. In: ISPRS – International Archives of the Photogrammetry, Remote Sensing and Spatial Information Sciences. XL-1-W5, pp. 43–46. https://doi.org/10.5194/isprsarchives-XL-1-W5-43-2015
5. Smith, R.: An overview of the Tesseract OCR engine. In: Ninth International Conference on Document Analysis and Recognition (ICDAR 2007), September, vol. 2, pp. 629–633 (2007)
6. Landge, R.Y., Sharma, R.: Blur detection methods for digital images – a survey. Int. J. Comput. Appl. Technol. Res. **2**, 495–498 (2013). https://doi.org/10.7753/IJCATR0204.1019
7. Matsumoto, K., Tajima, Y., Saito, R., Nakata, M., Sato, H., Kovacs, T., Takadama, K.: Learning classifier system with deep autoencoder. In: 2016 IEEE Congress on Evolutionary Computation (CEC), July, pp. 4739–4746 (2016)
8. Vincent, P., Larochelle, H., Lajoie, I., Bengio, Y., Manzagol, P.A.: Stacked denoising autoencoders: learning useful representations in a deep network with a local denoising criterion. J. Mach. Learn. Res. **11**, 3371–3408 (2010)
9. Redmon, J., Divvala, S., Girshick, R., Farhadi, A.: You only look once: Unified, real-time object detection (2015). CoRR, abs/1506.02640
10. Al-Najdawi, N., Bez, H., Singhai, J., Edirisinghe, E.: A survey of cast shadow detection algorithms. Pattern Recogn. Lett. **33**, 752–764 (2012). https://doi.org/10.1016/j.patrec.2011.12.013
11. Sharma, P., Sharma, R.: Shadow detection and its removal in images: a review. Res. Cell **17**, 2229–6913 (2016)
12. Turchenko, V., Chalmers, E., Luczak, A.: A deep convolutional auto-encoder with pooling–unpooling layers in caffe (2016). CoRR, abs/1701.04949
13. Nazari, Z., Kang, D., Asharif, M.R., Sung, Y., Ogawa, S.: A new hierarchical clustering algorithm. In: 2015 International Conference on Intelligent Informatics and Biomedical Sciences (ICIIBMS), November, pp. 148–152 (2015)
14. Beaudoin, J.E.: Content-based image retrieval methods and professional image users. J. Assoc. Inf. Sci. Technol. **67**(2), 350–365 (2016)
15. Moulon, P., Monasse, P., Perrot, R., Marlet, R.: OpenMVG: Open multiple view geometry. RRPR@ICPR (2016)

Improving Landmark Recognition Using Saliency Detection and Feature Classification

Akash Kumar, Sagnik Bhowmick, N. Jayanthi, and S. Indu

Abstract With increasing tourism and democratization of data, image landmark recognition has been one of the most sought-after classification challenges in the field of vision and perception. After so many years of generic classification of buildings and monuments from images, people are now focusing on fine-grained problems—recognizing the category of each building or monument and indexing information to it. In this chapter, we propose an ensemble network for the classification of Indian landmark images. To this end, the proposed method gives a robust classification by ensembling the predictions from the Graph-Based Visual Saliency (GBVS) network along with supervised feature-based classification algorithms such as K-nearest neighbor (kNN) and Random Forest. The final architecture is an adaptive learning of all the mentioned networks. The proposed network produces a decent score to eliminate false category cases. Evaluation of the proposed model was done on a new dataset, which involves challenges such as landmark clutter, variable scaling, and partial occlusion.

Keywords Visual saliency · Transfer learning · Feature classification · Supervised learning · Model ensemble

1 Introduction

The United Nations Educational, Scientific and Cultural Organization (UNESCO) World Heritage Center recognizes over 1500 monuments and landmarks as world heritage sites. The tourism industry valued at $7500 billion globally faces a major complication in data archiving for all these landmarks. Moreover, there are over 10K monuments and landmarks spread over the globe that serve as local tourist attractions and have a massive contribution to the history and culture of the location.

A. Kumar (✉) · S. Bhowmick · N. Jayanthi · S. Indu
Delhi Technological University, New Delhi, India
e-mail: akash_bt2k15@dtu.ac.in; sagnikbhomic_2k15ec133@dtu.ac.in; njayanthi@dtu.ac.in; s.indu@dtu.ac.in

© Springer Nature Switzerland AG 2021
J. Mukhopadhyay et al. (eds.), *Digital Techniques for Heritage Presentation and Preservation*, https://doi.org/10.1007/978-3-030-57907-4_9

Fig. 1 Overview of the dataset

However, it is impossible for humans to individually recognize and classify all monuments according to history and architecture. Recent developments in the computer vision and deep learning fields have played a pivotal role in overcoming this challenge.

Many convolutional neural networks (CNNs)-based deep learning frameworks have been shown to be handy in such a scenario, where classes have different features. Every landmark architecture style has some distinguishable features from other forms of architectures. These features play a pivotal role in the recognition of such landmark architectures. India, one of the most diverse countries in the world, is home to varied architectures. From classic dome-shaped architectures in Mughal designs to pillared halls in Dravidian designs, India hosts them all. We propose a framework to classify these landmarks based on the era they were constructed, considering their patterns and architectural styles. These varied architectural features make the classification of Indian monuments a challenging task. Moreover, these historic buildings are useful references for architects designing contemporary architecture. Thus information about the architectural styles of these monuments seems necessary. The overview of the dataset is shown in Fig. 1.

In this chapter, we use CNN to address the problem of landmark recognition. Our main contributions are:

1. We propose an end-to-end architecture to classify Indian monuments in the image. Experiments show that the proposed model surpasses the existing baseline on the dataset.
2. We employ convolutional architectures to learn the intra-class variations between different landmarks. The final prediction vector is calculated by an average ensemble of the following architectures: Graph-Based Visual Saliency, kNN, and Random Forest supervised classification algorithm.

The chapter is arranged as follows: Sect. 2 discusses the prevailing approaches using keypoint feature extraction, matching, and the use of CNNs to learn these discriminative features. Section 3 describes the challenges existing in the domain of landmark classification, and Sect. 4 analyzes the distribution of the dataset. In Sect. 5, we describe the suggested approach to solve the problem of landmark classification. After that, in Sect. 6 we analyze what the suggested network is learning and which approach is boosting the proposed model accuracy. Finally, in Sect. 7, we lay out the future directions in which this area can be explored more.

2   Related Work

There are several recent papers that address the problem of landmark recognition [4, 14, 21]; most of them are based on deep learning except [1], which classifies landmarks using visual features such as Histogram of Gradients (HoGs) [6], Scale Invariant Feature Transform (SIFT) [14], and Speeded Up Robust Feature (SURF) [2]. SIFT extracts invariant local features from images. It comes handy due to its robustness in conditions when the images are rotated or scaled. SURF, an improvised implementation of SIFT, is much faster than SIFT. Both use feature descriptors to compare the similarities in images. While landmark recognition can be considered as descriptor matching, the proposed work relates to [21]. Using that, we learn to employ a visual saliency algorithm to focus on the most noticeable and significant regions and extract those features for classification.

Landmark recognition using CNN presents a competitive research, as there are so many small intra-class variations [3]. Chen et al. [4] considered the appearance and viewpoint changes in places over a short time like day–night cycles or long-time changes such as architectural changes over the years. They also employed a multiscale feature embedding to generate viewpoint invariant features for specific place recognition. Saini et al. [18] used local binary patterns and a gray-level co-occurrence matrix to match the pairs using pixel-wise information. Triantafyllidis and Kalliatakis [24] devised an architecture using visual descriptors and Bag-of-Words for image-based monument classification. Shukla et al. [21] used AlexNet to extract features and classified landmarks using supervised feature learning. Many works have been done on specific place recognition, but the area of using fine-grained features to recognize Indian landmarks has not been explored yet.

Taj Mahal   Khooni Darwaza

Fig. 2 Same class had varied architecture style

3   Problem Formulation

Landmark recognition in the Indian context is very different from the European and the American, due to the extreme variations that exist within each region in its diverse architecture. Approaches such as Bag-of-Words, HoG, and SIFT are constrained by database size. Other approaches based on the deep learning framework [20] face challenges in identifying different images in the same class (refer Fig. 2). Among all these methods, we need a more robust and dynamic framework that can learn these intra-class variations. Hence, the proposed architecture focuses on these explicit and implicit features of images.

4   Dataset

The manually accumulated Indian monument dataset consists of monument images majorly of four classes based on architecture types, i.e., Buddhist, Dravidian, Kalinga, and Mughal architectures. Among these four classes, each architecture has its characteristic features that need to be learned, to distinguish them from other classes. In Dravidian architecture, the shape of the monuments is pyramidal, whereas the Mughals always keep the main structure of their monument dome shaped. Kalinga temples are primarily made up of two parts: tower and hall. The monument structure of Kalinga temples is generally horseshoe shaped. Buddhist temples alone have three different types of stupas.

A total of 3514 dataset images have been divided into a ratio of 80:10:10 that indicates Training:Validation:Testing images, respectively. The exact distribution of images is shown in Table 1. Examples of each of the classes, in the dataset, are shown in Fig. 3.

Table 1 Categorical distribution of dataset among four classes

Class label	Train set	Validation set	Test set
Buddhist	647	81	81
Dravidian	657	83	82
Kalinga	881	111	110
Mughal	624	79	78
Total	2809	354	351

Fig. 3 Dataset: In this figure, the leftmost column shows examples for Buddhist architecture and the subsequent columns show examples for Dravidian, Kalinga, and Mughal architectures, respectively

5 Methodology

In this section, we discuss the proposed framework that is used for landmark classification. We devise two architectures to solve the problem of monument classification. These methods are described as follows.

5.1 Graph-Based Visual Saliency (GBVS)

Image saliency is what stands out and how fast we can focus on the most relevant parts of what we see. The regions where the human eye focuses at the very first glance are denoted as salient regions. Now, in the case of landmarks, the less salient region is a common background, which is the blue sky. The architectural design of the monuments is what differentiates between the classes. GBVS [9, 24] first finds feature maps and then applies nonlinear activation maps to highlight "significant" locations in the image. We used GBVS to detect five important locations per training image. Those generated images were used for multistage training (Fig. 4). It helped to enhance our accuracy by 3–4%. An example of a salient region detected using the GBVS algorithm is shown in Fig. 5.

Fig. 4 Salient map generated by graph-based visual saliency [24]. We can visualize the important regions identified by graph-based visual saliency

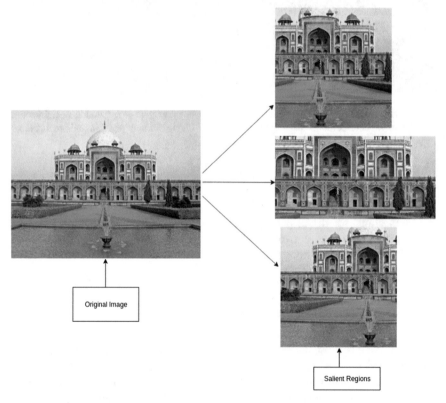

Fig. 5 Salient region detection using graph-based visual saliency [24]. From this picture, we can visualize that the saliency model crops out the important parts of an image

5.2 Transfer Learning

Transfer learning is a technique in which a model trained on one task is remodeled to use on another task. Here, we used models pretrained on the ImageNet [7] dataset.

These models are trained from scratch on a dataset that contains 1.2 million images varied over 1000 classes. We can utilize these pretrained models on datasets, where the number of images is insufficient. In our case, the dataset contains only 2800 images for training. Therefore, we unfroze the final few layers of these models and trained them on our dataset. In the initial few layers, the model grasps the basic structures such as lines, circles, squares, and triangles. In the final layers, the model looks into the complex shapes of the images.

Moreover, freezing the weights of initial layers leads to a reduction of million trainable parameters in the model. Otherwise, these models would overfit on our dataset, and the test time accuracy would be compromised. Now, coming to the models, we used Inception V3 and Inception ResNet V2 as base models to extract features. We will briefly discuss the basic architecture of these models.

Inception V3 This architecture is developed on the idea that most of the activations are redundant, and the use of a filter of multiple dimensions gathers global and local information more discreetly. It uses factorization and batch normalization, so that the convolutional operations are more efficient. All $n \times n$ convolutional operations are broken down into $n \times 1$ and $1 \times n$ operations.

Inception ResNet V2 On top of inception modules, it uses skip connection architecture, just like ResNet models. As these architectures are very deep, they face the problem of vanishing gradient. Thus, skip connections do not saturate the gradient flow during backpropagation. Compared to Inception V3, it also requires fewer epochs and achieves higher accuracy.

5.3   Supervised Feature Classification

The idea of supervised learning came from the notion of concept learning of human beings and animals. In concept learning, the agent learns by mapping the given input with the corresponding output. Each data points are a pair of an input object (feature vector) and the desired output (class or quantity depending on the problem). The algorithm analyzes the training dataset and generates an inferred function, which can be used to map new samples.

As a prestep before supervised learning, generally feature selection, transformation, and reduction are performed. As a rule of thumb, only independent features should be selected to categorize/predict. However, it is quite difficult to only select independent features from the feature space, so we opt for features providing most variances to make it more distinguishable among classes.

In this approach, we used fc layer features of ImageNet models to train supervised machine learning models such as kNN and Random Forest Classification. Among all the ImageNet models, Inception ResNet V2 performed best for landmark classification. Therefore, we extracted the representation from Inception Net of dimension 2048.

5.3.1 K-Nearest Neighbor Algorithm (KNN)

KNN is one of the elementary algorithms in the supervised learning domain. It is used for the purpose of both classification and regression. This general algorithm is based on how humans classify nearest feature similar objects. An analogy of KNN can be taken from real-world problems. Let us consider the binary classification of objects based on n-features in two classes (Class A and Class B) (Fig. 6):

$$X_1 1, X_1 2, \ldots X_1 n \subseteq Y_1,$$

$$X_2 1, X_2 2, \ldots X_2 n \subseteq Y_2,$$

for N data points the dimension of axis for feature space visualization is n.

According to the KNN algorithm, the classification of an unknown data point depends on the K-nearest objects. Suppose we consider a scenario of K = 3, the algorithm will take three nearest neighbors of the unknown sample and predict on the basis of the maximum votes among the three.

Now that we have a fair understanding of how KNN works, we should ponder on two main points:

– Distance metric used
– The value of K

To measure the distance between two or more points, various distance metrics have been used in the past. Some of the popular ones are as follows:

1. Euclidean distance: Let A and B be represented by feature vectors $A = (x_1, x_2, \ldots, x_m)$ and $B = (y_1, y_2, \ldots, y_m)$, where m is the dimensionality of the feature space. To calculate the distance between A and B, the normalized Euclidean metric is generally used by

$$dist(A, B) = \sqrt{\Sigma_{i=1}^{m}(x_i - y_i)^2/m}$$

Fig. 6 K-nearest neighbor

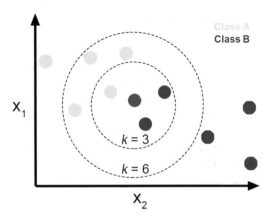

2. Minkowsky distance:

$$dist\_Minkowsky = (\Sigma_{i=1}^{m}|x_i - y_i|^r)^{1/r}$$

Other distances include Mahalanobis distance, cosine similarity, Chi-squared distance, etc. The most common among all is Euclidean distance; hence, we opted for the same to find the distance between the nearest features.

Now using the second scenario, we can choose the value for K, to decide how big or small the value may be. K determines the number of nearest neighbors in consideration. Let us analyze the situation by the following steps:

1. Considering K = 1: In such a scenario, the algorithm is highly flawed since it considers only one nearest neighbor, and in a real-world scenario where linearly separable data is a myth, it is highly correlated. Having K = 1 may be the fastest (due to fewer calculations involved); however, it fails the sole purpose of general prediction of the algorithm. Hence, it provides a biased result based on the nearest points.
2. Considering K to be large: As we learned, K cannot be too small; now let us analyze K to be on the other side of the spectrum. This may give an overall generalized prediction, but this involves a large number of points. Hence the more the computations, the slower the results will be. It is an inefficient solution.

Hence, there is always a trade-off between the speed of predictions and the quality of predictions. Here, we want the value to be neither too high nor too low; it should be moderate somewhere near the lower side.

5.3.2 Random Forest Algorithm

As the name suggests, it consists of a large number of decision trees that work as an ensemble. Each tree in Random Forest generates a class prediction, and the class with the maximum votes becomes the model's prediction. The basic concept of Random Forest is a simple yet powerful one—the wisdom of crowds. The flowchart of the Random Forest algorithm for class prediction is shown in Fig. 7.

A large number of almost independent and uncorrelated trees operating as a group always outperform any of the individual subset trees. The low correlation between models is the key to better predictions. The reason for this commendable effect is that the submodels (trees) protect each other from their error contribution (as long as they do not constantly generate all errors in the same direction). The predictions of subset trees as a collective group helps the model to predict the right class. Therefore, the prerequisites for Random Forest to perform well are as follows:

1. To avoid random guess, extracted features should contain important information.
2. The predictions (including both errors and perfect ones) made by the individual trees need to have low correlations with each other.

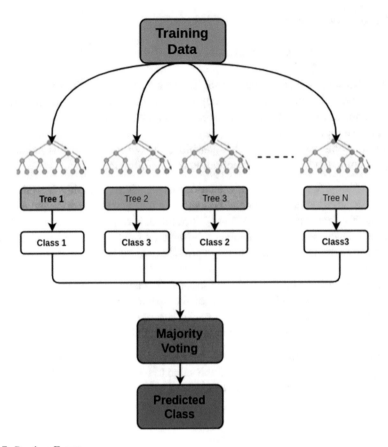

Fig. 7 Random Forest

Random Forest acts both as a classifier and as a regressor, depending on the use case.

5.4 *Architecture*

Our final architecture comprises average ensembling of different approaches [19]. The test image is passed first from the GBVS algorithm to create a batch of five images. The batch prediction is made using Inception ResNet V2 [22]. Similarly, the test image is also passed through the Inception ResNet model for feature extraction.

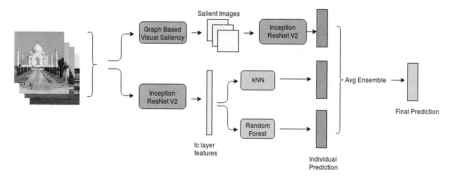

Fig. 8 Proposed architecture

These features were used to learn and predict classes using the kNN and Random Forest classifiers. The final prediction is made using the average of predictions from the three models described above. Ensemble learning boosts the accuracy by approximately 2–3%. The final architecture is diagrammatically explained in Fig. 8.

6   Experiments

6.1   Implementation Details

Training We trained the proposed model, first on original images that were resized to 416 × 416. After that, we trained it on salient regions extracted using a Graph-Based Visual Saliency algorithm. The salient images helped us to learn local discriminative features between various classes. Original images assisted in the learning of global spatial features. We used ImageNet pretrained weights to train Inception ResNet V2 [22] architecture on original and salient images. We modified the top *fc* layer accordingly. The loss function used for training is categorical cross-entropy [27]. The value of loss function over the training period on validation data is depicted in Fig. 9. It shows that the proposed model does not overfit the data.

Testing At the testing time, we used the trained weights to generate a 512-dimensional feature vector. The proposed architecture has two parallel workflows. The first part takes an image and passes it through a saliency model to generate five salient regions of a test image. Then, we create a batch of those images and predict trained Inception ResNet V2 weights. It focuses on the local artifacts of the monument. In the second part, we use those trained weights to generate a feature vector. These feature vectors are classified using the kNN and Random Forest algorithms. This part helps us to concentrate on global features. After that, we use the average ensembling method to boost the accuracy of the proposed model (Figs. 10, 11, 12, and 13).

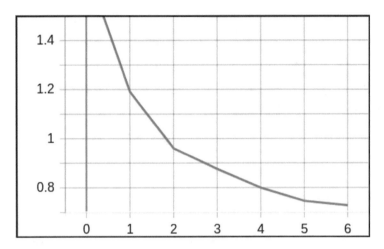

Fig. 9 With the increase in epochs, the training loss decreases

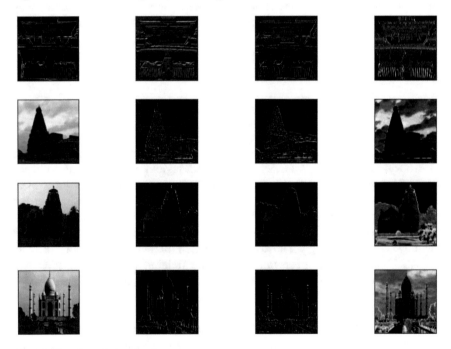

Fig. 10 Conv layer 1 visualization

6.1.1 Parameters

In the proposed model, we used the ADAM ($lr = 0.0001$) [10] optimizer and the ReLU [15] activation function. The model was trained for seven epochs using the

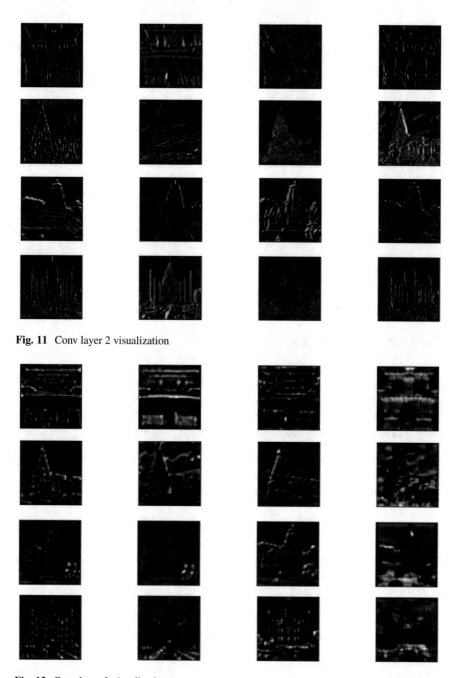

Fig. 11 Conv layer 2 visualization

Fig. 12 Conv layer 3 visualization

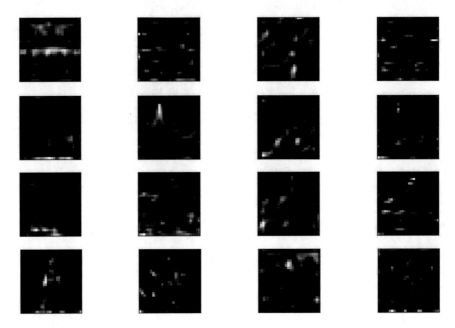

Fig. 13 Conv layer 4 visualization

pretrained ImageNet weights as initialization for transfer learning. We trained the proposed models for more epochs, but the increase in accuracy was not substantial. We also evaluated the proposed model with the Swish [17] activation function. In our case, however, ReLU outperformed Swish by a margin of 2–3%.

7 Performance Analysis

The experimental results on the landmarks dataset are presented in Table 2. The scores obtained are from different architectures trained on salient crops and original images during multistage training. The proposed model was able to classify images in complex cases, as shown in Fig. 14. In these cases, the images are rotated or they consist of very small parts of the monument, but the proposed architecture learns

Table 2 Accuracy during multistage training on Inception V3 and Inception ResNet V2 models

Model architecture	Data subset	Train	Validation	Test
Inception V3 [23]	Original images	90.1	77.23	75.42
	Original + salient	91.81	80.3	78.91
Inception ResNet V2 [22]	Original images	91.76	77	76.35
	Original + salient	92.29	81	80

Fig. 14 Difficult cases

Fig. 15 Cases in which the proposed model failed to classify images. As we can see from the figure, each image is a small part of its respective temple. It does not contain any architectural characteristics that could be helpful for classification

the parameters that help to classify these images. The outlined approach failed in certain cases; for example, the approach could not identify images that contain only prayer wheels, a case of Buddhist architecture. The approach also failed to identify pictures of deities that do not quantify any information about the architecture of the monument. The cases in which the approach failed to classify the images are depicted in Fig. 15.

Table 3 compares the accuracy scores for all the models on the training, validation, and testing dataset. The final prediction is done by the average ensembling of three models to get the final architecture with low variance and low bias (Fig. 16).

Table 4 compares the results of the existing dataset. It is clear that the proposed approach outperforms the existing models by 8% (Fig. 17).

Table 3 Evaluation comparison (in %) of different models

Model architecture	Train	Validation	Test
GBVS + Inception ResNet V2	92.61	89.65	86.18
Inception ResNet V2 + kNN	93.62	90.72	86.94
Inception ResNet V2 + Random Forest	91.58	89.8	88.23
Average ensemble	**94.58**	**93.8**	**90.08**

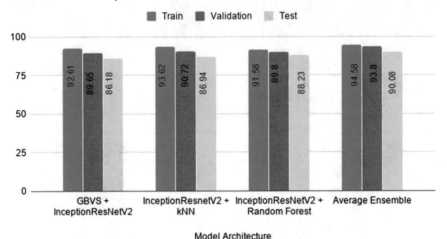

Fig. 16 Visualization based on different models used

Table 4 Comparison of the best-proposed model with competing methods [20]

Framework	Test
SIFT + BoVW	51%
Gabor transform + Radon barcode	70%
Radon barcode	75%
CNN	82%
Average ensemble (ours)	**90%**

8 Conclusion and Future Work

This chapter presented two approaches on which extensive experiments were done to classify Indian architectural styles. The landmark recognition problem presents some unique solutions, as there are no training data available for less famous landmarks. The proposed solution focuses on the most noticeable region of the image to classify landmarks accurately. The outlined approach targets the fine-grained features as well as the global features of monuments. Previous works lack the attention mechanism to differentiate models based on fine-grained features. The proposed model outperforms the existing approach by 8%.

Result Visualization

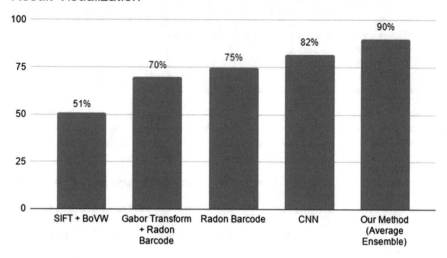

Fig. 17 Different architecture performance on the basis of accuracy

In the future, the authors aim to use Attentive Deep Local features [16] and Visual Attention mechanisms such as Multi-Head Attention [26] to further improve the accuracy of the model and learn more substantial features. We will also try to incorporate AutoAugment [5], which helps to find the best data augmentation policies for a particular dataset. AutoAugment reviews all types of data augmentation using the Reinforcement Algorithm and then selects the best policies among them. We also aim to incorporate unsupervised domain adaptation [8, 11–13, 25] so that we can classify images across datasets without using any labels. It will be helpful to annotate images in domains where the labels are mostly unavailable.

References

1. Amato, G., Falchi, F., Bolettieri, P.: Recognizing landmarks using automated classification techniques: Evaluation of various visual features. In: 2010 Second International Conferences on Advances in Multimedia, June, pp. 78–83 (2010). https://doi.org/10.1109/MMEDIA.2010. 20
2. Bay, H., Ess, A., Tuytelaars, T., Van Gool, L.: Speeded-up robust features (surf). Comput. Vis. Image Underst. **110**(3), 346–359 (2008). https://doi.org/10.1016/j.cviu.2007.09.014
3. Blog, G.A.: Google-landmarks: A new dataset and challenge for landmark recognition. https:// ai.googleblog.com/2018/03/google-landmarks-new-dataset-and.html. Accessed 28 Sept 2019
4. Chen, Z., Jacobson, A., Sünderhauf, N., Upcroft, B., Liu, L., Shen, C., Reid, I.D., Milford, M.: Deep learning features at scale for visual place recognition (2017). CoRR abs/1701.05105. http://arxiv.org/abs/1701.05105
5. Cubuk, E.D., Zoph, B., Mané, D., Vasudevan, V., Le, Q.V.: Autoaugment: Learning augmentation policies from data (2018). CoRR abs/1805.09501. http://arxiv.org/abs/1805.09501

6. Dalal, N., Triggs, B.: Histograms of oriented gradients for human detection. In: Proceedings of the 2005 IEEE Computer Society Conference on Computer Vision and Pattern Recognition (CVPR'05) – Volume 1 – Volume 01, pp. 886–893. CVPR '05. IEEE Computer Society, Washington (2005). https://doi.org/10.1109/CVPR.2005.177

7. Deng, J., Dong, W., Socher, R., Li, L.J., Li, K., Fei-Fei, L.: ImageNet: A large-scale hierarchical image database. In: CVPR09 (2009)

8. Ganin, Y., Ustinova, E., Ajakan, H., Germain, P., Larochelle, H., Laviolette, F., Marchand, M., Lempitsky, V.S.: Domain-adversarial training of neural networks. J. Mach. Learn. Res. **17**, 59:1–59:35 (2015)

9. Harel, J., Koch, C., Perona, P.: Graph-based visual saliency. In: Schölkopf, B., Platt, J.C., Hoffman, T. (eds.) Advances in Neural Information Processing Systems 19, pp. 545–552. MIT Press, Cambridge (2007). http://papers.nips.cc/paper/3095-graph-based-visual-saliency.pdf

10. Kingma, D.P., Ba, J.: Adam: A method for stochastic optimization (2014). Preprint. arXiv:1412.6980

11. Laradji, I.H., Babanezhad, R.: M-adda: Unsupervised domain adaptation with deep metric learning (2020). arXiv abs/1807.02552

12. Long, M., Cao, Y., Wang, J., Jordan, M.I.: Learning transferable features with deep adaptation networks. In: ICML (2015)

13. Long, M., Zhu, H., Wang, J., Jordan, M.I.: Deep transfer learning with joint adaptation networks. In: ICML (2016)

14. Lowe, D.G.: Distinctive image features from scale-invariant keypoints. Int. J. Comput. Vision **60**(2), 91–110 (2004). https://doi.org/10.1023/B:VISI.0000029664.99615.94

15. Nair, V., Hinton, G.E.: Rectified linear units improve restricted Boltzmann machines. In: Proceedings of the 27th International Conference on International Conference on Machine Learning. ICML'10, Omnipress, pp. 807–814 (2010). http://dl.acm.org/citation.cfm?id=3104322. 3104425

16. Noh, H., Araujo, A., Sim, J., Weyand, T., Han, B.: Large-scale image retrieval with attentive deep local features. In: Proc. ICCV (2017). https://arxiv.org/abs/1612.06321

17. Ramachandran, P., Zoph, B., Le, Q.V.: Searching for activation functions (2017). CoRR abs/1710.05941. http://arxiv.org/abs/1710.05941

18. Saini, A., Gupta, T., Kumar, R., Gupta, A.K., Panwar, M., Mittal, A.: Image based Indian monument recognition using convoluted neural networks. In: 2017 International Conference on Big Data, IoT and Data Science (BID), December, pp. 138–142 (2017). https://doi.org/10. 1109/BID.2017.8336587

19. Sainin, M.S., Alfred, R., Adnan, F., Ahmad, F.: Combining sampling and ensemble classifier for multiclass imbalance data learning. In: Alfred, R., Iida, H., Ag. Ibrahim, A.A., Lim, Y. (eds.) Computational Science and Technology, pp. 262–272. Springer Singapore, Singapore (2018)

20. Sharma, S., Aggarwal, P., Bhattacharyya, A.N., Indu, S.: Classification of Indian monuments into architectural styles. In: Rameshan, R., Arora, C., Dutta Roy, S. (eds.) Computer Vision, Pattern Recognition, Image Processing, and Graphics, pp. 540–549. Springer Singapore, Singapore (2018)

21. Shukla, P., Rautela, B., Mittal, A.: A computer vision framework for automatic description of Indian monuments. In: 2017 13th International Conference on Signal-Image Technology Internet-Based Systems (SITIS), December, pp. 116–122 (2017). https://doi.org/10.1109/ SITIS.2017.29

22. Szegedy, C., Ioffe, S., Vanhoucke, V., Alemi, A.A.: Inception-v4, Inception-ResNet and the impact of residual connections on learning. In: ICLR 2016 Workshop (2016). https://arxiv.org/ abs/1602.07261

23. Szegedy, C., Vanhoucke, V., Ioffe, S., Shlens, J., Wojna, Z.: Rethinking the inception architecture for computer vision. In: Proceedings of IEEE Conference on Computer Vision and Pattern Recognition (2016). http://arxiv.org/abs/1512.00567

24. Triantafyllidis, G., Kalliatakis, G.: Image based monument recognition using graph based visual saliency. ELCVIA Electron. Lett. Comput. Vis. Image Anal. **12**(2), 88–97 (2013). https://elcvia.cvc.uab.es/article/view/v12-n2-triantafyllidis-kalliatakis

25. Tzeng, E., Hoffman, J., Saenko, K., Darrell, T.: Adversarial discriminative domain adaptation. In: 2017 IEEE Conference on Computer Vision and Pattern Recognition (CVPR), pp. 2962–2971 (2017)
26. Vaswani, A., Shazeer, N., Parmar, N., Uszkoreit, J., Jones, L., Gomez, A.N., Kaiser, L.u., Polosukhin, I.: Attention is all you need. In: Guyon, I., Luxburg, U.V., Bengio, S., Wallach, H., Fergus, R., Vishwanathan, S., Garnett, R. (eds.) Advances in Neural Information Processing Systems 30, pp. 5998–6008. Curran Associates, Red Hook (2017). http://papers.nips.cc/paper/7181-attention-is-all-you-need.pdf
27. Zhang, Z., Sabuncu, M.R.: Generalized cross entropy loss for training deep neural networks with noisy labels (2018). CoRR abs/1805.07836. http://arxiv.org/abs/1805.07836

Part III
Applications of Modern Tools in Digital Heritage

Bharatanatyam Dance Transcription Using Multimedia Ontology and Machine Learning

Tanwi Mallick, Patha Pratim Das, and Arun Kumar Majumdar

Abstract Indian classical dance is an over 5000-year-old multimodal language for expressing emotions. Preservation of dance through multimedia technology is a challenging task. In this chapter, we develop a system to generate a parseable representation of a dance performance. The system will help preserve intangible heritage, annotate performances for better tutoring, and synthesize dance performances. We first attempt to capture the concepts of the basic steps of an Indian classical dance form, named *Bharatanatyam Adavu*s, in an ontological model. Next, we build an event-based, low-level model that relates the ontology of *Adavu*s to the ontology of multimodal data streams (RGB-D of Kinect in this case) for a computationally realizable framework. Finally, the ontology is used for transcription into Labanotation. We also present a transcription tool for encoding the performances of *Bharatanatyam Adavu*s to Labanotation and test it on our recorded data set. Our primary aim is to document the complex movements of dance in terms of Labanotation using the ontology.

Keywords Multimedia ontology · Dance transcription · Machine learning · *Bharatanatyam Adavu* · Laban XML · Labanotation

1 Introduction

Dance is a form of art that may tell a story, set a mood, or express emotions. Indian classical dance (ICD) is an ancient heritage of India, which is more than 5000 years old. With the passage of time, the dance form has been performed, restructured, reformulated, and re-expressed by several artists. New choreography has been composed using basic forms. Hence, the dance forms have been associated with a rich set of rules, formations, postures, gestures, stories, and other artifacts.

T. Mallick · P. P. Das (✉) · A. K. Majumdar
Indian Institute of Technology Kharagpur, Kharagpur, India
e-mail: ppd@cse.iitkgp.ac.in; akmj@cse.iitkgp.ac.in

© Springer Nature Switzerland AG 2021
J. Mukhopadhyay et al. (eds.), *Digital Techniques for Heritage Presentation and Preservation*, https://doi.org/10.1007/978-3-030-57907-4_10

179

But, to date it has been passed on to the student by the teacher, from one generation to the next, through the traditional method of *Guru–Shishya Parampara*, which is the typically acknowledged Indian style of education where the teacher (*Guru*) personally trains her/his disciple (*Shishya*) to keep up a continuity (*Parampara*) of education, culture, learning, or skills. Hence, there is a need to preserve the intangible heritage of dance artifacts.

Recently, many significant systems have been developed to preserve cultural heritage through digital multimedia technology. The preservation of tangible heritage resources like monuments, handicrafts, and sculpture can be done through digitization and 2D and 3D modeling techniques. The preservation of intangible resources like language, art and culture, music, and dance is more complex and requires a knowledge-intensive approach. Therefore, not much work has been carried out for the preservation of dance heritage.

These dance forms embody a collection of knowledge that can be preserved either by creating a digital transcription of the performances or by annotating the video recordings of performances. Analysis of dance can help convert the audio-visual information of dance into a graphical notation. Dance transcription, still a rarity, can be handy in preserving the heritage of a country like India that boasts of diverse types of classical dance forms. Transcription can also help in exchanging dance ideas between performers. Another way of preserving the intangible heritage of dance is dance media annotation or to attach conceptual metadata to the collection of digital artifacts. The collection of digital artifacts with conceptual metadata can help in semantic access to the heritage collection.

Mallik et al. [7] present an ontology-based approach for designing a cultural heritage repository. A Multimedia Web Ontology Language (MOWL) is proposed to encode the domain knowledge of choreography. The suggested architectural framework includes a method to construct the ontology with a labeled set of training data and the use of the ontology to automatically annotate new instances of digital heritage artifacts. The annotations enable the creation of a semantic navigation environment in the repository. The efficacy of the approach is demonstrated by constructing an ontology for the domain of ICD in an automated fashion and with a browsing application for semantic access to the heritage collection of ICD videos.

The use of notation is another way of recording dance for future use. A system of notation is required for recording the details of postures and movements in the domain of dance. Labanotation [3] is a widely used notation system for recording human movements in terms of graphical primitives and symbols. Karpen [4] first attempted to manually encode the movements of *Bharatanatyam* on paper using Labanotation. It has been demonstrated through examples that the body movement, space, time, and dynamics of the ICD, in particular *Bharatanatyam*, can be described through Labanotation. Hence it is argued that Labanotation, coupled with video filming, is a good way to record ICD. According to the author, hand gestures can also be easily implemented in Labanotation together with palm facing and specification of the quality of movement. However, no attempt was made in this paper to automate the process, and for the next three decades no work was done in transcribing ICD in Labanotation. Some research on dance preservation using notation has been carried out in other dance forms like Thai dance, contemporary dance, etc. Raheb et al. [1] use *Web Ontology Language* (OWL) to encode the knowledge of dance. The semantics of the Labanotation system is used to build elements of the ontology. Tongpaeng et al. [9] propose a system to archive the knowledge of Thai dance using Labanotation and then use the score of the notation to represent the dance in 3D animation. To date, automatic generation of Labanotation from the recorded dance video has not been attempted.

This work has been inspired by the idea of musical notations. Similar dance transcription systems may be useful in several ways. The system can generate parseable representation of a dance performance, help to preserve intangible heritage, help to annotate performances for better tutoring, and can be used as a front end for dance synthesis. We first attempt to capture the concepts of *Bharatanatyam Adavu*s in an ontological model. At the top level, a *Bharatanatyam Adavu* can be expressed as a dance (a sequence of visual postures) accompanied by music. Further, we identify the concepts of audio and video structures of *Bharatanatyam Adavu*. We next build an event-based, low-level model that relates the ontology of *Adavu*s to the ontology of multimodal data streams (RGB-D of Kinect in this case) for a computationally realizable framework. An event denotes the occurrence of an activity (called *Causal Activity*) in the audio or the video stream of an *Adavu*. The events of audio and video and their synchronization, thus, are related to the corresponding concepts of the ontological model. We use this ontology and event characterization for transcription into Labanotation using Laban ontology. We also present a transcription tool for encoding the performances of *Bharatanatyam Adavu*s to Labanotation and test it on our recorded data set. Our aim is to examine the ways in which Labanotation can be used for documenting the dance movements.

2 Indian Classical Dance: *Bharatanatyam* and Its *Adavu*s

We introduce the domain of *Bharatanatyam Adavu* in the context of knowledge capture and heritage preservation scheme in this section.

Bharatanatyam is one of the eight[1] Indian classical dance forms. Like most dance forms, *Bharatanatyam Adavu* too is deeply intertwined with music. It is usually accompanied by instrumental (*Tatta Kazhi*,[2] *Mridangam*, Flute, Violin, *Veena*, etc.) and/or vocal music (Carnatic style—with or without lyrics) called *Sollukattu*. *Adavu*s are the basic units of *Bharatanatyam* that are combined to create a dance performance. An *Adavu* involves various postures and gestures of the body including the torso, head, neck, hands, fingers, arms, legs and feet, and eyes. While

---

[1]ICD has eight distinct styles as recognized by the Ministry of Culture, Government of India: namely, *Bharatanatyam, Kathak, Odissi, Kathakali, Kuchipudi, Manipuri, Mohiniyattam, and Sattriya.*

[2]A wooden stick is beaten on a wooden block to produce instrumental sound.

performing *Adavu*s, the dancer stamps, rubs, touches, and slides on the ground in different ways in synchronization with the *Sollukattu*. There are 15 basic *Adavu*s in *Bharatanatyam*—most having one or more *Variant*s. In total, we deal with 58 *Adavu* variants. There exists a many-to-one mapping from the *Adavu*s to the *Sollukattu*s.

2.1   Sollukattu *and* Bols: *The Music of* Adavus

Bharatanatyam is deeply intertwined with music. It is usually accompanied by instrumental (*Tatta Kazhi, Mridangam*, Flute, Violin, *Veena*, etc.) and/or vocal music (Carnatic style—with or without lyrics). The music is strung together in sequences to create different rhythmic patterns, called *Taalam*,[3] to accompany dance performances. A repeated cycle of *Taalam* consists of a number of equally spaced beats, which are grouped into combinations of patterns. Time interval between any two beats is always equal. The specific way they mark the beats (by tapping their laps with their fingers, palm, and back of the hand or by a specific instrument) is determined by these patterns of the beats or the *Taalam*.

*Taalam*s necessarily synchronize the movements of various parts of the body with the music through a structured harmonization of four elements, namely, (a) rhythmic beats of *Taalam*, (b) *Mridangam* beats from percussion, (c) musical notes or *Swaras*,[4] and (d) steps of the *Adavu*s. It may be noted that a number of different *Taalam*s are used in *Bharatanatyam*. The *Taalam*s[5] commonly used in *Adavu* are *Adi taalam* (8 beat pattern) and *Roopakam taalam* (6 beat pattern). Finally, a *Taalam* is devoid of a physical unit of time and is acceptable as long as it is rhythmic in some temporal units. With a base time unit, however, *Bharatanatyam* deals with three speeds, called *Kaalam* or *Tempo*. The *Taalam*s are played mainly in three different tempos: *Vilambitha Laya* or slow speed, *Madhya Laya* (double of *Vilambitha Laya*) or medium speed, and *Drutha Laya* (quadruple of *Vilambitha Laya*) or fast speed.

A phrase of rhythmic syllables (*Sollukattu*) is linked to specific units of dance movement in an *Adavu*. A *Sollukattu*[6] is a specific rhythmic musical pattern created by a combination of instrumental and vocal sounds. Traditionally, a *Tatta Kazhi* (wooden stick) is beaten on a *Tatta Palahai* (wooden block) for the instrumental sound, and an accomplice of the dancer speaks out a distinct vocalization of rhythm, like *tat, tei, ta*, etc., called *Bols*.[7] In a *Sollukattu*, both the instrument and the voice follow in sync to create a pattern of beats. Every beat is usually marked by a synchronous beating (instrumental) sound, though some beats may be silent. In

---

[3]*Taalam* is the Indian system for organizing and playing metrical music.

[4]*Swara*, in Sanskrit, connotes a note in the successive steps of the octave.

[5]*Adavu*s can be performed in all seven *taalam*s as well, but the rest are less popular.

[6]*Sollukattu* = *sollum* (syllables) + *kattu* (speaking). A *Sollukattu* refers to a phrase of rhythmic syllables linked to specific units of dance movement (*Adavu*).

[7]*Bols* (or *bolna* = *to speak*) are mnemonic syllables for beats in the *taalam*.

Table 1 List of *Sollukattu*s with *bol* compositions

Sollukattu	# Beats	Description of *Bol*s
Joining A	8	tat dhit ta [B] tat dhit ta [B]
Joining B	6	[dhit dhit] tei [dhit dhit] tei [dhit dhit] tei [dhit dhit] tei
Joining C	8	tei tei [dhit dhit] tei tei tei [dhit dhit] tei
KUMS	6	[tan gadu] [tat tat] [dhin na] [tan gadu] [tat tat] [dhin na]
Mettu	8	tei hat tei hi tei hat tei hi
Nattal A	8	tat tei tam [B] dhit tei tam [B]
Nattal B	8	[tat tei] tam [dhit tei] tam [tat tei] tam [dhit dhit] tei
Tattal	8	tat tei ta ha dhit tei ta ha
Natta	8	[tei yum] [tat tat] [tei yum] ta [tei yum] [tat tat] [tei yum] ta
Paikkal	8	[dhit tei da] [ta tei] [dhit tei da] [ta tei] [dhit tei da] [ta tei] [dhit tei da] [ta tei]
Pakka	8	ta tei tei tat dhit tei tei tat
Sarika	8	tei a tei e tei a tei e
Tatta A	8	[tei ya] tei [tei ya] tei [tei ya] tei [tei ya] tei
Tatta B	6	tei tei tam tei tei tam
Tatta C	8	[tei ya] [tei ya] [tei ya] tei [tei ya] [tei ya] tei
Tatta D	8	tei tei [tei tei] tam tei tei [tei tei] tam
Tatta E	8	tei tei tam [B] tei tei tam [B]
Tatta F	8	tei tei tat tat tei tei tam [B]
Tatta G	6	tei tei tei tei [dhit dhit] tei
TTD	8	[tei tei] [dhat ta] [dhit tei] [dhat ta] [tei tei] [dhat ta] [dhit tei] [dhat ta]
Tirmana A	12	ta [tat ta] jham [ta ri] ta [B] jham [ta ri] jag [ta ri] tei [B]
Tirmana B	12	[tat ding] [gin na] tom [tak ka] [tat ding] [gin na] tom [tak ka] [dhi ku] [tat ding] [gin na] tom
Tirmana C	12	[ki ta ta ka] [dha ri ki ta] tom tak [ki ta ta ka] [dha ri ki ta] tom [tak ka] [dhi ku] [ki ta ta ka] [dha ri ki ta] tom

Multiple *bol*s at the same beat are enclosed within []. [B] stands for a beat without any *bol*s—typically called stick beat. KUMS, Mettu, Nattal, Tattal, and TTD stand for Kartati–Utsanga–Mandi–Sarikkal, Kuditta Mettu, Kuditta Nattal, Kuditta Tattal, and Tei Tei Dhatta, respectively

some cases, there may be beating (instrumental) sounds at positions that are not beats (according to the periodicity). The list of *Sollukattu*s is given in Table 1. As *Adavu*s are performed along with the rhythmic syllables of a *Sollukattu* that continues to repeat in cycles, the rhythm performs the role of a timer (with beats as temporal markers). Between the interval of beats, the dancer changes her posture.

2.2   Adavus: *The Postures and Movements*

*Adavu*s are the basic units of Bharatanatyam that are combined to form a dance sequence in Bharatanatyam. *Adavu*s form the foundation stone on which the entire *Nritta* rests. It involves various postures and gestures of the body, hand, arms, feet, and eyes.[8] While performing *Adavu*s, the dancer stamps, rubs, touches, and slides on the ground in different ways in synchronization with the *Sollukattu* (bol) or the syllables used. The *Adavu*s are classified according to the rhythmic syllables on which they are based and the style of footwork employed. According to the *Kalakshetra* school of training, there are 15 *Adavu*s. Most *Adavu*s have two or more *variants*. Variants of an *Adavu* bear a similarity of intent and style but differ in details. A total of 58 *Adavu*s and 23 *Sollukattu*s are used in *Kalakshetra*.[9] The details are listed in Table 2. Every (variant of an) *Adavu* uses a fixed *Sollukattu*, while a given *Sollukattu* may be used in multiple *Adavu*s. Each posture of *Adavu*s is a combination of leg support (*Mandalam*), legs position (*Pada Bheda*), arms position (*Bahu Bheda*), head position (*Shiro Bheda*), hand position (*Hasta Mudra*s), neck position (*Griba Bheda*), and eyes position (*Drishti Bheda*).

Since *Adavu*s are elementary units and used for training, each *Adavu* has a specific purpose (as shown is Table 3). For example, *Tatta Adavu*s focus on *striking of the floor with foot*. The body remains in a posture called *Araimandi*, and the feet, by rotation, strike the floor alternately with the sole. There are eight variants of *Tatta Adavu*. The features of Variant 1 of *Tatta Adavu* (say, *Tatta* 1) are (a) strike on the floor, (b) heel to touch hip during strike, (c) no hand gesture, and (d) no movements. The *Sollukattu* used in *Tatta* 1 is *tei a tei* (say, *Tatta_A*). This follows the *Adi Taalam* or 8 beat pattern as shown in Table 4. The *bol*s on each beat are shown in three different tempos.

The posture of a dancer is synchronized with the beats. The synchronized postures with beats are shown in Fig. 1. Here, the dancer strikes her left and right foot with the beats in rotation.

Like *Tatta* 1, all *Adavu*s are combinations of:

- **Position of the legs (*Sthanakam*)/posture of standing (*Mandalam*)**: *Adavu*s are performed in the following postures (Fig. 2): (a) *Samapadam*, or the standing position; (b) *Araimandi/Ardha Mandalam*, or the half-sitting posture; and (c) *Muzhumandi*, or the sitting posture.
- **Jumps (*Utplavana*)**: Based on the mode of performances, *Utplavana*s are classified into *Alaga*, *Kartari*, *Asva*, *Motita*, and *Kripalaya*.

---

[8]Current work does not consider hand and eye movements for limitations of sensors.

[9]There are four major styles of *Bharatanatyam*: *Thanjavur*, *Pandanallur*, *Vazhuvoor*, and *Mellatur*. *Kalakshetra*, promulgated by the *Kalakshetra Foundation* founded by Rukmini Devi, is the modern style of *Bharatanatyam* and is reconstructed from the *Pandanallur* style.

Table 2 List of *Adavu*s with accompanying *Sollukattu*

#	Adavu		Taalam	Sollukattu
	Name	Variants		
1	Joining	Joining 1	Adi	Joining A
		Joining 2		Joining B
		Joining 3		Joining C
2	Kati or Kartari	Kati or Kartari 1	Roopakam	KUMS
3	Kuditta Mettu	Kuditta Mettu 1–4	Adi	Kuditta Mettu
3	Kuditta Nattal	Kuditta Nattal 1–3	Adi	Kuditta Nattal A
		Kuditta Nattal 4–5		Kuditta Nattal B
		Kuditta Nattal 6		Kuditta Nattal A
5	Kuditta Tattal	Kuditta Tattal 1–5	Adi	Kuditta Tattal
6	Mandi	Mandi 1–2	Roopakam	KUMS
7	Natta	Natta 1–8	Adi	Natta
8	Paikkal	Paikkal 1–3	Adi	Paikkal
9	Pakka	Pakka 1–4	Adi	Pakka
10	Sarika	Sarika 1–4	Adi	Sarika
11	Sarrikkal	Sarrikkal 1–3	Roopakam	KUMS
12	Tatta	Tatta 1–2	Adi	Tatta A
		Tatta 3	Roopakam	Tatta B
		Tatta 4	Adi	Tatta C
		Tatta 5		Tatta D
		Tatta 6		Tatta E
		Tatta 7		Tatta F
		Tatta 8	Roopakam	Tatta G
13	Tei Tei Dhatta	Tei Tei Dhatta 1–3	Adi	Tei Tei Dhatta
14	Tirmana	Tirmana 1	Roopakam	Tirmana A
		Tirmana 2		Tirmana B
		Tirmana 3		Tirmana C
15	Utsanga	Utsanga 1	Roopakam	KUMS

KUMS stands for Kartati–Utsanga–Mandi–Sarikkal

- **Walking movement (*Chari*)**: *Chari* are used for gaits. According to *Abhinayadarpana*, there are eight kinds of *Chari*s: *Chalana, Chankramana, Sarana, Vehini, Kuttana, Luhita, Lolita,* and *Vishama Sanchara*.
- **Hand gestures (*Nritta Hastas*)**: *Bharatanatyam* primarily uses two types[10] of *Hasta Mudra*s that play a significant role in communication—28 single hand gestures (*Asamyutha Hasta*) and 23 combined (both) hand gestures (*Samyutha Hasta*). There are twelve major hand gestures for *Adavu*s: *Pataka, Tripataka, Ardhachandra, Kapittha, Katakamukha, Suchi, Musthi, Mrigasirsha, Alapadma, Kaetarimukha, Shikhara,* and *Dola*.

---

[10]Few other types like *Nritya Hasta* are used at times.

Table 3 Purpose of various *Adavu*s

Adavu	*Purpose of the* Adavu
Joining	Simple connecting of *Adavu*s to be used while building longer sequences of postures
Kati or Kartari	*Paidhal* itself includes a variety of leaps and may also be coupled with spins (*Bramhari*). It also includes the famous *Kartari* (scissors) *adavu* where the movement of the hand and feet traces crisscross patterns in space
Kuditta Mettu	Jumping on the toes and then striking the heels
Kuditta Nattal	Striking the floor with feet, jumping on toes, stretching legs and hands, and also circular movement of hand
Kuditta Tattal	Striking the floor, jumping on toes, stretching hands, circular movements of hands, neck, and head with the bending of torso and waist, and hand movements defining different planes in space
Mandi	*Mandi* in some Indian languages refers to the area around the thigh and knee. In some instances, it can refer to a bent knee. For example, *Araimandi* is where the knee is half bent. *Muzhumandi* or *Poorna Mandala* is where the knee is fully bent. In *Mandi adavu*s, we make use of the *Muzhumandi* position often. Steps could vary from jumps in *Poorna Mandala* to jumping and touching one knee on the floor
Natta	Stretching of legs
Paikkal	*Paikkal* (*Paidhal* or *Paichal*) is a Tamil term that means **to leap**. It differs from the *Kuditta Mettu*, in the sense that the dancer while doing the *Paikkal* covers space, whereas in *Kuditta Mettu* she/he jumps on the same spot. A very graceful step in itself, *Paikkal* is usually seen at the end of Korvai (a string of *Adavu*s) as part of *Ardhi*s
Pakka	Moving toward sides
Sarika	*Sarika* means a thing of beauty or nature
Sarrikkal	*Sarrikkal* means **to slide**. Here as one foot is lifted and placed, the other foot slides toward it
Tatta	Striking the floor with feet
Tei Tei Dhatta	Use of half and full sitting, stretching legs and hand, jumping with linear and circular movements of hands
Tirmana	*Tirmana* (or *Teermanam*) means **to conclude** or an ending or a final stage. Thus the steps in these *adavu*s are used to end a dance sequence or *jathi*s. It is done in a set of three steps or repeated thrice
Utsanga	Use of different hand positions to enhance the stretching on half sitting, straight standing, jump on heels, and striking the floor. Also use of linear and circular movements of waist and stretching of hands

Source: Vasudevan and Kavanagh [10] and personal communication with Debaldev Jana

In *Bharatanatyam*, **Adavu** is used in dual sense. It either denotes just the dance part (postures and movements) or the dance and the accompanying music together. To maintain clarity of reference, in this chapter, we refer to the dance simply as *Adavu* and the composite of dance and music as *Bharatanatyam Adavu*.

Table 4 Beat pattern of *Tatta* 1 (*Tatta Adavu* Variant 1) in *Adi Taalam*

Speed	Beats							
	1	2	3	4	5	6	7	8
First	tei a	tei	tei a	tei	tei a	tei	tei a	tei
Second	tei a tei	tei a tei	tei a tei	tei a tei	tei a tei	tei a tei	tei a tei	tei a tei
Third	tei a tei	tei a tei	tei a tei	tei a tei	tei a tei	tei a tei	tei a tei	tei a tei
	tei a tei	tei a tei	tei a tei	tei a tei	tei a tei	tei a tei	tei a tei	tei a tei

Time Measure: *Adi Taalam*

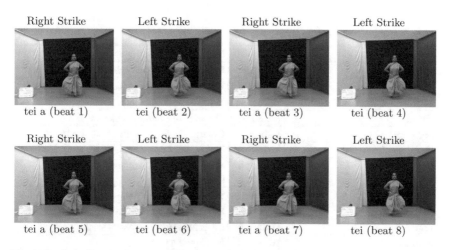

Right Strike	Left Strike	Right Strike	Left Strike
tei a (beat 1)	tei (beat 2)	tei a (beat 3)	tei (beat 4)
Right Strike	Left Strike	Right Strike	Left Strike
tei a (beat 5)	tei (beat 6)	tei a (beat 7)	tei (beat 8)

Fig. 1 Example performance of *Tatta* 1 (*Tatta Adavu* Variant 1)

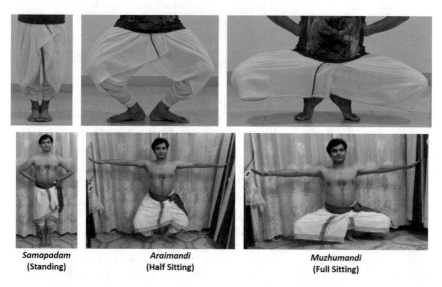

Samapadam
(Standing)　　**Araimandi**
(Half Sitting)　　**Muzhumandi**
(Full Sitting)

Fig. 2 Three *Mandalam*s (types of leg support) of *Bharatanatyam* as performed by the dancer Dr. Debaldev Jana

3   Object-Based Modeling of *Adavus*

To express the ontology, we follow an extended object-based modeling framework comprising a set of classes (Table 5), a set of instances (Table 6), and a set of relations (Table 7). Classes are used to represent generic as well as specific concepts. These can be *Abstract* or *Concrete*. A concrete class has one or more instances, while an abstract class has one or more specialized classes. Relations are usually binary and are defined between two classes, between a class and an instance, or between two instances.

Table 5 List of classes for the ontology of *Bharatanatyam Adavu*

Class	Type	Remarks
Sollukattu	Concrete	The music (audio) of *Adavus* (Table 1)
Adavu	Abstract	The movements (video) of *Adavus* (Table 2)
Tatta Adavu, Natta Adavu, ⋯	Concrete	Types of *Adavus* (Table 2)
Carnatic Music	Abstract	The style of *Bharatanatyam* music
Sequence	Abstract	Ordered list of elements of one kind
Beat	Abstract	Basic unit of time—an instance on timescale
Bol	Concrete	Mnemonic syllable or vocal utterances (Table 8)
Posture	Abstract	Standing or sitting position of a dancer
Taalam	Concrete	Rhythmic pattern of beats
Tempo	Concrete	Beats per minute—defines speed
Instrumental Strike	Concrete	Beating of a percussion
Position (Time Stamp)	Concrete	Instant of time
Key Posture	Concrete	Momentarily stationary posture (Fig. 1)
Transition Posture	Abstract	Nonstationary posture
Trajectorial Transition Posture	Concrete	Transitions along a well-defined trajectory
Natural Transition Posture	Concrete	Natural posture transitions by the dancer
Leg Support (*Mandalam*)	Concrete	Ways to support the body (Fig. 2)
Legs Position (*Pada Bheda*)	Concrete	Positions of both legs in *Bharatanatyam*
Arms Position (*Bahu Bheda*)	Concrete	Positions of both arms in *Bharatanatyam*
Head Position (*Shiro Bheda*)	Concrete	Positions of head in *Bharatanatyam*
Neck Position (*Griba Bheda*)	Concrete	Positions of neck in *Bharatanatyam*
Eyes Position (*Drishti Bheda*)	Concrete	Eye movements depicting *navarasa*
Hands Position (*Hasta Mudra*)	Abstract	Positions of both hands in *Bharatanatyam*
Single Hand Gesture	Concrete	*Asamyukta Hasta Mudras*
Double Hand Gesture	Concrete	*Samyukta Hasta Mudras*
Left Leg (Formation)	Concrete	Left leg in *Pada Bheda* (Table 9)
Right Leg (Formation)	Concrete	Right leg in *Pada Bheda* (Table 9)
Left Arm (Formation)	Concrete	Left arm in *Bahu Bheda* (Table 10)
Right Arm (Formation)	Concrete	Right arm in *Bahu Bheda* (Table 10)
Left Hand (Formation)	Concrete	Left hand in *Hasta Mudra* (Table 12)
Right Hand (Formation)	Concrete	Right hand in *Hasta Mudra* (Table 12)

Table 6 List of instances for the ontology of *Bharatanatyam Adavu*

Class:Instance	Remarks
Sollukattu: *Tatta_A, ⋯, Tatta_G, Natta, Kuditta Mettu*	23 types of *Sollukattu*s (Table 1)
Adavu: *Tatta 1, ⋯, Tatta 8, Natta, Kuditta Mettu*	58 types of *Adavu*s (Table 2)
Bol: *tei, yum, tat, ⋯,*	31 types of *Bol*s (Table 8)
Taalam: *Adi Taalam, Roopakam Taalam*	2 of the 7 types of *Taalam*s
Tempo (*Laya*): *Vilambit Laya, Madhya Laya, Drut Laya*	3 types of *Laya*s (speed) or tempo
Spinal bending (Boolean)	Spine may or may not be bent
Key postures: *Natta1P1, Natta1P2, Natta1P3, ⋯*	Key postures of *Natta Adavu* Variant 1
Leg support: *Samapadam* (Standing), *Araimandi* (Half Sitting), *Muzhumandi* (Full Sitting)	3 types of leg support
Legs position: *Aayata* **[S]**, *Prenkhanam* **[M]**, ⋯	Types of both legs positions
Arms position: *Natyarambhe* **[S]**, *Natyarambhe* **[M]**, ⋯	Types of both arms positions
Head position: *Samam, Left Paravrittam, Right Paravrittam, ⋯*	Types of head positions (Table 11)
Hands position: *Tripataka* **[S]**, ⋯	Types of both hands gestures
Left/right leg (Formation): *Aayata, Anchita, ⋯*	Types of single leg formations (Table 9)
Left/right arm (Formation): *Natyarambhe, Kunchita Natyarambhe, ⋯*	Types of single arm formations (Table 10)
Left/right hand (Formation): *Tripataka, ⋯*	Types of single hand gestures

[S]: Denotes symmetric (**[S]**) positions between the left and right limbs. **[M]**: Denotes asymmetric positions between the left and right limbs and its mirror (**[M]**). Instances of neck position, eye position, and double hand gestures are not considered

3.1 Ontology of Bharatanatyam Adavus: Top Level

At the top level, a *Bharatanatyam Adavu* can be expressed simply as a dance (*Adavu*) accompanied and driven by (*isAccompaniedBy*) music (*Sollukattu*) (Fig. 3). In other words, the musical *meter*[11] of an *Adavu* is called a *Sollukattu*, which is a sequence of beats/*bol*s. An *Adavu* is a sequence of postures. We also note that *Sollukattu* is a form of Carnatic music.

Elaborating on the basic concept of *Adavu*s, we show in Fig. 4 that there are several specializations of *Adavu*s like *Tatta Adavu* or *Natta Adavu* having instances of *Tatta Adavu 1, ⋯, Tatta Adavu 8*, etc. and there are several instances of *Sollukattu*s like *Tatta A, ⋯ Kuditta Mettu*, etc. Specifically, every *Adavu* is synchronized with (*isSyncedWith*) a unique *Sollukattu*.

---

[11] The *meter* of music is its rhythmic structure.

Table 7 List of (binary) relations for the ontology of *Bharatanatyam Adavu*

Relation	Domain	Co-domain	Remarks
is_a	Class	Class	Specialization/generalization or *is_a* hierarchy of object-based modeling. This is used to build the *taxonomy*. For example, *Tatta Adavu is_a Adavu*
has_a	Class	Class/ instance	Composition or *has_a* hierarchy of object-based modeling. This is used to build the *partonomy*. For example, *Sollukattu has_a Taalam*
isInstanceOf	Instance	Class	Distinct instances of a class
isAccompaniedBy	Class	Class	*isAccompaniedBy* captures the association between video and audio streams. Hence, *Adavu isAccompaniedBy Sollukattu*
isSyncedWith	Class	Class	Expresses high-level synchronization—between audio and video streams. Every *Adavu isSyncedWith* a unique *Sollukattu*
isSequenceOf	Class	Class	*isSequenceOf* builds a sequence from elements of the same type. For example, every *Sollukattu* (*Adavu*) *has_a* sequence of beats (postures) constructed from beat (postures) by *isSequenceOf* relation. *isFollowedBy* is a dual of this relation
isAccentedBy	Class	Class	A beat *isAccentedBy* a *bol*
isFollowedBy	Class	Class	Ordering of audio events (like *beats*) or video events (like *postures*)—Event E_1 *isFollowedBy* event E_2. *isSequenceOf* is a dual of this relation
triggers	Instance	Instance	Expresses low-level synchronization—between audio and video events. Hence, a beat *triggers* a posture as the dance is driven by the music
repeats	Class	Class	Once a *taalam* completes a bar, it may repeat itself

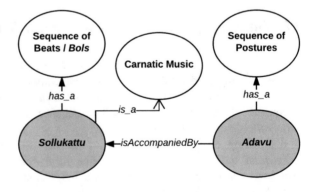

Fig. 3 Ontology of *Bharatanatyam Adavu* at the abstract level

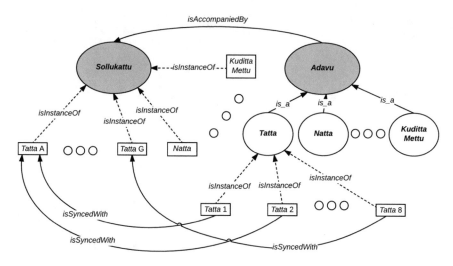

Fig. 4 Ontology of *Bharatanatyam Adavu* with specializations and instances

3.2 Ontology of Sollukattus

Next, we elaborate the ontology of a *Sollukattu* (Sect. 2.1) in Fig. 5. A *Sollukattu* is performed in a *Taalam* that designates a specific pattern of rhythm. A *Taalam* is composed of a sequence of beats (*isSequenceOf*) going at a certain tempo (speed). At the end of the sequence of beats (or the bar), the *Taalam repeats* itself. A tempo corresponds to the speed of the rhythm, which may be carried out in one of the three speeds (*Laya*): slow, medium, and fast. *Adi Taalam* and *Roopakam Taalam* are the typical rhythms used in *Bharatanatyam*.

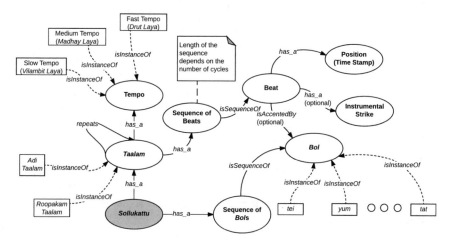

Fig. 5 Ontology of *Sollukattu*s

Table 8 *Bol* vocabulary of
Sollakattus

Sl. #	Bol	Sl. #	Bol	Sl. #	Bol
1	a	12	ha	23	tak
2	da	13	hat	24	tam
3	dha	14	hi	25	tan
4	dhat	15	jag	26	tat
5	dhi	16	jham	27	tei
6	dhin	17	ka	28	tom
7	dhit	18	ki	29	tta
8	ding	19	ku	30	ya
9	e	20	na	31	yum
10	gadu	21	ri	32	*Stick Beat*
11	gin	22	ta		

Stick Beat is treated as a pseudo-*bol*. The *bols* shown in the table are typical as *Bharatanatyam* does not follow a strictly fixed set of *bol*.

A beat is an instant in time that may be marked by the beating of a stick and optionally accented by a *bol*. Hence, it *has_a* temporal position (time stamp), an instrumental strike (e.g., beating of *Tatta Kazhi*), and a *bol* like *tei, yum, tat,* ··· (a vocabulary of *Bols* by *Bharatanatyam* experts is given in Table 8).

3.3 Ontology of Adavus

We elaborate the ontology of an *Adavu* (Sect. 2.2) in Fig. 6. An *Adavu* is created by a sequence of *postures* and intervening *movements* like *Utplavana* (jumps), *Chari* (walking), or *Karana*[12] (synchronized movement of the hands and feet). A posture may be a *Key Posture* or a *Transition Posture*. A Key Posture is defined as a momentarily stationary pose taken by the dancer with well-defined positions for the *Legs* (*Pada Bheda*), the *Arms* (*Bahu Bheda*), the *Head* (*Shiro Bheda*), the *Neck* (*Griba Bheda*), the *Eyes* (*Drishti Bheda*), and the *Hands* (*Hasta Mudra*). Every Key Posture is also defined with a specific *Leg Support* and *Spinal Bending* to support and balance the body. A Transition Posture, in turn, is a transitory pose (ill-defined, at times) between two consecutive Key Postures in a sequence or a pose assumed as a part of a movement. It may be *Trajectorial* or *Natural*. While a *Trajectorial Transition Posture* occurs in a well-defined trajectory path of body parts, a *Natural Transition Posture* may be suitably chosen by a dancer to move from one Key Posture to the next.

In the current work, we focus only on Key Postures and do not model and/or analyze movements and transitions. Hence, we do not elaborate the ontology for *Transition Postures* or movements. However, the concept of Key Postures is detailed in Fig. 7.

---

[12] *Karana*s (*doing* in Sanskrit) are the 108 key transitions described in *Natya Shastra*.

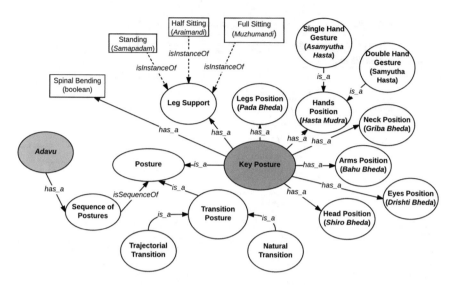

Fig. 6 Ontology of *Adavu*s

3.3.1 Vocabulary of Positions and Formations

To elaborate the ontology for a Key Posture, we introduce the notions of *positions* and *formations* of constituent limbs or body parts. A *formation* describes the specific manner in which a body part is posed in the posture. For body parts that occur in pairs (like the legs, arms, hands, eyes), the combined formation of the individual (left and right) parts defines a *position*. For the rest (like the head, neck), *position* and *formation* are taken to be synonymous. An accepted nomenclature (as identified by experts) exists for many positions/formations of most of the body parts in *Bharatanatyam*. Naturally, we adopt those. For the rest, we assign names based on crisp descriptors of the positions. We observe that the postures mostly are distinguishable based on the four major body parts: the leg, arm, head, and hand. Hence, we have not considered the eyes and the neck in building the posture ontology.

In Table 9, we list the vocabulary for formations of the left and right legs as well as their combined legs positions. Some of the positions are asymmetric in which the left and the right leg assume different formations. For example, if the left leg is in the *Anchita* formation and the right leg is in the *Samapadam* formation, the combined legs position is named as *Ardha Prenkhanam*. Naturally, every asymmetric position has a position that is a mirror image of the other one, marked by **[M]** (Mirror), where the formations of the legs are swapped. That is, in *Ardha Prenkhanam* **[M]**, the right leg is in the *Anchita* formation and the left leg is in the *Samapadam* formation. In the table, we have listed only one of these mirrored positions. The remaining leg positions are symmetric in which both legs assume the same formation. In such cases, the position is marked with an **[S]** (Symmetric), and the same name is used

Table 9 Vocabulary for the formations and positions of legs (*Pada Bheda*)

Left leg formation	Right leg formation	Leg position
Asymmetric positions		
Anchita	*Samapadam*	*Ardha Prenkhanam*
Aayata	*Back Swastikam*	*Back Swastikam*
Agratala Sanchara	*Samapadam*	*Chalan Chari*
Aayata	*Diagona Anchita*	*Diagonal Prenkhanam*
Bend On Knee	*Support*	*Ekapadam*
Aayata	*Front Anchita*	*Front Prenkhanam*
Aayata	*Front Swastikam*	*Front Swastikam*
Aayata	*Prerita*	*Prerita*
Parsasuchi	*Bisamasuchi*	*Garudamandalam*
Aayata	*Forward/Side Low*	*Lolita Chari*
Aayata	*Anchita*	*Prenkhanam*
Aayata	*Side Middle/Low*	*Prenkhanam Above Floor*
Aayata	*Kunchita*	*Aaleeda* (**[M]** = *Pratyaaleeda*)
Kunchita	*Aayata*	*Pratyaaleeda*
Symmetric positions		
Aayata	*Anchita*	*Ekapadam Bhramari*
Samapadam	*Motita Mandal*	*Side Chankramanang*
Muzmandi	*Slip With Left Knee*	*Chankramanang*
Kuttana	*Slip With Right Knee*	*Back Chankramanang*
Parswa Aayata		

Table 10 Vocabulary for the formations of arms (*Bahu Bheda*)

Above Head Natyarambhe	*Diagonal High*	*Kunchita Natyarambhe*
Above Head Natyarambhe	*Diagonal Middle*	*Left Diagonal High*
(*Joined*)	*Elbow Down Anchita*	*Natyarambhe*
Anchita	*Forward High*	*Right Diagonal High*
Anchita Above Left Ear	*Forward High Above Head*	*Right Diagonal Middle*
Anchita Above Right Ear	*Forward Low*	*Side High*
Ardha Vithi	*Forward Middle*	*Side High Natyarambhe*
Backward High	*Front Natyarambhe*	*Side Low*
Backward Low	*Katyang Behind Waist*	*Side Middle*
Backward Middle	*Kunchita*	*Utsanga*
Cross Kunchita	*Kunchita Above Shoulder*	

for the formation and the position. Hence in *Aayata* **[S]** position, both legs are in the *Aayata* formation.

In Table 10, we list the vocabulary for the formations of the arms. Either arm can assume any of these formations. In the case of the arms, no specific names are used for combined arms positions. Hence, they are referred to with the names of both the formations if they are different. For example, if the left arm is in the *Kunchita Natyarambhe* formation and the right arm is in the *Natyarambhe* formation, the

Table 11 Vocabulary for positions/formations of the head (*Shiro Bheda*)

Samam	Left Adhomukham	Right Adhomukham
Adhomukham	Left Ardha Paravrittam	Right Ardha Paravrittam
Back Paravrittam	Left Paravrittam	Right Paravrittam
Udvahitam	Left Utshiptam	Right Utshiptam
Ardha Aalolitam		

Table 12 Vocabulary for formations of the hands (*Hasta Mudra*)

Alapadma	Kartarimukha	Mushti	Suchi
Avahitya	Katakamukha	Pataka	Tripataka
Dola	Mrigashirsha	Shikhara	

combined arms position is named as *Natyarambhe–Kunchita Natyarambhe*. If, however, both formations are the same, we name the position with an **[S]**. Hence *Natyarambhe* **[S]** has the *Natyarambhe* formation for both arms. In Table 11, we list the vocabulary for the formations of the head. Naturally, there is no position descriptor here. Next we list the vocabulary for the formations of the hands (*hasta mudra*) in Table 12. Like the arms, these are also denoted with formations of single hands only, and the combined hands position is similarly named. It may be noted that the vocabulary listed here is a subset of *Asamyutha Hasta* or single hand gestures as commonly observed in the *Adavu*s. We do not consider *Samyutha Hasta* or combined (both) hand gestures in building the vocabulary.

3.3.2 Ontology of Key Postures

We elaborate the ontology of Key Postures in Fig. 7. Consider the *Legs Positions*. For the *Prenkhanam* Legs Position in Natta1P2 in the figure, the left leg makes the *Aayata* (bent at the knee) and the right leg makes the *Anchita* formation (straight and stretched). *Prenkhanam* **[M]** is a mirror image position of *Prenkhanam* where the formations of the two legs are swapped. Natta1P3 is a mirrored posture of Natta1P2 and has *Prenkhanam* **[M]** for the legs positions. With symmetry, Natta1P1 has *Aayata* **[S]** legs position.

Consider instances of three key postures—Natta1P1, Natta1P2, and Natta1P3—of *Natta 1 Adavu*. For example, Natta1P1, we have *Legs Position = Aayata* **[S]**, *Arms Position = Natyarambhe* **[S]**, *Hands Position = Tripataka* **[S]**, and *Head Position = Samam*.

We identify 361 distinct postures and 48 distinct movements in the 58 *Adavu*s.

3.4 Ontology of Audio-Visual Sync Between Sollukattu and Adavu

With the ontology of music (*Sollukattu*) and (visual) sequence of postures (*Adavu*) of *Bharatanatyam*, we next capture the synchronization of the events. As the

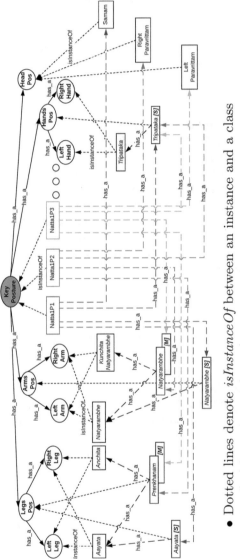

- Dotted lines denote *isInstanceOf* between an instance and a class
- Dashed lines denote *has_a* between two an instances

Fig. 7 Ontology of key postures. (1) Dotted lines denote *isInstanceOf* between an instance and a class. (2) Dashed lines denote *has_a* between two instances

postures are driven by and are synchronized with the beats of the music, and as the performance repeats after a bar of the rhythm, we capture the ontology of synchronization between an *Adavu* and its *Sollukattu* as in Fig. 8. Here specific instances of beats—Beat 1, Beat 2, $\cdots$, Beat n—form the sequence of beats in a *Sollukattu*. So we express that Beat 1 *isFollowedBy* Beat 2, Beat 2 *isFollowedBy* Beat 3, and so on. Finally, after Beat n, the bar *repeats*, and hence, Beat n *isFollowedBy* Beat 1. Similarly, instances of key postures—Posture 1, Posture 2, $\cdots$, Posture n—form the sequence of postures in an *Adavu* that also *repeats*. Being driven by music, every beat *triggers* the corresponding posture. In the figure, we show only one cycle (bar) of the *Taalam*. In an *Adavu*, usually 1, 2, 4, 6, 8, or more number of repetitions are performed by the dancer. Explicit instances of *bol*s and time instants are omitted on the diagram for better clarity.

In this section, we have captured the central concepts of *Bharatanatyam Adavu*s in terms of a set of object-based ontological models. These models identify the key items with their interrelationships and help the annotation of data sets for training as well as testing. Naturally, they lead to algorithms for the analysis and recognition of various items (like *bol*s and postures). However, these models are structural and, hence, are limited in their temporal specification.

4   Event-Based Modeling of *Adavu*s

The framework used so far is good for taxonomical and partonomical representation but lacks the expressibility in temporal terms. But dance is multimedia in nature with music driving the steps. In order to capture the dynamic association between music and video, we first tried to use the concept of triggers to model the synchronization of events. The progression of time is captured by simple sequences (*isFollowedBy*) of occurrences of *bol*s and beats. This approach is illustrated in Fig. 8. Since a simple sequence of *bol*s and beats misses the actual quantum of time slice, it cannot deal with triggers between beat and posture actions and cannot ensure equal time gap between beats. Temporal behavioral models are necessary to analyze and recognize such temporal and synchronization details in depth. Hence, we introduce an event-based modeling framework that, on the one hand, can relate to the key concepts as introduced above and is defined in terms of temporal relationships on the other.

This event-based framework treats a performance as a multimedia stream and takes the models closer to the structure of the data that we capture later by Kinect. A *Bharatanatyam Adavu*, therefore, consists of (1) a Composite **Audio Stream** (*Sollakattu*) containing (a) an *Instrumental Sub-stream* as generated by instrumental strikes and (b) a *Vocal Sub-stream* as generated by vocalizations or *bol*s; (2) a **Video Stream** of frames containing either (a) a Key Posture (called *K-Frame*) or (b) a Transition Posture (called *T-Frame*); and (3) a **Synchronization** (**Sync**) of Position, Posture, Movement, and Gesture of an *Adavu* as performed in synchronization among themselves and in synchronization with the rhythm of the music. In *Instrumental* and *Vocal Sub-streams* of a *Sollukattu*, beating and *bol*s

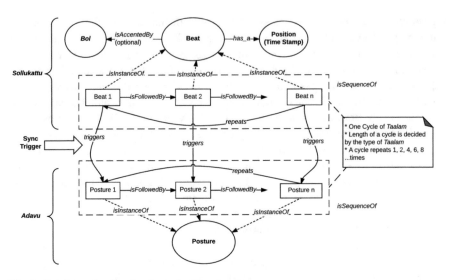

Fig. 8 Ontology of audio-visual sync in *Bharatanatyam*

are usually generated in sync. The rules or structure of synchronization have been defined for every *Sollakattu* in *Bharatanatyam*.

4.1 *Events of* Adavus

An *Event* denotes the occurrence of an activity (called *Causal Activity*) in the audio or the video stream of an *Adavu*. Further, sync events are defined between multiple events based on temporal constraints. Sync events may be defined jointly between audio and video streams. An event is described by:

1. *Category*: The nature of the event based on its origin (*audio*, *video*, or *sync*).
2. *Type*: Type relates to the causal activity of an event in a given category. Event types are listed in Table 13 with a brief description.
3. *Time stamp/range*: The time of occurrence of the causal activity of the event. This is the elapsed time from the beginning of the stream and is marked by a function $\tau(.)$. Often a causal activity may spread over an interval $[\tau_s, \tau_e]$, which will be associated with the event. For video events, we use a range of video frame numbers $[\eta_s, \eta_e]$ as the temporal interval. Since the video has a fixed rate of 30 fps, for any event we interchangeably use $[\tau_s, \tau_e]$ or $[\eta_s, \eta_e]$ as is appropriate in a context.
4. *Label*: Optional labels may be attached to an event for annotating details.
5. *ID*: Every instance of an event in a stream is distinguishable. These are sequentially numbered in the temporal order of their occurrence (Table 16).

The list of events is given in Table 13 and characterized in the next sections.

Table 13 List of events of *Adavu*s

Event category	Event type	Event description	Event label
Audio	α^{fb}	Full beat[a] with *bol*	*bol*[b], downbeat[c], upbeat[d]
Audio	α^{hb}	Half beat[e] with *bol*	*bol*
Audio	α^{qb}	Quarter beat[f] with *bol*	*bol*
Audio	α^{fn}	Full beat having no *bol*	upbeat
Audio	α^{hn}	Half beat having no *bol*	
Audio	β	*bol* is vocalized	*bol*
Video	v^{nm}	No-motion[g]	Range of Frames[h], Key Posture[i]
Video	v^{tr}	Transition Motion[j]	Range of Frames
Video	v^{tj}	Trajectory Motion[k]	Range of Frames, Trajectory
Sync	ϕ^{fb}	*bol* @ Full beat	*bol*
Sync	ϕ^{hb}	*bol* @ Half beat	*bol*
Sync	ψ^{fb}	No-motion @ Full beat[l]	Key Posture
Sync	ψ^{hb}	No-motion @ Half beat	Key Posture

[a] A (full) beat is the basic unit of time—an instance on the timescale
[b] Vocalized *bol*s accompany some beats
[c] The first beat of a bar
[d] The last beat in the previous bar that immediately precedes the downbeat
[e] Half beats are soft strikes at the middle of a tempo period
[f] Quarter beats strike at the middle of a Full-to-Half or a Half-to-Full beat
[g] Frames over which the dancer does not move (assumes a Key Posture)
[h] Sequence of consecutive frames over which the events spread
[i] A Key Posture is a well-defined and stationary posture
[j] Transitory motion to change from one Key Posture to the next
[k] Motion that follows a well-defined trajectory of movement for the limbs
[l] α^{fb} and v^{nm} in sync. That is, $\tau(\alpha^{fb}) \cap \tau(v^{nm}) \neq \phi$

4.2 Characterization of Audio Events

A *Sollukattu* is the musical *meter* of an *Adavu*. Traditionally, a *Tatta Palahai* (wooden stick) is periodically struck on a *Tatta Kozhi* (wooden block) in the rhythmic pattern of *Adi* or *Roopakam Taalam*s to produce the periodic beats (or α^{fb} events as defined in Table 13 and illustrated in Table 14). Usually beats repeat in a *bar*[13] of $\Lambda = 6$ or 8. The *tempo* of a meter is measured by beats per minute (bpm) and can be slow, medium, or fast. We use *Tempo Period* or *Period T* = (60/bpm) or the time interval between two consecutive beats in seconds as the temporal measure for a meter.

In this study, we use only the slow tempo. While there is no fixed definition for the *bpm* of a slow tempo (medium and fast progressively double relative to the slow one), it is typically found to be between 75 (period = 0.8 s) and 30 (period = 2 s) in most of the performances. Theoretically, the tempo period should not vary during the performance of a specific *Sollukattu* or across *Sollukattu*s. However, in reality it

---

[13] A *bar* (or *measure*) is a segment of time corresponding to a specific Λ number of beats. *Sollukattu*s also use longer bars (12, 16, 24, or 32).

does vary depending on the skill of the beat player. Naturally, the event model needs to take care of such variations.

Next let us consider two consecutive beats α_i^{fb} and α_{i+1}^{fb} in a bar of length Λ, where i denotes the ith ($1 \leq i < \Lambda$) period. The time stamps of the respective events are then related as $\tau(\alpha_{i+1}^{fb}) - \tau(\alpha_i^{fb}) \approx T$. Further, the bar repeats after an equal time interval of T. That is, $\tau(\alpha_{\Lambda*i+1}^{fb}) - \tau(\alpha_{\Lambda*i}^{fb}) \approx T$, $i \geq 1$. We refer to such beats as *full beats* and hence the superscript *fb* in α^{fb} events. The first beat α_0^{fb} (last beat $\alpha_{\Lambda-1}^{fb}$) of a bar is referred to as a *downbeat* (*upbeat*). We mark these on the events as labels. In many *Sollukattu*s, beating is also performed at the middle of a period. These are called *half beats* and produce the α_i^{hb} events in the ith period. Naturally, $\tau(\alpha_i^{hb}) - \tau(\alpha_i^{fb}) \approx \tau(\alpha_{i+1}^{fb}) - \tau(\alpha_i^{hb}) \approx T/2$.

Often in a *Sollukattu*, the beat player (an accomplice of the dancer) also utters *bol*s. These are done in sync with a full beat or a half beat. We represent *bol*s as labels of the respective α^{fb} or α^{hb} events. A *bol* is *optional* for an event.

It may be noted that a beat is actually an instant of time that occurs in every T seconds. So it is possible that a beat has no beating (and obviously no *bol*). Such cases, however, are not in the scope of this study, and we always work with a beating at a beat.

There are 23 *Sollukattu*s. We illustrate a few here to understand various meters. All *Sollukattu*s are shown in slow tempo or *Vilambit Laya*.

1. ***Kuditta Mettu*** ($T \approx 1.2$ s, $\Lambda = 8$): We show two bars in Table 14 with *bol*s and time stamps. In Fig. 9, we illustrate the signal for a *Kuditta Mettu* recording and highlighting various events, time stamps, and *bol*s. While this *Sollukattu* has only α^{fb} events by definition, some incidental α^{hn} events can still be seen in the signal. These will need to be later removed.

   Table 16 shows its relationship with the *Adavu*.

Table 14 Pattern of *Kuditta Mettu Sollukattu* (Fig. 9a)

Event	Time (s) $(\tau(\alpha))$	Beat offset (s) $(\tau(\alpha_{i+1}) - \tau(\alpha_i))$	Event	Time (s) $(\tau(\alpha))$	Beat offset (s) $(\tau(\alpha_{i+1}) - \tau(\alpha_i))$
α_1^{fb} (tei)	2.681		α_9^{fb} (tei)	12.271	1.207
α_2^{fb} (hat)	3.912	1.231	α_{10}^{fb} (hat)	13.386	1.115
α_3^{fb} (tei)	5.108	1.196	α_{11}^{fb} (tei)	14.512	1.126
α_4^{fb} (hi)	6.269	1.161	α_{12}^{fb} (hi)	15.603	1.091
α_5^{fb} (tei)	7.523	1.254	α_{13}^{fb} (tei)	16.764	1.161
α_6^{fb} (hat)	8.742	1.219	α_{14}^{fb} (hat)	17.902	1.138
α_7^{fb} (tei)	9.891	1.149	α_{15}^{fb} (tei)	19.028	1.126
α_8^{fb} (hi)	11.064	1.173	α_{16}^{fb} (hi)	20.178	1.150

$T = 1.2$ s, $\Lambda = 8$

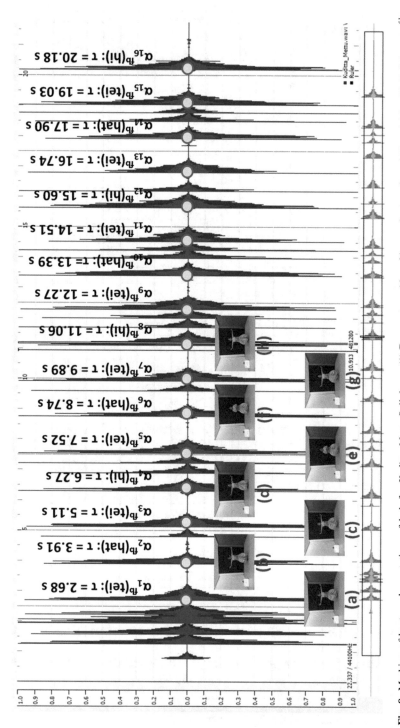

Fig. 9 Marking of beats and annotations of *bols* for *Kuditta Mettu Sollukattu*. (1) **Parameters**: No. of bars = 2, Λ = 8, and T = 1.16 s. (2) Full-beat (α^{fb}) event positions are highlighted (yellow blobs) and the corresponding *bols* and time stamps are shown (Table 14). Note that several α^{hn} are visible in the signals. These are rather incidental and not intended in the *Sollukattu*. Also, the beatings before the downbeat (α_1^{fb}) are ignored. Right-sided *Key Postures* (Fig. 11) are also shown for the first 8 beats. Left-sided *Key Postures* are performed for the next 8 beats

Table 15 Patterns of *Tatta_C Sollukattu* (Fig. 9b)

Event	Time (s) $(\tau(\alpha))$	Beat offset (s) $(\tau(\alpha_{i+1}^{fb}) - \tau(\alpha_i^{fb}))$	Half-Beat offset (s) $(\tau(\alpha_i^{hb}) - \tau(\alpha_i^{fb}))$
α_1^{fb}(tei)	6.571		
α_1^{hb}(ya)	7.395		0.82
α_2^{fb}(tei)	8.185	1.61	
α_2^{hb}(ya)	8.962		0.78
α_3^{fb}(tei)	9.752	1.57	
α_3^{hb}(ya)	10.565		0.81
α_4^{fb}(tei)	11.366	1.61	
α_5^{fb}(tei)	13.003	1.64	
α_5^{hb}(ya)	13.815		0.81
α_6^{fb}(tei)	14.628	1.63	
α_6^{hb}(ya)	15.441		0.81
α_7^{fb}(tei)	16.184	1.56	
α_7^{hb}(ya)	17.031		0.85
α_8^{fb}(tei)	17.809	1.63	

$T = 1.6$ s, $\Lambda = 8$

Table 16 Variations in the patterns of *Sollukattus* with *Adavus*

Sollukattu	Description of Bol/*Adavus*
Kuditta	α_1^{fb}(tei) α_2^{fb}(hat) α_3^{fb}(tei) α_4^{fb}(hi)
Mettu	α_5^{fb}(tei) α_6^{fb}(hat) α_7^{fb}(tei) α_8^{fb}(hi)
	Adavu: Kuditta_Mettu 1, 2, 3, 4
Kuditta	α_1^{fb}(tat) α_2^{fb}(tei) α_3^{hn} α_3^{fb}(tam) α_4^{fn} α_4^{hn}
Nattal A	α_5^{fb}(dhit) α_6^{fb}(tei) α_6^{hn} α_7^{fb}(tam) α_8^{fn} α_8^{hn}
	Adavu: Kuditta_Nattal 1, 2, 3, 6
Tatta E	α_1^{fb}(tei) α_2^{fb}(tei) α_3^{fb}(tam) α_4^{fn} α_4^{hn}
	α_5^{fb}(tei) α_6^{fb}(tei) α_7^{fb}(tam) α_8^{fn} α_8^{hn}
	Adavu: Tatta 6
Joining B	α_1^{fb}(dhit) α_2^{fb}(dhit) α_3^{fb}(tei)
	α_4^{fb}(dhit) α_5^{fb}(dhit) α_6^{fb}(tei)
	Adavu: Joining 2

2. **Tatta_C** ($T \approx 1.6$ s, $\Lambda = 8$): It has α^{fb} as well as α^{hb} events (Table 15 and Fig. 10).

3. **Kuditta Nattal_A** and **Tatta_E** ($T \approx 1.0$ s, $\Lambda = 8$): In addition to α^{fb}, α^{fn} and α^{hn} events are also found (Table 16) where there is only beating and no *bol*.

4. **Joining_B** ($T \approx 1.5$ s, $\Lambda = 8$): As such it uses only α^{fb}s (Table 16).

All *Sollukattus* in terms of the *Bols* are listed in Table 1.

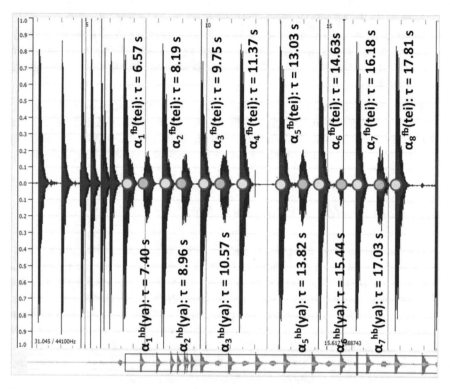

Fig. 10 Marking of beats and annotations of *bols* for *Tatta_C Sollukattu*. (1) **Parameters**: No. of bars = 2, $\Lambda = 8$, and $T = 1.56$ s. (2) Full-beat (α^{fb}) (yellow blobs) and half-beat (α^{hb}) (green blobs) event positions are highlighted and the corresponding *bols* and time stamps are shown (Table 15)

4.3 Characterization of Video Events

While performing an *Adavu*, the dancer closely follows the beats of the accompanying music. At a beat, the dancer assumes a *Key Posture* and holds it for a little while before quickly changing to the next *Key Posture* at the next beat. Consequently, while the dancer holds the key posture, she stays almost stationary, and there is no or very slow motion in the video. This leads to v^{nm} no-motion events. Further, while the dancer changes to the next key posture, we observe the v^{tr} (transition) or v^{tj} (trajectory) motion events. Since a frame is an atomic observable unit in a video, we can classify the frames of the video of an *Adavu* into two classes:

1. **K-frames or Key Frames**: These frames contain key postures where the dancer *holds* the posture. Evidently, a v^{nm} has the sequence of *K-frames* as labels. All *K-frames* of an v^{nm} contain the same key posture.
2. **T-frames of Transition Frame**: These are transition frames between two *K-frames* while the dancer is rapidly changing posture to assume the next key

posture from the previous one. *T-frames* contain *Natural Transition Postures* (leading to v^{tr} events) or *Trajectorial Transition Postures* (leading to v^{tj} events). A v^{tr} or v^{tj} event has the corresponding sequence of *T-frames* as labels. In this study, we do not deal with movements and transitions. Hence, we ignore *T-frames*.

In Fig. 11, we show the key postures of *Kuditta Mettu Adavu* at every beat of the first bar of *Kuditta Mettu Sollukattu*. The corresponding video and audio events are marked in Table 17 with *K-/T-frames*. These are also marked on the *Sollukattu* in Fig. 9. Note that only the right-sided half of the postures is shown in both figures.

4.4 Characterization of Synchronization

A *Bharatanatyam* dancer intends to perform the key postures of an *Adavu* in synchronization with the beats. Hence various audio events like α^{fb} and corresponding video events like v^{nm} should be in sync. Every *Adavu* has a well-defined set of rules that specifies this synchronization based on its associated *Sollukattu*. For example, in Fig. 11, we show how different key postures of *Kuditta Mettu Adavu* should be assumed at every beat of the *Kuditta Mettu Sollukattu*, that is, how the α^{fb}s of a bar in the audio should sync with the v^{nm}s of the video. Other *Adavus* require several other forms of synchronization between the audio and the video events including sync between beats and trajectory-based body movements v^{tj}.

We assert a sync event ψ^{fb} if a key posture (v^{nm}) should sync with a corresponding (full) beat (α^{fb}). In simple terms, a ψ^{fb} occurs if the time intervals of α^{fb} and v^{nm} events overlap. That is, $\tau(\alpha^{fb}) \cap \tau(v^{nm}) \neq \phi$. Similar sync events may be defined between other audio and video events according to the rules of *Adavus*.

Perfect synchronization is always intended and desirable for performance. However, we often observe the lack of it due to various reasons. The beating instrument, vocal *bols*, and body postures each have a different latency. If a posture is assumed *after hearing* the beat, v^{nm} will lag α^{fb}. If the dancer assumes the posture in *anticipation*, v^{nm} may lead to α^{fb}. Lack of sync may also arise due to the imperfect performance of the dancer, the beater, or the vocalist. Hence, analysis and estimation of sync are critical for processing *Adavu*.

While sync between the audio and video streams is fundamental to the choreography, there are a variety of other synchronization issues that need to be explored. These include sync between beating (instrumental) beats and (vocalized) *bols*, uniformity of time gap between consecutive beats, sync between different body limbs while changing from one key posture to the next, and so on.

Fig. 11 Right-sided key postures of *Kuditta Mettu Adavu* (Variant 2). (**a**) v_1^{nm}, α_1^{fb}(tei). (**b**) v_2^{nm}, α_2^{fb}(hat). (**c**) v_3^{nm}, α_3^{fb}(tei). (**d**) v_4^{nm}, α_4^{fb}(hi). (**e**) v_5^{nm}, α_5^{fb}(tei). (**f**) v_6^{nm}, α_6^{fb}(hat). (**g**) v_7^{nm}, α_7^{fb}(tei). (**h**) v_8^{nm}, α_8^{fb}(hi). (1) *Sollukattu* = *Kuditta Mettu* with *bol*s for Bar 1. (2) From a *tei* to the next *hat* or *hi*, the dancer sharply lowers her raised feet. (3) Further, eight left-sided Key Postures are performed for the next 8 beats in Bar 2

Table 17 Patterns of *Kuditta Mettu Adavu* (Fig. 11)

Events	K-/T-Frames		Events	K-/T-Frames	
	Range	# of		Range	# of
v_1^{nm} [α_1^{fb}(tei)]	70–99	30	v_9^{nm} [α_9^{fb}(tei)]	359–386	28
v_1^{tr}	100–103	4	v_9^{tr}	387–390	4
v_2^{nm} [α_2^{fb}(hat)]	104–124	21	v_{10}^{nm} [α_{10}^{fb}(hat)]	391–410	20
v_2^{tr}	125–145	21	v_{10}^{tr}	411–429	19
v_3^{nm} [α_3^{fb}(tei)]	146–172	27	v_{11}^{nm} [α_{11}^{fb}(tei)]	430–451	22
v_3^{tr}	173–176	4	v_{11}^{tr}	452–455	4
v_4^{nm} [α_4^{fb}(hi)]	177–191	15	v_{12}^{nm} [α_{12}^{fb}(hi)]	456–470	15
v_4^{tr}	192–214	23	v_{12}^{tr}	471–492	22
v_5^{nm} [α_5^{fb}(tei)]	215–245	31	v_{13}^{nm} [α_{13}^{fb}(tei)]	493–521	29
v_5^{tr}	246–249	4	v_{13}^{tr}	522–525	4
v_6^{nm} [α_6^{fb}(hat)]	250–262	13	v_{14}^{nm} [α_{14}^{fb}(hat)]	526–542	17
v_6^{tr}	263–287	25	v_{14}^{tr}	543–564	22
v_7^{nm} [α_7^{fb}(tei)]	288–314	27	v_{15}^{nm} [α_{15}^{fb}(tei)]	565–587	23
v_7^{tr}	315–317	3	v_{15}^{tr}	588–590	3
v_8^{nm} [α_8^{fb}(hi)]	318–345	28	v_{16}^{nm} [α_{16}^{fb}(hi)]	591–620	30
v_8^{tr}	346–358	13	v_{16}^{tr}	621–	–

5   Ontology of Events and Streams

We have captured the structural models of *Sollukattu*s and *Adavu*s in Sect. 3 and then
the temporal behavioral models in Sect. 4 based on these structures. Now, we would
like to relate these to the actual recording data of the performances. For the current
work, we capture the performances of *Bharatanatyam Adavu*s using Kinect XBox
360 (Kinect 1.0) sensor. So in this section, we model the relationships between the
events and the Kinect streams to facilitate the formulation of the algorithms later.

Kinect 1.0 is an RGBD sensor that captures a multichannel audio stream with
three video streams, RGB, Depth, and Skeleton, in its data file. The video streams
are captured at 30 frames per second (fps). The RGB stream comprises frames
containing color intensity images. The depth stream comprises frames containing
depth images. And the skeleton stream comprises frames containing images of 20
skeleton joints of human beings in the view. The video streams are synchronized
between themselves. Hence for any RGB frame, the corresponding depth and
skeleton frames carry the same frame number. The audio is also synchronized with
the video by the same clock. Hence, any time t on the audio stream corresponds to
an RGB (depth, skeleton) frame by $t/30$.

We now present a combined ontology for the events (as introduced in the last
section) and the streams (of a Kinect data file) and capture their interrelationships.
For this we identify sets of classes (Table 18), instances (Table 19), and relations
(Table 20).

The ontology is presented in Fig. 12. The following points about the ontology
may be noted:

- The event side is shown in blue and the stream side is shown in black.
- A *K-frame* is a semantic notion that is instantiated as a triplet of an RGB, Depth,
  and Skeleton frames. Also, it actually represents a sequence of consecutive
  frames in the video having *no-motion*. *T-frame*s are treated similarly.
- *isExtractedFrom* represents the processes of extraction (or detection, estimation,
  etc.) of audio (video) events from audio (video) streams. These are not directly
  available from the Kinect streams and need to be computationally determined.
  Specific algorithms required include:

  - Beat detection to produce α^f or α^h
  - *Bol* recognition to produce $\alpha^{fb}(< bol >)$ or $\alpha^{hb}(< bol >)$
  - *No-Motion* detection to produce ν^{nm} events

- *isInSync* represents the fact that streams in Kinect are synchronized by the sensor.
- In contrast *isSyncedWith* denotes the explicit attempt of the dancer to synchronize
  her/his moves and postures with the beats and *bol*s. These are ψ^{fb} or ψ^{hb} events.
  To estimate *isSyncedWith*, *K-frame*s and *T-frame*s need to be extracted (Fig. 12).

Table 18 List of classes for the ontology of events and streams

Class	Type	Class	Type
Kinect data file	Concrete	Audio-event stream	Concrete
Audio stream	Concrete	Video-event stream	Concrete
Video stream	Concrete	Audio event	Abstract
RGB stream	Concrete	Video event	Abstract
Depth stream	Concrete	Beat event	Abstract
Skeleton stream	Concrete	*Bol* Event	Concrete
RGB frame	Concrete	Full-beat event	Concrete
Depth frame	Concrete	Half-beat event	Concrete
Skeleton frame	Concrete	Full beat with *bol* (FB+B) event	Concrete
K-frame	Concrete	Half beat with *bol* (HB+B) event	Concrete
T-frame	Concrete	No-motion event	Concrete
		Transition event	Concrete

Table 19 List of instances for the ontology of events and streams

Class:Instance	Remarks
Full Beat Event: FBB1, FBB2, $\cdots$	Instances of full beat with *bol* events
Half Beat Event: HBB1, HBB2, $\cdots$	Instances of half beat with *bol* events
No-Motion Event: NM1, NM2, $\cdots$	Instances of *no-motion* events
K-Frame: $I.p, I \cdots, I.p + u, \cdots$	Intensity (RGB) image frames from no. p to $p + u$
T-Frame: $I.q + 1, I \cdots, I.q + v, \cdots$	Intensity image frames from no. $q + 1$ to $q + v$, where $q = p + u$
$:D.p, D \cdots, \cdots$	Depth image frames from number p
$:S.p, S \cdots, \cdots$	Skeleton image frames from number p

Table 20 List of relations for the ontology of events and streams

Relation	Domain	Co-domain	Remarks
is_a	Class	Class	As in Table 7
has_a	Class	Class	As in Table 7
isInstanceOf	Instance	Class	As in Table 7
isSyncedWith	Instance	Instance	Expresses low-level synchronization—between audio/video events and video frames. For example, an audio event FBB1 (instance of "full-beat with bol") *isSyncedWith* a unique K-Frame
isSequenceOf	Class	Class	As in Table 7
isExtractedFrom	Class	Class	An event *isExtractedFrom* Kinect video
isInSync	Relation over three instances		Expresses the inherent synchronization in data—between audio and multiple video streams—RGB, Depth, and Skeleton. Every *RGB Frame isInSync* with a corresponding *Depth Frame* or *Skeleton Frame*

All relations, with the exception of "isInSync," are binary

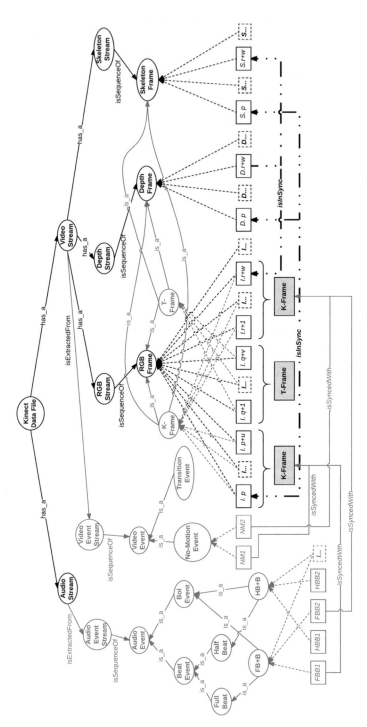

Fig. 12 Ontology of Kinect data file, streams, and audio–video events

6 Representation of *Adavu*s in Labanotation

We intend to represent *Bharatanatyam* ontology according to the ontology of a parseable standard notation. Labanotation [2] (often referred to as *Laban Encoding* or simply *Laban*) is a standard notation system used for recording human movements. To record a movement, the Laban system symbolizes *space, time, energy,* and *body parts*. Here, we introduce a limited set of symbols that are particularly used for representing the posture of *Bharatanatyam Adavu*s. A posture encoded in Laban is called frame, and the Laban frames are stacked in laban staff as shown in Fig. 13. When there is a sequence of postures or gestures changing over time, we stack their symbols on the staff vertically to show the progression over time. The centerline of the staff indicates the time. The symbols are read from the bottom to the top of the staff.

The *Staff* represents the body. The *Centerline* divides the body into two parts: left and right. Immediately next to the centerline is *Support Columns*. The symbols placed in these columns indicate the body parts that carry the weight of the body. Other columns represent the gestures of other body parts such as the *leg, body* (torso), *arm,* and *head*. Except the head, other body parts have left and right columns. Labanotation captures the movements of human body parts in terms of the *directions* and *levels* of the movement. The direction symbols are used to indicate in which direction in space the movements occur and in any direction can have three different levels, namely, *upward or high, horizontal or middle,* and *downward or low*. Every body part can be expressed in terms of the direction and level by placing respective symbols in the designated columns (Fig. 14).

The arms and the legs do not always remain straight while performing an *Adavu*. Few joints of the body like the knee and the elbow can get folded. Hence *degree of folding* is useful for these joints. There are a total of six degrees of folding. *Bharatanatyam* also involves a lot of footwork. Hence, we need to encode the type of touch between the foot and the ground and also which part of the foot is in contact with the ground. Labanotation system has symbols to diagrammatically illustrate

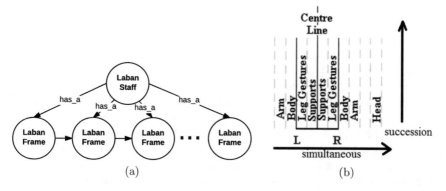

Fig. 13 Ontology of Labanotation: (**a**) component and sequence diagram and (**b**) Laban staff

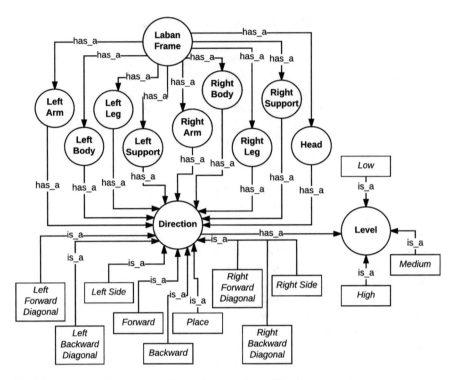

Fig. 14 Ontology of Labanotation illustrating direction and level

the specific part of the foot that contacts the ground. This attribute is called *touch* in Labanotation. There are 11 parts of the foot that can touch the ground. The concepts are shown in Fig. 15.

We use the concepts of Labanotation to transcribe the data captured by the sensor into a machine-parseable form. We map the Kinect data to the concepts of *Bharatanatyam* in Fig. 14. Now, we intend to map the concept of *Bharatanatyam* to the concept of Labanotation as our goal is to generate a parseable XML descriptor of *Bharatanatyam Adavu*. The ontology is shown in Fig. 16. There are four layers in the ontology:

1. **Input or Sensor Layer**: This layer contains the data captured by the sensor. We capture the video of the dance using the Kinect sensor. The data contains the *K-frames* as well as *T-frames*. Here we intend to transcribe only the *K-frames*.
2. **Dance Layer**: According to the ontology shown in Fig. 14, the *K-frames* contain No-Motion events. The No-Motion events are nothing but the Key postures of *Bharatanatyam Adavu* as shown in Fig. 7. Here, we map the key posture in terms of direction, level, degree of folding, and touch concept of Labanotation. The leg, arm, and head of a key posture are mapped into the Laban concept.
3. **Laban Descriptor Layer**: Each key posture has a corresponding Laban frame in the Laban staff. The legs are described in terms of leg and support of Laban-

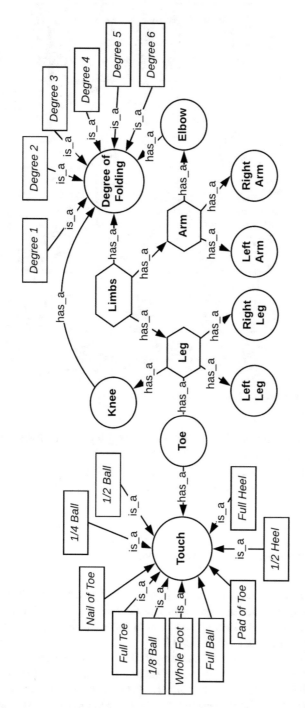

Fig. 15 Ontology of Labanotation illustrating touch and degree of folding

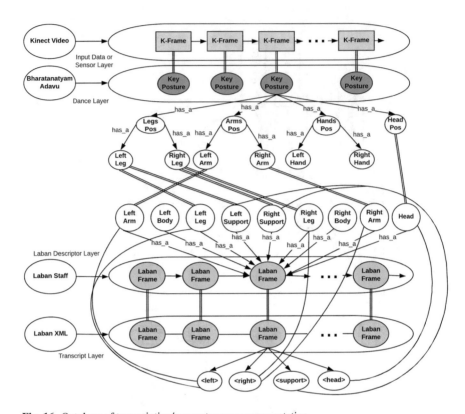

Fig. 16 Ontology of transcription/sensor to parser representation

otation. The arm and head have one-to-one mapping between *Bharatanatyam*
ontology and Laban ontology.

4. **Transcript Layer**: Finally, the Laban ontology gets encoded into a parseable
   XML format so that the Labanotation can be visualized or animation can be
   generated from the XML.

7   Laban Encoding of an *Adavu* Posture

We represent *Adavu* as a sequence of key postures. To transcribe an *Adavu*, we need
to transcribe every key posture that occurs in the *Adavu*. For the purpose of use,
we encode the symbols of direction and level in Table 21, the degree of folding in
Table 22, and the touch attribute in Table 23.

The sequence of key postures occurring in the first four beats of *Natta Adavu
Variation 1* is shown in Table 24. A posture is described in terms of the legs, arms,
head, and hands using the vocabulary (Sect. 3.3.1) for the annotation of the limbs.
Now, we want to transcribe the posture. Hence, we need to encode the body parts

Table 21 Encoding of directions and levels in Labanotation

Direction	Place	Left side	Right side	Left forward	Right forward	Left backward
Encoding	1	2	3	4	5	6

	Right	Left	Right	Left	Right
Direction	backward	forward diagonal	forward diagonal	backward diagonal	backward diagonal
Encoding	7	8	9	10	11

Level	High	Mid	Low
Encoding	1	2	3

Table 22 Degree of folding

	No fold	Fold degree 1	Fold degree 2	Fold degree 3	Fold degree 4	Fold degree 5	Full fold
Degree of folding							
Encoding	0	1	2	3	4	5	6

Table 23 Type of touch with floor

Foot parts	Full heel	One half heel	Whole foot	One eighth ball	One fourth ball	One half ball
Encoding	1	2	3	4	5	6

Foot parts	Full ball	Pad of toe	Full toe	Nail of toe	No touch
Encoding	7	8	9	10	0

Table 24 Annotation of the video of *Natta Adavu Variation 1*

Posture name (a)	Start frame (b)	End frame (c)	Beat number (d)	Bols (e)
Natta1P1	70	89	0	No Bol
Natta1P2	101	134	1	*tei yum*
Natta1P1	144	174	2	*tat ta*
Natta1P3	189	218	3	*tei yum*
Natta1P1	231	261	4	*ta*

from the *Bharatanatyam* terminology to the Labanotation descriptor. For example, consider the key posture Natta1P1 *Natta Adavu Variation 1*. Let us describe the posture using the Labanotation symbols. The posture is shown in Fig. 18. The different body parts of the posture are marked in different colors, like the arm is marked yellow. Annotation of the body parts of postures Natta1P1 is given in Table 25 (we exclude *Hasta Mudra* from the transcription work).

The next challenge is to map the *Bharatanatyam* ontology to the Labanotation ontology. As an example, we encode the posture Natta1P1 (Fig. 17, Table 25) to Laban in Table 26 and Fig. 18.

Table 25 Annotation of the body parts of postures in *Natta Adavu 1*

Body part	Position	Formation		Vocab
		Left	Right	
Posture = Natta1P1				
Leg	*Aayata* **[S]**	*Aayata*	*Aayata*	Table 9
Arm	*Natyarambhe* **[S]**	*Natyarambhe*	*Natyarambhe*	Table 10
Head	*Samam*			Table 11

	Foot		Arm	⬤ Elbow
	Support		Head	◔ Knee

Fig. 17 Natta1P1 posture annotated for Laban encoding

1. **Leg**: The leg is in *Aayata* position, which means:

   - The weight of the body is on both legs. So the legs are in support (as both legs are taking the weight of the body). The Support Direction and Support Level are encoded accordingly in Table 26.
   - The left (right) foot is in the left (right) direction. The legs are not stretched in any direction, so the legs are in place.
   - The folding of the legs indicates that the level of the leg is low.
   - The legs are not crossing each other, so Leg Crossing = 0.
   - We mark the symmetric position of both the legs using Mirror = 1. If Mirror = 1, then the direction of the right leg will just be in the opposite of the left leg.

Table 26 Laban encoding of leg, arm, and head for Natta1P1 posture

Leg vocab	Support direction	Support level	Leg direction	Leg level	Leg crossing	Mirror
Aayata	1	3	0	0	0	1

Hip support	Knee folding	Touch
0	3	3

Arm vocab	Arm direction	Arm level	Arm crossing	Elbow folding	Body inclusion	Mirror
Natyarambhe	2	2	0	1	0	1

Head vocab	Direction	Level
Samam	1	2

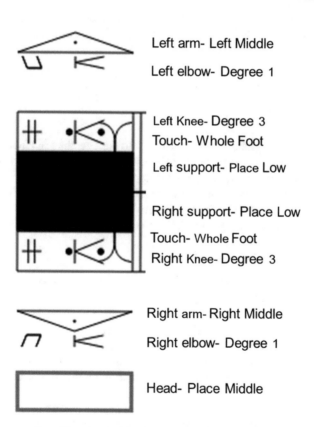

Left arm- Left Middle

Left elbow- Degree 1

Left Knee- Degree 3
Touch- Whole Foot

Left support- Place Low

Right support- Place Low

Touch- Whole Foot
Right Knee- Degree 3

Right arm- Right Middle

Right elbow- Degree 1

Head- Place Middle

Fig. 18 Laban encoding of leg, arm, and head for Natta1P1 posture

- The body weight is not on the hip, so Hip Support = 0.
- Both legs are folded at the knee. The knee is folding in around 90°, so Knee Folding = 3 (Fig. 22).
- The whole feet are touching the ground, so Touch = 3 (Fig. 23).

2. **Arm**: The arms are in *Natyarambhe*, which means:

   - The hands are stretched out on the left and right side of the body at the shoulder level and are slightly folded at the elbow. So, Arm Direction = 2, Arm Level = 2, and Elbow Folding = 1.
   - The arm is not occluding with the body (Body Inclusion = 0).
   - Both arms are similar (Mirror = 1).

3. **Head**: The head is in *Samam*, which means:

   - The head is straight and forward (Head Direction = 1 and Level = Middle).

The complete Laban encoding for Natta1P1 is shown in Table 26. In a similar manner, we have encoded the other postures used in *Bharatanatyam Adavu*. This has been done with the help of the experts.

7.1 LabanXML

While the graphical symbolization of Laban and our encoding in tabular formats as above are both forms of transcription, neither is amenable to machine processing. To visualize the postures and to build further applications based on the transcripts, we need a searchable and parseable representation. So we adopt LabanXML [8]—an *eXtensible Markup Language* (XML) design for Labanotation. LabanXML bundles columns of the staff in four groups: left, right, support, and head. Left and right, in turn, contain the arm and leg.

The tags of LabanXML are as follows:

- `<laban>`: This is the root tag which includes `<attribute>` and `<notation>` tags.
- `<attribute>`: This includes tag `<title>` used to name the XML file.
- `<notation>`: This includes the tag `<measure>`.
- `<measure>`: Which gives position of current pose on the time line.
- `<left>`: Contains tags for columns appearing on the left side of Labanotation.
- `<right>`: Contains tags for columns appearing on the right side of Labanotation.
- `<support>`: Describes the support element in Labanotation columns. It has an attribute *side* having the value *left* or *right* indicating the side of the support.
- `<arm>`, `<leg>`, `<foot>`, `<head>`, and `<support>`: These tags include `<direction>` and `<level>` tags of the respective limb.
- `<elbow>`, `<knee>`: These tags include `<degree>` for degree of folding.

Table 27 LabanXML of posture Natta1P1

```
-<laban>                                            -<elbow duration="1">
   -<attribute>                                        <Degree>1</Degree>
      <title>natta_1</title>                         </elbow>
   </attribute>                                      -<foot>
   -<notation>                                          <touch>3</touch>
      -<measure num="0">                              </foot>
         -<left>                                      -<knee duration="1">
            -<arm duration="1">                          <Degree>3</Degree>
               <direction>2</direction>               </knee>
               <level>2</level>                    </right>
            </arm>                                 -<support side="left">
            -<elbow duration="1">                     <direction>1</direction>
               <Degree>1</Degree>                     <level>3</level>
            </elbow>                                </support>
            -<foot>                                 -<support side="right">
               <touch>3</touch>                       <direction>1</direction>
            </foot>                                    <level>3</level>
            -<knee duration="1">                    </support>
               <Degree>3</Degree>                   -<head>
            </knee>                                    <direction>1</direction>
         </left>                                       <level>2</level>
         -<right>                                    </head>
            -<arm duration="1">                     </measure>
               <direction>3</direction>          </notation>
               <level>2</level>               </laban>
            </arm>
```

— `<touch>`: This tag is included in the `<support>` tag and `<leg>` tag. It describes how the foot is hooked on to the floor.

Using the above tags, we represent the information from Table 26 in XML format in Table 27. The graphical representation of Laban encoding is shown in Fig. 18. The symbols described earlier are used to write the XML tags in Laban staff.

7.2 Tool Overview

To build the *Adavu* Transcription Tool, we first encode our ontological models of *Adavu*s, especially the key postures and their sequences, and the video annotations in Laban ontology following the approach as illustrated in Sect. 7. This cross-ontology of concepts (called *Posture Ontology*) is then represented in a mapping database indexed by the posture ID. This is used by the *Adavu* Transcription Tool as given in Fig. 19. We explain the modules in Fig. 19.

7.2.1 Posture Recognizer

This is a machine learning-based system [6] that helps to recognize a unique posture ID when the RGB frame of the key posture is given. We first extract the human figure, eliminate the background, and convert the RGB into a grayscale image. We next compute the *Histograms of Oriented Gradient* (HOG) descriptors for each

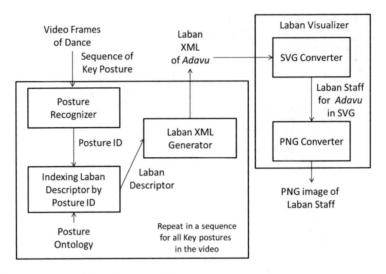

Fig. 19 Architecture of the *Adavu* transcription tool

posture frame. Finally, we use the HOG feature to train the same SVM classifier. There are a total of 23 key postures in *Natta Adavu*s. To recognize the postures into 23 posture classes, we use the *One vs. Rest* type of multi-class SVM. The data set shown in Table 28 is used for training and testing the SVM. For testing we use the trained SVM models to predict the class labels. Our accuracy of the posture recognition is 97.95%.

Table 28 Data set for posture recognition using 23 posture classes in Fig. 20

Posture ID	Training data	Test data	Posture ID	Training data	Test data
C01	6154	1457	C13	235	80
C02	3337	873	C14	393	117
C03	3279	561	C15	404	121
C04	1214	219	C16	150	48
C05	1192	268	C17	161	51
C06	1419	541	C18	323	81
C07	1250	475	C19	175	46
C08	284	112	C20	168	43
C09	306	133	C21	19	6
C10	397	162	C22	21	6
C11	408	117	C23	118	61
C12	229	84			

Numbers indicate the number of *K-frame*s. Each *K-frame* is given by the frame number of the RGB frame in the video. Associated depth and skeleton frames are used as needed. Various position and formation information on body parts are available for every *K-frame* from the annotation

Fig. 20 23 Key postures of *Natta Adavu*s with class/posture IDs

Now we use the trained classifier to recognize the input sequence of key postures. The key posture recognizer extracts the sequence of key postures in terms of their posture IDs from the video of an *Adavu* performance.

7.2.2 Indexing Laban Descriptor by Posture ID

Given a posture ID, we look up the *Posture Ontology* to get the Laban descriptor values for the different limbs in terms of a database record.

7.2.3 LabanXML Generator

From the database record of Laban descriptors, an equivalent LabanXML file is generated using the definition of tags as in Sect. 7.1.

7.2.4 Laban Visualizer

Since Labanotation is graphical, it is important to visualize it in terms of its icons. So we implement a converter from LabanXML to Scalable Vector Graphics (SVG). SVG is an XML-based vector image format for two-dimensional graphics with support for interactivity and animation. Like XML, SVG images can also be created and edited with any text editor, as well as with drawing software. The SVG converter is written in C++ on cygwin64 using libxml xml parser. SVG images are also rendered in PNG (using Inkscape) for easy-to-use offline notation.

7.3 Results and Discussion

Our tool is able to generate transcription for a sequence of key frames. For a given sequence of RGB frames, Posture Recognizer generates their posture IDs. These posture IDs are mapped to corresponding cluster IDs in the laban ontology. By using the posture IDs and ontology, a Laban transcription for all frames is encoded in LabanXML. By using LabanXML, a stack of Laban frames for *BN Adavu* key postures is generated. The Laban XML and stack of postures in Laban Staff, as generated by our tool for the sequence of key postures of *Natta Adavu* variation 1, are shown in Fig. 21 along with the transcription. The RGB frames are shown on the left, and the corresponding Laban descriptors are shown on the staff on the right. An initial part of the LabanXML is given in the middle.

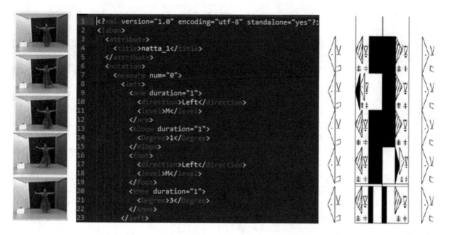

Fig. 21 Key postures of *Natta Adavu Variant 1* with transcription in LabanXML (a part) and depiction in Laban Staff by our tool

8   Conclusion

In this chapter, we demonstrate a system to generate parseable representation of *Bharatanatyam* dance performance and document the parseable representation using Labanotation. The system uses a unique combination of multimedia ontology and machine learning techniques. To the best of our knowledge, this is the first work toward automatic documentation of dance using any notation.

In the process of developing the system, we have also presented a detailed ontology for *Bharatanatyam Adavu*s, which is a maiden attempt for any Indian classical dance. Finally, we have captured and annotated a sizable data set for *Adavu*s, part of which is also available for use at [5].

In the future, we intend to extend our work to document a more fine description of each posture. We are also interested to capture the movements that we have used for this study. Finally, we also want to extend our work to generate the ontology automatically guided by the grammar of the dance form.

Acknowledgments The authors would like to thank Tata Consultancy Services (TCS) for providing the fund and support for this work.

References

1. El Raheb, K., Ioannidis, Y.: A labanotation based ontology for representing dance movement. In: International Gesture Workshop, pp. 106–117. Springer, Berlin (2011)
2. Guest, A.H.: Labanotation the system of analyzing and recording movement, vol. 487. Routledge, New York (2005)

3. Guest, A.H.: Labanotation: The System of Analyzing and Recording Movement. Routledge, New York (2014)
4. Karpen, A.P. Labanotation for Indian classical dance, in particular Bharatanatyam. In 11th European Conference on Modern South Asian Studies (1990)
5. Mallick, T., Das, P.P., Majumdar, A.K.: Annotated *Bharatanatyam* data set (2017). http://hci. cse.iitkgp.ac.in/. Online; Accessed 13 Feb 2020
6. Mallick, T., Das, P.P., Majumdar, A.K.: Posture and sequence recognition for Bharatanatyam dance performances using machine learning approach (2019). Preprint. arXiv:1909.11023
7. Mallik, A., Chaudhury, S., Ghosh, H.: Nrityakosha: preserving the intangible heritage of Indian classical dance. J. Comput. Cult. Herit. (JOCCH) **4**(3), 11 (2011)
8. Nakamura, M., Hachimura, K.: An xml representation of labanotation, labanxml, and its implementation on the notation editor labaneditor2. Rev. Natl. Center Digit. **9**, 47–51 (2006)
9. Tongpaeng, Y., Sureephong, P., Rattanakhum, M., Yu, H.: Thai dance knowledge archive framework based on labanotation represented in 3d animation. In: International Conference on Digital Arts, Media and Technology (ICDAMT), pp. 66–70. IEEE, Piscataway (2017)
10. Vasudevan, P., Kavanagh, B.: *Bharatanatyam* – dancing for the gods (2017). http://www. dancingforthegods.org. Online; Accessed 14 May 2017

Evolution and Interconnection: Geometry in Early Temple Architecture

Sambit Datta

Abstract This chapter addresses the evolution and interconnection of temple-building traditions across South and Southeast Asia. The remains of early temple architecture are mapped through the comparative analysis of temple geometry through 3D reconstruction. The chapter presents the 3D reconstruction pipeline for combining image-based analysis methods with flexible generative modelling techniques. These 3D schematic reconstructions of individual temples capture the architectural form of the temple as well as the knowledge of temple production and their architectural lineage. Drawing upon canonical descriptions and previous scholarship on temple geometry, the chapter presents schematic reconstructions of four individual temples. A comparative analysis of the similarities and differences between the temples reveals the role of canonical constructive mechanisms underlying these temples. The computational reconstruction of temple geometry is described in the chapter. First, canonical geometry identified from early Indian temple texts is formalized into 3D geometric constructions called scaffolds. Photo-based structure-from-motion (SfM) techniques are used to develop digital point datasets of temple remains. Dissections represent horizontal and vertical profiles that capture attribute features of a temple from field measurements and surveys. Geometric scaffolds and dissections are then combined to propose conjectural reconstructions. The chapter outlines the results and contributions of the work in developing the geometric modelling of early temples. It concludes with an overview of how such digital reconstructions can assist in the conservation of digital cultural heritage in South and Southeast Asia. More broadly, the methods posit a broader understanding of how individual buildings of a particular historical and philosophical lineage may be compositionally connected through computational means to provide a symbolic view of variance in architectural production over time.

Keywords 3D reconstruction · Temple architecture · Geometric modelling · Digital heritage · Cultural informatics

S. Datta (✉)
Curtin University, Perth, WA, Australia
e-mail: Sambit.Datta@curtin.edu.au

© Springer Nature Switzerland AG 2021
J. Mukhopadhyay et al. (eds.), *Digital Techniques for Heritage Presentation and Preservation*, https://doi.org/10.1007/978-3-030-57907-4_11

1 Introduction

This chapter addresses the evolution and interconnection of temple-building traditions across South and Southeast Asia. The remains of early temple architecture are mapped through the comparative analysis of temple geometry through 3D reconstruction. The chapter presents the 3D reconstruction pipeline for combining image-based analysis methods with flexible generative modelling techniques. These 3D schematic reconstructions of individual temples capture the architectural form of the temple as well as the knowledge of temple production and their architectural lineage. Drawing upon canonical descriptions and previous scholarship on temple geometry, the chapter presents schematic reconstructions of four individual temples. A comparative analysis of the similarities and differences between the temples reveals the role of canonical constructive mechanisms underlying these temples.

The computational workflow of the reconstruction process of temple geometry is described in the chapter. First, canonical geometry identified from early Indian temple texts is formalized into 3D geometric constructions called scaffolds. Second, photo-based structure-from-motion (SfM) techniques are used to develop point datasets of temple remains from site surveys. Shape analysis and geometric modelling methods provide intermediate hybrid representations that combine elements from scaffolds and pointset data. From these representations, dissections are produced representing horizontal and vertical profiles of a temple. Geometric scaffolds and dissections are then combined to propose conjectural reconstructions that capture both the attribute features at the geometric and semantic levels.

The chapter outlines the background of a long-standing project to develop suitable methods, reconstruction workflow and results of the work in modelling six representative case studies. It concludes with an overview of how such digital reconstructions can assist in the conservation of digital cultural heritage in South and Southeast Asia. More broadly, the methods posit a broader understanding of how individual buildings of a particular historical and philosophical lineage may be compositionally connected through computational means to provide a symbolic view of variance in architectural production over time.

2 Background

2.1 Indian Temple Architecture

The early temple architecture of Southeast Asia presents a remarkable and intriguing body of evidence in support of inter-Asian connections [2]. Seen as a collective corpus, these sites establish a consistent pattern of religious, cultural and techno-logical ideas that transcend national or geographic boundaries [16]. The temples of Southeast Asia are obviously derivative from Indian canon and yet profoundly original and different from the corpus of the subcontinent. Further, the regional nuances of these temples, whether in Java, Cambodia or Champa, defy obvious and linear connections within these traditions and with the pan-Indian corpus. While epigraphists, Sanskritists and historians have made significant connections between these temple-building traditions, much work remains to be done on the compositional and architectural linkages along the trading routes of South and Southeast Asia.

Individual temples owe their compositional characteristics to the interpretation of canonical treatises by priest-architects [20] and the usage of earlier examples as architectural models for later ones [15]. In the absence of local textual records, the evidence embedded in the geometric and material composition of the surviving monuments is the main, and sometimes the only, evidence by which a more conclusive understanding of the relation between theory and practice in these buildings might be developed [7]. The motivations for the reconstruction and recovery of the reconstruction are to develop three-dimensional digital datasets of early temples and conduct comparative analysis of temple geometry across exemplars from India, Cambodia and Java. By focusing on digital methods of spatio-temporal geometry mapping through plans, layout and proportion of wall ensembles, superstructure form and constructional and ornamental motifs, the evolution and interconnection of the earliest Southeast Asian temples can be traced to their genesis in the archetypal Brahmanic/Hindu temple. The next sections explain the process of digital codification and methods of preservation covering documentation and recording of physical heritage sites and individual monuments as well as linkages and connections between monuments.

2.2   Digital Archetypes

The Digital Archetypes Project [8] develops a computational approach to preservation covering the spread and adaptation of early temple architecture from its early beginnings in India. The aim of the project is to model and reconstruct temple sites across a geographic and temporal space (500–900 CE). The project covers a broad spatio-temporal area of early temple architecture extending from the salt ranges of Pakistan to the eastern coastline of Vietnam. The key sites from the fifth century to the tenth century are indicated with reference to their proximity to present-day urban centres. In this chapter, we focus on four key sites in Java, Cambodia and India as highlighted in Fig. 1.

Advances in image-based modelling [10], combined with developments in computational generation of architectural geometry [22] and accessible means for virtual simulation and visualization, have contributed to the rapid development of heritage reconstruction from multiple sources of evidence integrated through digital means. One area of work that has received relatively less attention is the virtual re-assembly of historic structures from deformed and partial datasets. In particular, the assumptions of accuracy and ambiguity in recovering robust geometric information from acquired point cloud datasets remain a significant problem. The fragmented

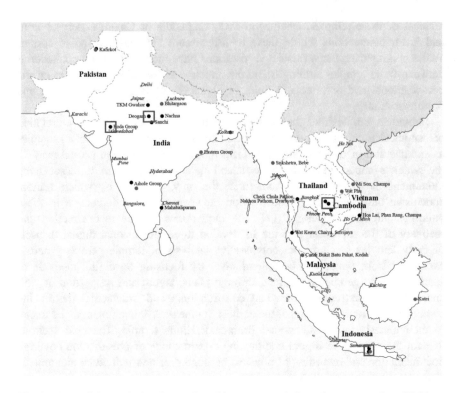

Fig. 1 The spatial spread of early temple architecture extends from the western edge of Pakistan to the eastern coastline of Vietnam. The key sites from the fifth century to the tenth century are indicated with reference to their proximity to present-day urban centres. A selected sample of four temple sites discussed in this chapter is highlighted (source: Author)

discontinuity of textual accounts, lack of graphical representations and heavily eroded early remains render the process of establishing the formal continuity and correspondences between canon and reconstruction difficult. This is further compounded in temple architecture, where missing information, fragmented and heavily eroded remains and loss of structural and formal integrity over time are common problems. In this context, the process of establishing formal continuity between artefact and 3D reconstruction becomes challenging.

These problems are addressed by exploiting domain knowledge of temple design and construction recorded in the vast literature on temple building. The mathematical and geometric similarities between temples and text are used to identify taxonomies between temples, generate architectural elements and detect salient features and principal geometric attributes of temples. Modelling the archetypal temple form based on textual descriptions from treatises of temple building forms a central contribution of the project. Computational techniques that can reassemble fragmentary evidence, provide robust and empirical methods to fill in missing information and generate and test the accuracy and ambiguities in the digital reconstruction of geometry are developed.

The architectural rules of composition, vocabulary of elements and principal features of temples are identified from canonical descriptions. These models are used to extract shapes, profiles and features of interest from temple datasets. Another challenge faced in digital 3D reconstruction is the recovery of sharp edges from pointsets [3]. Virtual reconstruction models play a key aspect in establishing the architectonic ideas underlying the earliest Indian, Javanese and Khmer temples and their relationships to canonical texts [4–8]. To recover the constructive principles underlying these temples, field measurements and close-range photogrammetry were combined with rule-based abstraction and parameterized models. Two- and three-dimensional reconstructed geometries are analysed and compared to measure their geometric similarities and differences to establish the compositional and architectural linkages between the temple-building traditions of South and Southeast Asia.

The problem of 3D reconstruction of the original shape and form of each historic monument from the temple data is addressed through computational modelling and analysis. This approach is used to derive a consistent mechanism for the reconstruction of temple geometry. In the case of Indian temples, Datta and Beynon [6] demonstrate the application of a hybrid computational approach to the problem of recovering the surface geometry of early temple superstructures. The approach combines field measurements of temples with close-range architectural photogrammetry. The datasets are processed with rule-based generation and parametric modelling techniques. This work contextualizes these methods through an examination of how digital modelling methods and workflows can afford and extend the classical tools of architectural analysis and comparison. For detailed descriptions of the spatio-temporal studies, the reader is referred to [8]. The next sections describe the following:

- **3D Reconstruction.** Workflow for the recovery of the architectural geometry of ruined temples through scaffolds and dissections
- **Case Studies.** Reconstruction of the geometric, structural and ornamental features of individual temples from India, Cambodia and Java
- **Spatio-temporal Mapping.** Comparative analysis of the evolution and interconnection of temple sites

3   3D Reconstruction

This section presents the reconstruction workflow for generating scaffold and dissection geometry for explaining the evolution of and interconnections between the earliest temples in India, Java and Cambodia. 3D reconstruction is a well-established methodology in art, architecture and archaeology. Such reconstructions play an important role in the scholarly study of the past architecture, formulation of

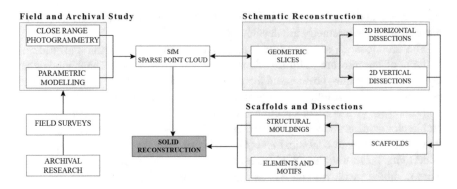

Fig. 2 Solid reconstruction workflow. Surface reconstruction is developed from field measurements and close-range photogrammetry. A sparse point cloud is developed using the structure-from-motion (SfM) technique. A set of horizontal and vertical dissections is developed from the raw point data. Extruded profiles are used to generate solid elements of the temple geometry. The elements are assembled into a flexible reconstruction (source: Author)

theoretical positions, conservation and physical restoration of monuments as well as serving as representations of the original artefacts for galleries and museums. Computer-generated 3D reconstructions have become increasingly common in the field, and a wide range of methods, datasets, workflows and outputs has been proposed to fit these applications. The digital workflow comprising modelling and reconstruction of models from raw datasets acquired from historic buildings is shown in Fig. 2. The digital reconstruction requires bringing together fragments of evidence from field measurements, relating these to mathematical and geometric descriptions in canonical geometry and proposing best-fit models. The 3D reconstruction comprises the following steps:

- **Parametric Scaffolds.** Drawing upon the previous studies of geometry and mathematical schema, parametric models are developed from the mathematical and geometric descriptions in early Indian temple texts. These models are analysed to measure and reconstruct 2.5D parametric constructions called scaffolds [5, 9].
- **Raw Surface Reconstruction.** The form and shape of the temple is determined from field measurements and close-range photogrammetry. Structure-from-motion (SfM) algorithms are used to develop digital point datasets from temple photographs, recovering the salient architectural features of the temple surfaces and interiors [10, 13].
- **Planar Dissections.** Formal scaffold geometry is combined with point datasets through model fitting and shape correlation methods. This process is used to generate closest-fit horizontal and vertical planar dissections that eliminate noise and deformation from the raw pointsets without loss of constructive geometry. Dissections are structured collections of planar two-dimensional points, lines, curves and planes that are oriented in three-dimensional space and form the building blocks for reconstruction. Dissections provide a new theoretical and

methodological bridge to clean and reduce the complexity of raw point cloud data and generate the planar-oriented control geometries for the reconstruction of temple architecture.

- **Canonical Adaptations.** Solid structural blocks and architectural elements are adapted from surface and dissection data to create extruded solid parts for the simulation of conjectural reconstruction. The simulation of archetypal form is developed theoretically through the combination of scaffolds and dissections. Scaffolds and dissections are used to bring together fragments of partial surface reconstruction, relating these to mathematical and geometric descriptions in canonical texts and proposing best-fit constructive and parametric profiles.
- **Prototyping.** Finally, virtual prototypes of temples are developed. These virtual reconstructions are then converted into physical prototypes using 3D printing techniques [4, pp. 447–449].

The translation or inverse modelling of the temple from existing conditions to a conjectural reconstruction rests on a number of important assumptions to quantify the accuracy of the translation process as well as address the ambiguities involved in working with deformations and missing information. The elements of the hybrid approach to 3D reconstruction are illustrated in Fig. 3 through the digital reconstruction of the temple of Ranakdevi in Wadhwan, India, built in the tenth century.

At one end of this spectrum is the raw model, a direct representation of the current temple as a dense point cloud or surface mesh with textures. The accuracy provided by such an approach is valid in cases where the veracity and integrity of the site are preserved and for visualization. At the other end of the spectrum is a conjectural representation as a three-dimensional reconstruction based on primary or fragmentary secondary sources. This approach is mostly used in cases of insufficient or missing information. Between the raw and speculative representations lie a number of intermediate or hybrid representations that combine elements from both and develop a stepwise strategy for 3D architectural reconstruction based on domain knowledge.

4 Case Studies

The computational approach to 3D reconstruction described above is demonstrated through six temple reconstructions from the following ancient sites:

- **Deogarh, Uttar Pradesh, India.** The sixth-century Daśāvatāra Temple at Deogarh in Uttar Pradesh is one of the earliest surviving stone temples from the Gupta period. The datasets comprise image data and site surveys, generated point cloud information and manually reconstructed 3D geometry.
- **Hanchey, Kampong Cham, Cambodia.** Two pre-Angkorian seventh-century temples in Hanchey are the earliest surviving stone temples from Cambodia. Temple B is a temple in a cuboidal cella with a flat roof. The Kuk Preah Thiet Temple has a stepped superstructure in a state of partial collapse. The noisy

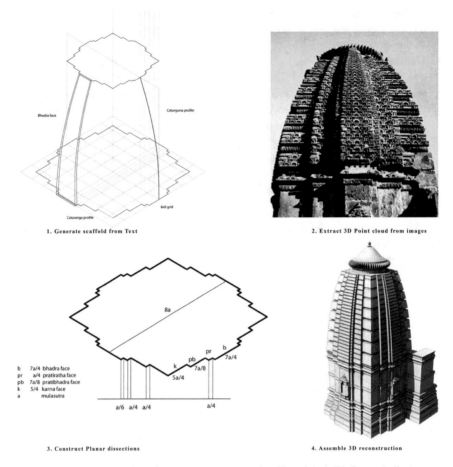

1. Generate scaffold from Text   2. Extract 3D Point cloud from images

3. Construct Planar dissections   4. Assemble 3D reconstruction

Fig. 3 The 3D reconstruction of the tenth-century temple of Ranakdevi, Wadhwan, India (source: Author)

datasets are utilized to demonstrate the reconstruction approach to the recovery of well-formed geometry from ill-formed datasets.

- **Dieng Plateau, Central Java, Indonesia.** Two central Javanese temples from the late seventh- and eighth-century Candi Arjuna and Candi Gatotkaca represent the earliest surviving temples in Indonesia. Although reconstructed from rubble, they present examples demonstrating the evolution of temple form during the eighth century.

- **Roda, Gujarat, India.** The eighth-century Temple 1 at Roda represents the Nāgara style of temple building. The geometry of this stone temple is a faceted cube with curvilinear superstructure. The datasets of this temple comprise detailed image data and reconstructed 3D geometry. The Roda temple reconstruction demonstrates the application of canonical geometry and use of curvature in temple superstructures.

4.1 Daśāvatāra Temple at Deogarh, Central India

Classical Gupta temples are the earliest known structural temples in India. These temples reveal the beginnings of stone experimentation as well as superstructure development, capped by pyramidal tiers, probably in imitation of wooden roofs. Scholars of Gupta temple architecture distinguished three general types [1]. The first of these is the temple with a square garbhagrha and flat roof, generally provided with a porch (such as Temple No. 17 at Sanchi and the Kankali Devi Temple at Tigowa). The second type is provided with a superstructure or Sikhara, examples being the Daśāvatāra Temple at Deogarh and the brick temple at Bhitargaon. In addition to these two, attention has been drawn to a third type of temple with a covered circumambulatory path, best illustrated by the Parvati temple at Nachna-Kuthara discovered by Cunningham in 1883. The significance of the temple reconstruction lies in the early date of the architectural composition, beginnings of its superstructure and a pyramidal composition in three tiers, known as Phāṃsanā in the literature, contemporaneous with the development of the majestic temple complexes of the Gupta period.

Dedicated to Viṣṇu, the Daśāvatāra Temple at Deogarh, Central India, is among the earliest extant structural temple from the Gupta period in South Asia. The cuboidal cella sits on a solid jagati (platform) with a distinctive vedībandha moulding, which is partially buried and yet to be analysed. The jangha or wall portion of the sanctuary is largely bare and simple. The distinctive candraśālā motif appears on the superstructure tiers.

The Daśāvatāra Temple at Deogarh is analysed through field measurements and dense point cloud generation of external surface geometry (Fig. 4, top centre). A conjectural sectional drawing of the east–west axis is generated from this analysis (Fig. 4, bottom right). The reconstructed plan profile at skandha of the Viṣṇu temple in Deogarh today (Fig. 4, bottom left) is developed from the analysis of the sparse point cloud.

The Vamana temple at Marhia and the Siva temple at Bhumara have similar bases, treatment of walls and motifs. However, the most significant aspect of this

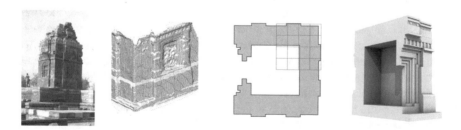

Fig. 4 The Daśāvatāra Temple at Deogarh (left), dense point cloud of external surface geometry (centre left). The reconstructed plan profile at skandha level of the Daśāvatāra Temple today (centre right). Conjectural sectional drawing of the east–west axis (right) (source: Author)

sanctuary is the (tiered pyramidal) superstructure with a distinctive moulding. In contrast to flat-roofed temples and the more developed superstructures at Sambor Prei Kuk and at Phnom Kulen in Cambodia [7], this temple is surmised to have had a tiered pyramidal form of superstructure, known from earlier wooden temples adopted in stone.

4.2   Hanchey, Kampong Cham, Cambodia

The two temples are located in Hanchey (Han Chei) about 20 km north of Kampong Cham, occupying a prominent hilltop on the west bank of the Mekong River in Cambodia. While presently dominated by a modern wat, Hanchey is significant as the location of three pre-Angkorian shrines, each in a distinctly different idiom, as well as the remains of several other buildings that have yet to be fully investigated.

The two inscriptions on the inner door pillars of the old brick sanctuary at Hanchey, just above Kampong Cham on the Mekong, were among the first discovered and were long considered as the most ancient in Cambodia [7]. Historically, Hanchey seems to have been an area where different Khmer polities converged in the fifth to eighth centuries, though never a major centre of power itself. Attributed to the ruler Bhavavarman (though dateable to well after his death), these inscriptions indicate that the site, if not the temples themselves, dates back to the second half of the sixth century.

4.2.1   Temple B, Hanchey, Cambodia

Temple B is located within the present-day monastery of Hanchey on the banks of the Mekong River in Cambodia. Hanchey B is an example of the maṇḍapikā type [19], made of thin structural stone slabs. Early stone use in India was associated with the idea of the temple-as-cave and rock excavated architecture rather than structural temples. Temple B at Hanchey appears to follow the same lineage, showing the use of timber construction techniques in stone.

The cella is a square infilled with single panels of sandstone, each 200 mm thick. The temple sits on a pithā platform with rectilinear mouldings, and the main features are aedicules, four evenly spaced on the north, west and south sides, and two flanking pillars on the east doorway. The east wall has a rectangular doorway entered through a step-over threshold. Its flat roof with projecting eave and candraśālā motifs has a curvilinear profile.

The superstructure of temple B is flat roofed and constructed out of interlocked stone slabs, shown in our reconstruction in Fig. 5. The roof edge is also punctuated by candrasalas, four on each side to match the aedicules on the platform. The plasticity of timber composition, construction and details are evident in this small shrine and may have been inspired by wooden structural temples using a similar

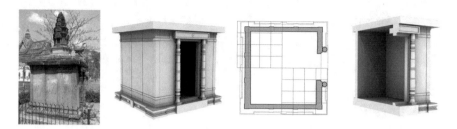

Fig. 5 Temple B at Hanchey (left) and reconstruction (centre left). Plan profile with superposition of the ritual grid (centre right). Sectional reconstruction of the east–west axis (right) (source: Author)

technique as in the Gupta temple at Marhia in Central India and the upper shrine of the Lad Khan Temple in Aihole [7].

4.2.2   Kuk Preah Thiet, Hanchey, Cambodia

Down the hill and closer to the banks of the Mekong is the temple of Kuk Preah Thiet. The pre-Angkorian shrine of Kuk Preah Thiet, therefore, represents one of the earliest known stone temples in Southeast Asia. The early date of the temple, its well-developed superstructure and its dressed basalt construction make it a seminal example of the pre-Angkorian temple corpus of Cambodia.

The form of the temple is lithic in its conception, is constructed of dressed stone and has a storeyed pyramidal superstructure composed of tiers as shown in Fig. 6. A cubic temple with a pyramidal roof, Kuk Preah Thiet is constructed of dressed basalt blocks. The elements of this shrine can be traced to many antecedents in the Gupta period [7]. Kuk Preah Thiet is in an advanced state of collapse, making dimensional correlation very difficult. Structural deformation, missing elements and surface erosion of the soft volcanic basalt stone contribute to the difficulties in establishing accurate measures.

To investigate the inherent ambiguity in establishing accurate measures, the virtual reconstructions, in particular the recovery of schematic profile information, play a key role in establishing the architectonic ideas underlying the temple (Fig. 6). However, Parmentier's 1927 seminal report [21] provides a comprehensive account of the temple as well as structural measures before deformation. In addition, close-range architectural photogrammetry combined with ritual grid information, a measured plan with dimensions from 1927 and a conjectural elevation of Kuk Preah Thiet is critical to the conjectural reconstruction (Fig. 6, top left).

Comparing the temple, 90 years later, there is considerable structural deformation and separation of the basalt blocks. The geometry of the temple is reconstructed by fitting schematic geometries from image-based analysis to sparse structure-from-motion datasets (Fig. 6, bottom centre, bottom right). Establishing the ground plane and the vertical and horizontal axes of the temple using three-point correlation is the first stage of reconstruction. The basic symmetries of the temple are assumed to be

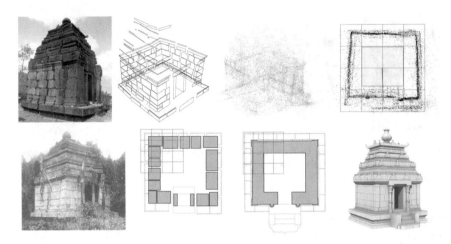

Fig. 6 Parmentier's 1927 photograph of the original temple ensemble (top left); measured drawing of the plan of Kuk Preah Thiet Temple, Hanchey, Cambodia (top centre); and conjectural drawing of the east facade [21]. The Kuk Preah Thiet Temple in Hanchey, Cambodia, today (bottom left). The geometry of the temple is reconstructed (bottom right) by fitting schematic geometries from image-based analysis to sparse structure-from-motion datasets (bottom centre) (source: Author)

regular around the established axes. In the case of plans, the entrance doorway and the wall extents and axial constraints are used to fit planar rectangular grids around both axes. Manual field measurements are used to scale the proportions of parts and establish proportionate ratios for alignment and fitting of parts. The deformation of the basalt block construction is assumed to be dry wall masonry with a nominal 2 mm joint. The blocks are assumed to be regular cuboids and aligned to fit the assumed orientations in both directions. Offsets are handled with proportionate ratios, usually integer ratios, unless field evidence for alternate systems is available. Complex elemental features such as lintels and door frames are simplified to simple geometric profile extrusions. Detailed carvings and relief motifs are abstracted to simple profile extrusions.

4.3 Temples in the Dieng Plateau, Central Java

The remains of many temples have been found in various locations in Central and Western Java. The three major temple locations in Central Java are the Dieng Plateau, the northern slopes of Mount Ungaran and the Prambanan Plain [12]. More recently, interest in Javanese temple sites has shifted again, partially to a reassessment of their cultural and social contexts. Veronique Degroot's study "*Candi, Space and Landscape*" on the distribution, orientation and spatial organization of Central Javanese temple remains has been most useful in combining extensive survey

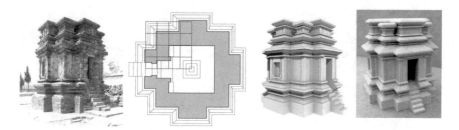

Fig. 7 Candi Gatotkaca, Dieng Plateau, Java. Surface reconstruction is developed from field measurements and close-range photogrammetry (left). A set of horizontal plan dissections is developed from the raw data correlated with site measurements and the ritual 8 × 8 grid maṇḍala (centre left). Extruded profiles are used to generate solid elements of the temple geometry (centre right). The elements are assembled into a physical prototype model (right) (source: Author)

material with a discussion of contextual issues [11]. Candi Gatotkaca and Arjuna are within a group of temples at the Dieng Plateau in Central Java, Indonesia.

4.3.1 Candi Gatotkaca, Dieng Plateau, Central Java

It has been surmised that Candi Gatotkaca represents a unique variation found at Dieng, an amalgam of the prevalent square and cruciform shape of early Javanese Candis (Fig. 7). Candi Gatotkaca and Candi Arjuna are two such examples discussed in this context within a group of temples at the Dieng Plateau in Central Java, Indonesia. There is evidence of the remains of a lower base level or jagati embedded in the ground forming a square about a metre wider than the temple (Fig. 7, top left). Surface reconstruction is developed from field measurements and close-range photogrammetry. A set of horizontal plan dissections is developed from the raw data correlated with site measurements. Extruded profiles are used to generate solid elements of the temple geometry. The elements are assembled into a physical prototype model (Fig. 7, right).

4.3.2 Candi Arjuna, Dieng Plateau, Central Java

Candi Arjuna is attributed to the eighth century and constructed of grey granite blocks. The temple is about 5000 mm square in plan and consists of a cubic cella sitting on top of a square pithā and topped with a tiered pyramidal superstructure. Overall, the top of the platform forms a flat ledge around the body of the cella. Inside is a simple cubic space with a pyramidal corbelled ceiling, dominated by a pithika. The interior space is about 2500 mm square and is accessed from the west through an entry stair via a narrow antechamber. Other than the entry, the main expressive elements at the wall level are niches, placed in the middle of the north, east and south walls, and flanking the entry porch on the west wall. Each of the walls, jaṅghā, is also divided into three panels by pilasters. The tall and narrow niches are expressed as doorways, despite being contained by the wall surface. Each has an elaborated base, expressed as a miniature version of the main wall (Fig. 8).

 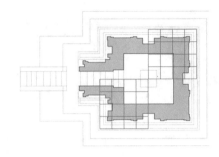

Fig. 8 Candi Arjuna, Dieng Plateau, Central Java. Tiered superstructure on a square plan with an embedded ritual grid (source: Author)

The superstructure of the temple is in pyramidal form and is composed of three tiers of evenly decreasing breadth and height, topped with a simple cylindrical finial. The main forms of these tiers are expressed as part-storeys, taking the same expression as the walls of the cella below to form a prāsāda composition. At the corners of each mini-platform are aedicular forms, like tiny versions of the temple with their own little bases, walls and tiered roofs. After three levels of these diminishing elements, the temple is topped with a tapering finial, square in plan. The heights of each part-storey are similarly proportioned in relation to the height of the main cella, and the platform also has a similar relationship, which combined with its surface expression means it could also be read as a part-storey. The niches also bear closer attention. While the niches in the main body of the temple are contained entirely within its wall surfaces, those of the upper part-storeys maintain their proportions by interrupting both the base and entablature of their respective levels. Combined with their kalamakara surrounds, they appear more like doorways than niches, and in being so equally and emphatically expressed on all sides, they provide the effect of a caturmukha.

4.4 Temple 1, Roda, Sabarkantha, Gujarat

The eighth century represents a time of great architectural experimentation in India. The Nāgara style of temple architecture emerges as adaptive forms based on and derived from the early Gupta temples. The principal form of adaption observed in these temples is the progressive development of plan typologies and a proliferation of distinctive superstructures. The Latina mode of Nāgara temple exhibits a tower of curved profile and a central band of continuous arch forms [14]. The origin and early development of this form of temple are traced in [17, p. 108].

Temple 1 base mouldings' reconstruction is shown in Fig. 9 (right). The base composition mouldings, wall and superstructure are correlated in a vertical

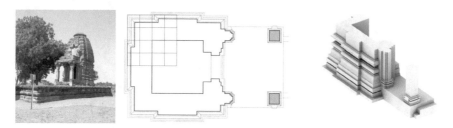

Fig. 9 Temple 1, Roda, Gujarat (left), showing a plan/scaffold grid with subdivisions (centre) and 3D reconstruction of base mouldings (right) (source: Author)

direction. The base mouldings are sequentially structured following the horizontal offsets reaching up to the niche level and terminating clearly at the porch. The jaṅghā wall section above the mouldings is left undecorated except for a niche on each bhadra marking the cardinal directions.

The Latina superstructure is clearly curvilinear and unified as a formal model of upward expression. The porch is clearly discernible as a four-pillared composition with a trabeated structural aesthetic topped by a separate roof form. The Śikhara is carved with a bold jāla pattern and intricately finished. The prāggrīva-type maṇḍapā is roofed with a phāṁsanā class superstructure.

5 Spatio-temporal Mapping

This section demonstrates how the 3D reconstructions explained in the previous sections can uncover compositional and architectural linkages. 3D digital recon-struction methods present new possibilities for interpreting the formal and geometric basis of temple form and form collections across time and space as well as urban and settlement aggregations. Through spatio-temporal mapping of the salient features of these temples, the common elements in plan form, base mouldings and architectural composition are established. The context, mapping and techniques used present an interesting series of findings.

The digital reconstruction models and their analysis present new and extensible possibilities for interpreting the formal and geometric basis of the built environment and its transformation. This temporal mapping demonstrates the compositional connections between South and Southeast Asian temple architecture over 500 years. The canonical adaptations of the plan form through 500 years of development across various sites in South and Southeast Asia are shown in Fig. 10.

The Gupta temples of the sixth century, such as the Daśāvatāra Temple at Deogarh, are raised on significant plinths, have an ambulatory and follow a trabeated form of construction in imitation of timber construction. These temples show only the beginnings of superstructure and are flat roofed or capped by pyramidal tiers, probably in imitation of wooden roofs. These elements are persistent over a

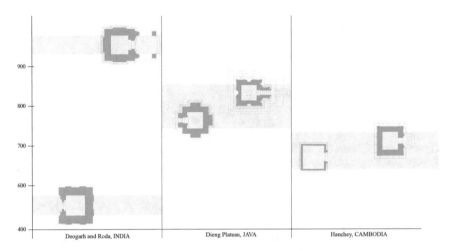

Fig. 10 Temporal distribution map of six temples spread over four ancient sites in India, Indonesia and Cambodia. The dataset is based on archival research, field measurements, virtual modelling and an analysis of plan geometry (source: Author)

century later in the two shrines presented from Cambodia. Temple B in Hanchey is a trabeated, flat-roofed temple, while the superstructure of Kuk Preah Thiet in Hanchey is a pyramidal composition in three tiers that closely resembles the Phāṁsanā style seen in India. The presence of flat-roofed and vedi superstructure structural stone cellas in Cambodia, only seen in the Gupta period in India, raises questions about the early genesis and development of Southeast Asian temples. These trends are continued in the seventh century as exemplified by the two Candis presented from Central Java.

The comparison and analysis of digital reconstructions of Indian temples across South and Southeast Asia underscore the common evolution and interconnection of these temples. These common elements are seen in the formal layout and geometry of the plan; the structuring, sequence and shape of the base mouldings; the elaboration of the tiered superstructure; the design of the entrance doorways; and the use of distinctive motifs. Figure 11 presents a comparative matrix of the principal features of temple form and their presence and variation in the six temples presented in this chapter. The three-dimensional models of temple architecture permit the tracking and analysis of architectural evolution at both individual and collective scales over large time periods. The interconnection of these temples are embodied in the following architectural features:

- **Ritual Grid.** All the temples presented in this chapter from South and Southeast Asia exhibit the systemic use of an ideal architectural canon. The use of canon in the formal composition of the temple is evident in the formal layout and geometry of the plan; the structuring, sequence and shape of the base mouldings; the elaboration of the tiered superstructure; the elements of the entrance doorways; and the use of distinctive motifs such as the candrasalas. Further work is

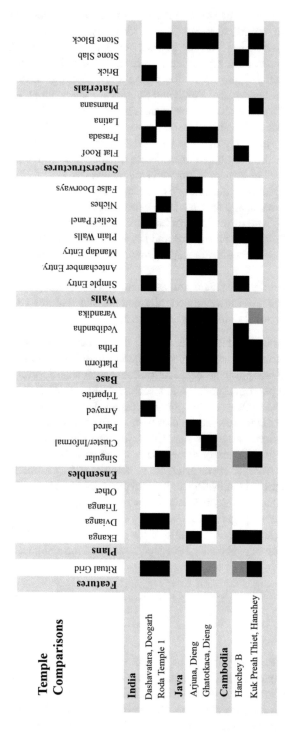

Fig. 11 Comparison matrix of principal features of the six temples spread over four sites in India, Indonesia and Cambodia (source: Author)

necessary in the systematic study of module and measure in these early temples and their relation to particular treatises and ideal composition.

- **Plan Offsets.** Piecing together the genesis and evolution of the ground plan of temples shows consistent adherence to canonical prescriptions for developing plan offsets based on the subdivision of the 8×8 ritual grid. All the temples presented in this chapter from South and Southeast Asia exhibit the systemic use of plan offsets. The plan offset mechanisms described in this chapter demonstrate the compositional connections between parts of South and Southeast Asia and present an intriguing body of evidence regarding the flow of architectural ideas during the sixth and eighth centuries. More detailed studies on the systems of measure employed in Java and Cambodia are necessary.
- **Ensembles.** Explaining the complex linkages and interconnections between architectural elements and features from geometric datasets through novel shape analysis methods reveals the logic of base and wall composition.
- **Superstructure.** Testing automated and semi-automated techniques for detecting, extracting and classifying superstructures and features from geometric datasets.
- **Materiality.** Testing automated and semi-automated techniques for detecting, extracting and classifying architectural elements and features from geometric datasets through novel shape analysis methods.

The results described in this chapter recover the geometric basis of this architecture. First, parametric scaffolds are pieced together based on traditional diagrams, grids and textual descriptions in classical building manuals. Second, using close-range architectural photogrammetry and structure-from-motion techniques, temple surfaces are captured as three-dimensional pointsets. Third, scaffolds and pointsets are combined to generate rule-based closest-fit horizontal and vertical planar 2D dissections. Dissections provide a new theoretical and methodological bridge to clean and reduce the complexity of raw point cloud data and generate consistent control geometries for the reconstruction of temple architecture. Finally, these dissections are combined to develop digital and physical prototypes. The advantage of this process of stepwise reconstruction is partly a matter of speed, both of data collection and of making geometric comparisons, and partly a new experimental method for interrogating the architecture of the past, focusing on analysis of plans, layout and proportion of wall ensembles, superstructure form and constructional and ornamental motifs.

6 Discussion

Digital reconstructions of Indian temples across South and Southeast Asia are presented in the chapter. The hybrid approach combining traditional survey methods with image-based methods presents comparable accuracy and reliability in the temple reconstructions. However, there remain numerous unique research challenges in modelling architectural ruins with these computational methods. The key challenges are in handling noise in datasets of Asian temples due to their poor state of preservation and remote location. The point clouds extracted using these two methods have different properties, e.g. noise level, artefacts and point density. This is often compounded by the complex nature of the scene captured for recording, making hard to extract information in a readily usable format. The ease of feature extraction depends on the well-formedness of digital models generated from raw data. The process of model construction remains intuitive, manual and ambiguous and requires considerable domain expertise. The accuracy of metrical 3D information, the sufficiency and consistency of images and the incorporation of aerial imagery in correlating measured data with canonical scaffolds are critical to our workflow. A crucial difficulty faced in digital reconstruction is the automated recovery of "features", that is, detection and classification of structural and architectural parts from digital datasets. This is further compounded in historic buildings, where information loss due to fragmented and heavily eroded remains is significant. Furthermore, loss of structural and formal integrity in such buildings render the process of establishing formal continuity between artefact and reconstruction difficult.

To address the above issues, new theoretical approaches to the problems of temple reconstruction from range-based, image-based and metrical surface models are needed. Improved techniques are needed for fusing together fragmented and incomplete architectural evidence, adjusting for erosion, missing parts and structural deformation. Therefore, computational techniques that can automatically reassemble fragmented data provide robust and empirical methods to fill in missing information and generate and test the accuracy and ambiguities in the digital reconstruction of geometry are necessary. The following techniques, as described in this chapter, summarize the case for continued development of 3D reconstruction methods from partial information for digital heritage applications:

- **Parametric Scaffolds.** Drawing upon the previous studies of geometry and mathematical schema, parametric models are developed from the mathematical and geometric descriptions in early Indian temple texts. These models are analysed to measure and reconstruct 2.5D parametric constructions called scaffolds [5, 9].
- **Raw Surface Reconstruction.** The form and shape of the temple is determined from field measurements and close-range photogrammetry. Structure-from-motion (SfM) algorithms are used to develop digital point datasets from temple photographs recovering the salient architectural features of the temple surfaces and interiors [10, 13].
- **Planar Dissections.** Formal scaffold geometry is combined with point datasets through model fitting and shape correlation methods. This process is used to generate closest-fit horizontal and vertical planar dissections that eliminate noise and deformation from the raw pointsets without loss of constructive geometry. Dissections are structured collections of planar two-dimensional points, lines, curves and planes that are oriented in three-dimensional space and form the building blocks for reconstruction.

- **Canonical Adaptations.** Solid structural blocks and architectural elements adapted from surface and dissection data to create extruded solid parts for simulation of conjectural reconstruction. Simulation of archetype from assembled solid parts.
- **Physical Prototyping.** In the physical reconstruction of temple architecture, dissections are also used to bring together fragments of partial surface reconstruction, relating these to mathematical and geometric descriptions in canonical texts and proposing best-fit constructive and parametric profiles. These reconstructions are then converted into physical prototypes using 3D printing techniques [4, pp. 447–449].

Through a comparison of the relationships between geometry and physical features in these early temple models, the generative role of geometry within the architectural historiography of Brahmanic temples can be clarified and more fully developed. The knowledge embedded in the architectural remains can be read through computational means to inform, posit or refute positions on their formal derivation. Finally, promoting a better understanding of Asia's shared cultural past can significantly enhance the socio-cultural and economic ties in the rapidly developing Asia-Pacific region. The increasing convergence of technological methods and the study of the built environment present new methods for understanding the architecture and urbanism of Asia as well as its prospects for its future. One such convergence is the virtualization of the material culture of the past [18]. Much of the computational work on point cloud processing has been in the manual creation of surface meshes and establishing ground truths. To further develop these experimental methods into a robust and reliable methodology for architectural analysis, new and automated ways of developing plan and section schematics will be explored in the future.

Acknowledgements This chapter is based on completed research of the author on the connections between the temple-building traditions of India and other parts of South and Southeast Asia. The author would like to acknowledge Dr. David Beynon, University of Tasmania, who was a co-investigator in an Australian Research Council-funded Discovery Project *The Influence of Indian Antecedents on Southeast Asian Temples* and co-author of the research monograph *Digital Archetypes: Adaptations of Early Temple Architecture in South and Southeast Asia*. Research students Stuart Hanafin, Michael Sharman, Greg Pitts, Holly Farley and Andrei Smolik assisted with digital modelling, photogrammetry and visual analysis of the temples.

References

1. Chandra, P.: A Vāmana Temple at Maṛhiā and Some Reflections on Gupta Architecture. Artibus Asiae **32**(2/3), 125–145 (1970). https://doi.org/10.2307/3249549
2. Chihara, D.: Hindu-Buddhist Architecture in Southeast Asia. Brill, Leiden (1996)
3. Daniels II, J., Ochotta, T., Ha, L.K., Silva, C.T.: Spline-based feature curves from point-sampled geometry. Visual Computer **24**(6), 449–462 (2008). https://doi.org/10.1007/s00371-008-0223-2

4. Datta, S.: Digital reconstructions and the geometry of temple fragments. In: Chang, L.H., Liu, Y.T., Hou, J.H. (eds.) Digital Applications in Cultural Heritage, pp. 443–452. The National Center for Research and Preservation of Cultural Properties (2007). http://dro.deakin.edu.au/view/DU:30031428

5. Datta, S.: Infinite sequences in the constructive geometry of tenth-century Hindu temple superstructures. Nexus Netw. J. Archit. Math. **12**(3), 471–483 (2010). http://link.springer.com/article/10.1007/s00004-010-0038-0

6. Datta, S., Beynon, D.: A computational approach to the reconstruction of surface geometry from early temple superstructures. Int. J. Archit. Comput. **3**(4), 471–486 (2005). http://multi-science.metapress.com/index/Q284066618382322.pdf

7. Datta, S., Beynon, D.: Compositional connections: temple form in early Southeast Asia. In: SAHANZ 2008: History in Practice: 25th International Conference of the Society of Architectural Historians Australia and New Zealand, pp. 1–11. Society of Architectural Historians, Australia and New Zealand, Perth (2008). http://dro.deakin.edu.au/view/DU:30018069

8. Datta, S., Beynon, D.: Digital Archetypes: Adaptations of Early Temple Architecture in South and Southeast Asia. Ashgate Publishing, Farnham (2014)

9. Datta, S., Beynon, D.J.: Scaffolds and dissections: computational reconstruction of Indic Temples and their architectural production. Archit. Theory Rev. **22**(3), 410–432 (2018). https://doi.org/10.1080/13264826.2018.1516682

10. Debevec, P.E., Taylor, C.J., Malik, J.: Modeling and rendering architecture from photographs: a hybrid geometry- and image-based approach. In: Proceedings of the 23rd Annual Conference on Computer Graphics and Interactive Techniques, SIGGRAPH '96, pp. 11–20. ACM, New York (1996). https://doi.org/10.1145/237170.237191

11. Degroot, V.: Candi, Space and Landscape: A Study on the Distribution, Orientation and Spatial Organization of Central Javanese Temple Remains. No. no. 38 in Mededelingen van Het Rijksmuseum Voor Volkenkunde, Leiden. Sidestone Press, Leiden (2009). OCLC: 617619171

12. Degroot, V.M.Y.: Temples and landscape in south Central Java. In: Haendel, A. (ed.) Old Myths and New Approaches: Interpreting Ancient Religious Sites in Southeast Asia, pp. 121–133. Monash University Publishing, Clayton (2012)

13. Dekeyser, F., Gaspard, F., Florenzano, M., De Luca, L., Chen, X., Leray, P.: Cultural heritage recording with laser scanning, computer vision and exploitation of architectural rules. Int. Arch. Photogrammetry Remote Sens. Spatial Inf. Sci. **34**, 145–149 (2003). http://www.isprs.org/proceedings/xxxiv/5-W12/proceedings/30.pdf

14. Dhaky, M., Meister, M., Deva, K.: Encyclopaedia of Indian Temple Architecture, North India: Foundations of the North Indian Style C.250 B.C. - A.D. 1100, vol. 2. Oxford University Press (1988)

15. Dumaray, J., Dumarcay, J., Smithies, M.: Architecture and Its Models in Southeast Asia. Orchid Press Publishing Limited, Bangkok (2008)

16. Haendel, A.: Old Myths and New Approaches: Interpreting Ancient Religious Sites in Southeast Asia. Monash University Publishing, Clayton (2012)

17. Hardy, A.: The Temple Architecture of India. Wiley, Chichester (2007)

18. Kalay, Y., Kvan, T., Affleck, J.: New Heritage: New Media and Cultural Heritage. Routledge, London (2007)

19. Meister, M.W.: Construction and conception of Maṇḍapikā shrines of Central India. East West New Series **26**, 409–418 (1976)

20. Meister, M.W.: Maṇḍala and practice in Nāgara architecture in northern India. J. Am. Orient. Soc. **99**(2), 204–219 (1979)

21. Parmentier, H.: L'art Khmér Primitif [Tome Premier]. G. Vanoest (1927). http://evols.library.manoa.hawaii.edu/handle/10524/12280

22. Pottmann, H., Bentley, D.: Architectural Geometry. Bentley Institute Press, Exton (2007)

Computer Vision for Capturing Flora

Vamsidhar Muthireddy and C. V. Jawahar

Abstract The identification of plant species by looking at their leaves, flowers, and seeds is a crucial component in the conservation of endangered plants. Traditional identification methods are manual and time consuming and require domain knowledge to operate. Owing to an increased interest in the automated plant identification system, we propose one that utilizes modern convolutional neural network architectures. This approach helps in the recognition of leaf images and can be integrated into mobile platforms like smartphones. Such a system can also be employed in aiding plant-related education, promoting ecotourism, and creating a digital heritage for plant species, among many others. Our proposed solution achieves a state-of-the-art performance for plant classification in the wild. An exhaustive set of experiments are performed to classify 112 species of plants from the challenging Indic-Leaf dataset. The best-performing model gives Top 1 precision of 90.08 and Top 5 precision of 96.90. We discuss and elaborate on our crowdsourcing web application that is used to collect and regulate data. We explain how the automated plant identification system can be integrated into a smartphone by detailing the flow of our mobile application.

Keywords Digital heritage of plant species · Plant classification · Convolutional neural network (CNN) · Gradient-weighted Class Activation Mapping (Grad-CAM) · Web application

1 Introduction

Biodiversity is an essential trait of organic life that maintains balance in an ecosystem. This delicate balance is often disturbed by direct or indirect human interventions [22] around the world. For conservation efforts to have positive results,

V. Muthireddy · C. V. Jawahar (✉)
International Institute of Information Technology, Hyderabad, Hyderabad, India
e-mail: vamsidhar.muthireddy@research.iiit.ac.in; jawahar.iiit.ac.in

© Springer Nature Switzerland AG 2021
J. Mukhopadhyay et al. (eds.), *Digital Techniques for Heritage Presentation and Preservation*, https://doi.org/10.1007/978-3-030-57907-4_12

245

the species should be geographically monitored by experts. However, the number of experts is limited and declining [12]. Even though they are more in number, nature enthusiasts cannot be employed for the task either since these conservation efforts rely on an accurate identification process, which is challenging apart from being time consuming. For instance, in the case of plant species that form a significant portion of biodiversity, the traditional identification process involves identifying the qualitative morphological characteristics of a plant to compare them with a discriminatory feature of known plants. An expert repeats this process until a matching species is found. This is a very long and tedious process requiring the involvement of domain experts. The traditional plant species identification process is challenging even for gardeners, farmers, or conservationists whose daily job involves dealing with plants. This process proves to be a hurdle as most nature enthusiasts are not equipped with the domain knowledge. This necessitates an automated plant species identification system for biodiversity conservation [7]. Such an identification system, apart from being accurate, also needs to be robust and simple enough for the general public to use (Fig. 1).

An enormous amount of work has been carried out in the development of automated approaches to plant species identification in the past decade. Most of these are based on computer vision and are considered promising. These automated identification systems can be integrated into a mobile tool, such as a smartphone. Such a smartphone application using image-based identification initiates the interaction between computer scientists and end users such as botanists, nature enthusiasts, and educators. With thousands of potential contributors, this application can act as a massive ecological monitoring system.

1.1 Motivation

Plant diversity plays a crucial role in the functioning of all ecosystems. Plants are important in Indian culture for their medicinal and spiritual values. Ayurveda is one of the ancient systems of plant-based treatments and is still widely practiced in modern times. It extensively involves the use of medicines derived from beneficial plant parts such as roots, shoots, leaves, bark, flowers, fruits, and seeds. Culturally, plants and their parts also play a significant role in many rituals and festivals, especially in rural areas. In a primarily agrarian society like India, farmers have to be provided with the most highly recommended practices for any specific crop to ensure that the national crop yield remains high. As such, they should be given the necessary information about the various diseases and pests that can affect crops. Further, knowing what a healthy plant looks like can help in the early detection of diseases. Therefore, preparing a systemic digital catalogue of the native species can have far-reaching benefits. First, this catalogue can be made a part of the digital bio-heritage to boost conservation efforts of various local plant species. It helps in differentiating between similar species and allows for selective cultivation of beneficial plants. It is also useful while setting up biodiversity parks to promote

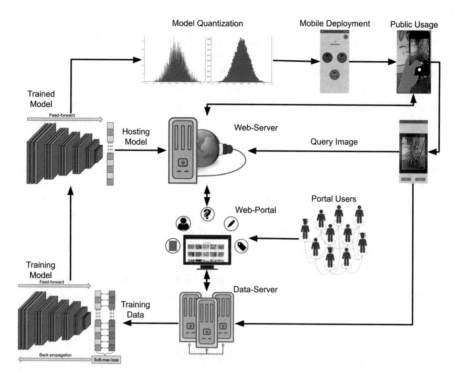

Fig. 1 The pipeline of our work is explained. Users add information on plant species to our web portal. Image data from the web portal is used to train leaf recognition models. Trained models are hosted on a web server, which can be accessed by the general public via our web portal. A quantized version of this trained model is integrated into a smartphone application to act as a standalone mobile plant species recognition system. Queried images are received by the web server, and the recognition results obtained are communicated to the relevant device. Each queried image is added to the data server to be used for further improvement of plant species recognition models

ecotourism. Further, having a digital platform piques the interest of the learners in our bio-heritage as well as makes plant-related education more accessible.

1.2 Related Works

Early work on plant species classification used handcrafted features to describe plant parts. Gu et al. [9] extract leaf skeleton from scan-like images and use it to classify leaf images. Some studies use the venation pattern of the leaves for the same [18, 23, 24]. Others utilize the texture of the leaf as a key feature [15]. The shape information is also used by the leaf-based identification methods [17, 31]. Several studies used the combination of texture and shape [4, 13], while other studies used the features from shape and veins [19]. Some used colour and polygon models to segment a leaf and extracted handcrafted shape features for leaf recognition [5]. Wäldchen and Mäder [30] in their extensive work provide an insight into the various handcrafted feature extraction methods designed to identify plants. Handcrafted features designed for leaf classification based on morphological characteristics often assume an image with a simple background of uniform colour. They fail in the context of images captured in the wild as it is often hard to capture an image containing only a single leaf with a uniform background in the cluttered natural environment.

In a neural network, each level/layer learns to transform its input data into a slightly more abstract and composite representation to obtain the desired output. This can be interpreted as a process to automate feature acquisition by learning an optimized representation of training data at each corresponding layer. Sun et al. [28] and Barré et al. [3] propose custom architectures for plant identification. The popular VGG model is modified [10] and used in classifying the PlantCLEF dataset [8]. Pl@ntNet, a plant identification system, has also shifted from using classic handcrafted features[16] to a CNN-based architecture for plant identification. We also take an approach of starting with pre-trained state-of-the-art convolutional neural networks and fine-tuning them on a challenging leaf classification dataset.

1.3   Existing Datasets: Problems and a Solution

An image-based dataset should capture features that help human experts identify the object of interest. For plant recognition, experts analyse foliage from various distances to take note of the plant shape, arrangement of leaves on the branch, and characteristics of the leaf. They study a plant from different levels of distance to identify it. Publicly available datasets such as Herbarium [1], Flavia [31], Swedish Leaf [27], Leafsnap [17], Middle European Woods (MEW) [21], MalayaKew (MK) Leaf, and PlantCLEF [8] have assisted in furthering the work in plant species classification. Other than PlantCLEF, all the others are composed of scan-like images in a lab-constrained environment. PlantCLEF, which captures plants in their natural environment, does not organize the images of the species according to the different distance levels mentioned above. Moreover, none of these datasets contain images specific to the Indian subcontinent. Keeping this in view, a new dataset named Indic-Leaf has been created. More details about this dataset are provided in Sect. 2. The following sections describe the methods and our experimental setup. The qualitative and quantitative analysis that we have carried out on the dataset to achieve a Precision@1 of 90.08 is also detailed.

2 Indic-Leaf Dataset

Data labelling has always been a bottleneck in deep learning-based tasks. ImageNet [6] alleviates this issue for neural network-based classification tasks to a large extent. But fine-grained tasks like plant classification require domain-specific data. For this purpose, the Indic-Leaf dataset composed of 27,000 images belonging to 112 Indian plant species has been created. It is divided into groups based on distance levels between the camera and the plant. This will allow for a broader set of tasks to be carried out using our dataset. As per our knowledge, this is the first dataset where the images are grouped according to different levels.

2.1 *Images*

The Indic-Leaf dataset contains 27K images belonging to 112 plant species found locally. This dataset in its original form is composed of images in an RGB colour space. For every image, there is an associated XML file that contains relevant annotations. Images from each species are further divided into groups: Level 0, Level 1, Level 2, and Level 3. Level 0 contains "scan-like" images. The rest of the groups contain "in the wild" images of the leaves. These groups are designed such that each one can be used as a separate smaller dataset to assist with more research problems. The above-mentioned groups are explained in detail below.

Level 0
Scan-like images in our dataset are grouped into this *level*. Leaves collected from a plant are pressed for a short time to make them relatively flatter. Each leaf is placed on a sheet of white paper; its picture is taken using a mobile phone camera at a fixed height with no flash. This *level* is designed taking into account the scenario where a plucked leaf needs to be identified. The top row of Fig. 2 shows Level 0 images of ten plant species from the dataset.

Fig. 2 Images from Level 0 and Level 1 of the Indic-Leaf dataset are shown. Each row indicates images from a different level. The top row shows images from Level 0 and the bottom row from Level 1. Each column shows images of different species

Fig. 3 Images from Level 2 and Level 3 of the Indic-Leaf dataset are shown. Each row shows images from a different level. The top row shows images from Level 2 and the bottom row from Level 3. Each column shows images of different species

Level 1

Leaves can be simple (a single leaf blade or lamina) or compound (with several leaflets). Level 1 contains images that capture a single leaf in its entirety so that the visibility of the blade area is maximized, as shown in the bottom row of Fig. 2. The process of capturing is easy in the case of simple-leaved plants that have one leaflet. However, for plants with compound leaves, where a leaf is divided into many small leaflets, this process is rather challenging. In such cases, the image is captured with a focus on these leaflets. Level 1 images capture the finer details of the leaf, such as its shape, colour, texture, and veins.

Level 2

Every individual plant species has evolved to survive in its native environment. The arrangement of leaves along a stem/branch is one such feature that helps in the sustenance of these species. Level 2 images capture these details of a leaf cluster. Different types of leaf clusters can be seen in the top row of Fig. 3. The second image in this figure shows leaves arranged in a notable rosette pattern.

Level 3

Plant species in their full-grown tree stage vary in their crown or shape. These features are developed by these species to counter the elements of nature, such as wind. Level 3 images of our dataset capture these features, as seen in the bottom row of Fig. 3. Images in this *level* capture the plant species in either partial or full view. The first species in this row, *Polyalthia longifolia*, has a "pyramidal" shape.

2.2 Image Tags

Each image in our dataset has an associated XML file that provides the annotations. They describe the morphological characteristics of the leaf along with other information related to the plant species captured in the image. The section that follows provides a detailed overview of these annotations.

Scientific Name

Every species is identified by a unique scientific name. It is a two-part name based on Latin. The first part of the name is the genus. The second part denotes a specific epithet that identifies the species within the genus. This tag is used to describe the scientific name of the plant species identified in the image. For example, the scientific name of the species in the first column of Fig. 2 is *Polyalthia longifolia*.

Common Name

Apart from the standardized scientific names, species acquire a different set of region-specific names. The populace in these regional communities uses common words in reference to these species in their day-to-day life. For a plant species captured in an image, its common names are provided in this tag. For example, the common names of the *Polyalthia longifolia* species in the first column of Fig. 2 include "Indian willow, Ashoka chettu, and Devdaru".

Family

In biological classification, family is given a higher taxonomic rank than species. Species are grouped into a family by expert biologists using the accessible information that ranges from physical characteristics to biological functionality. For plant species, the name of the family ends with "aceae". This tag is used to record the family of a plant species captured in an image. For example, the species *Polyalthia longifolia* in the first column of Fig. 2 belongs to the family "Annonaceae".

Picture Type

Every image in our dataset is assigned a *level* as mentioned in Sect. 2.1. This additional division of plant species is to understand the variance in identification features when studied in different image resolutions. For this purpose, each image is grouped into one of the four existing *levels*. For example, Figs. 2 and 3 show images from ten species in different *levels*. The top and bottom row images of Fig. 2 belong to Level 0 and Level 1, respectively. Similarly, the top and bottom row images of Fig. 3 belong to Level 2 and Level 3.

Leaf Shape

Leaves are the most abundant of the plant organs. They are widely used by biologists during the plant identification process. Their shape is one of the key visible features that makes this process swift. The shape of a leaf is unique to each plant species, but to make the cataloguing less exhaustive, it is associated with known geometric shapes. For the captured plant species in the image, this tag records the shape of its leaves. For example, the leaves belonging to *Polyalthia longifolia* in the first column of Fig. 2 have a "lanceolate" shape.

Leaf Margin/Edge

Leaf margin refers to the outside perimeter of a leaf. This is one of the visible characteristics of a leaf consistent within the same plant species. Leaf margins, along with their shape, are used in visual plant identification. This tag stores the type of leaf margin for a plant species captured in an image. For example, the leaves belonging to *Polyalthia longifolia* in the first column of Fig. 2 have an "entire" leaf margin.

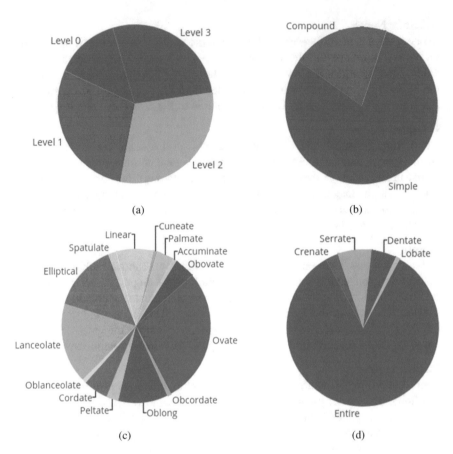

Fig. 4 The distribution of different dataset attributes. Contribution of each (**a**) level, (**b**) leaf division type, (**c**) leaf shape, and (**d**) margins

Leaf Division

Two basic forms of leaves can be described considering the way the blade (lamina) is divided. A leaf with simple division has a single undivided blade, and the one with complex division has several leaflets due to the fully subdivided blade. This tag describes whether the leaf division of the plant is simple or compound. For example, the fifth and sixth columns in Fig. 3 show the species with a "compound" leaf division, whereas the remaining columns have species with a "simple" leaf division (Fig. 4).

Picture Season

The physical characteristics of a plant change in accordance with the season. Every season has its importance in the growth of a plant. Some provide for the flowering of plants, while some cause wilting and falling of leaves. In essence, having seasonal variance in data will improve the understanding of the plant species. This tag contains the season in which the images in the dataset have been captured.

Disease

Plant diseases are one of the many ecological factors that sustain the balance between animals and plants. However, for agrarian communities, they are a hassle, hindering the normal state of plant growth. These diseases vary from season to season, depending on environmental conditions and crop varieties, among many factors. Early detection of such diseases will help in preventing them from their onset. In addition, every image in the dataset is tagged with possible diseases that the species captured might contain.

Description

The description tag provides detailed information about the species of the plant in the image. It contains a visual description of the species, detailing the height of the plant/tree, colour and size of flowers and fruits, etc. For example, *Polyalthia longifolia*, shown in the first column of Fig. 3, the Ashoka tree native to India, is a lofty evergreen tree, commonly planted due to its effectiveness in alleviating noise pollution. It exhibits symmetrical pyramidal growth with willowy weeping pendulous branches and long narrow lanceolate leaves with undulate margins. The tree is known to grow to over 10 m in height.

Utility

Plants and their products fuel the day-to-day life of a society in different forms. Such utilities of plant species captured in the images of our dataset are provided in this tag. For example, the leaves of the *Polyalthia longifolia* species shown in the first column of Fig. 3 are used for ornamental decoration during festivals. The tree is the main attraction in gardens throughout India. It can be cut into various shapes and maintained in the required sizes. In the past, communities in ship-building industries have used the trunks of this tree as masts for sailing ships due to its straight, flexible, and lightweight nature.

2.3   Challenges in Data Creation

Dataset creation is a demanding task, often with its challenges. During the creation of the Indic-Leaf dataset, we faced challenges while deciding on the shape of the leaves. The leaf shape of a species is defined by how similar it is to a predetermined geometrical shape such as "ovate" or "oblong". But leaves belonging to the same species do not always have a uniform shape, and more often their shape score lies in a range. For example, the third column of Fig. 2 shows a leaf of *Psidium guajava* L. Its shape is best defined as "oval" (ovate–elliptic or oblong–elliptic). This can be interpreted as ovate and elliptic or oblong and elliptic, all of which are known individual shapes. This situation is not uncommon and can be seen in a significant portion of the plant species that were collected. Since each species is to be assigned a single shape for its leaf, it is decided based on relevant Level 0 and Level 1 leaf images.

2.4 Other Datasets

To show the complex nature of the proposed Indic-Leaf dataset, we compare it with five other existing leaf datasets. These datasets are detailed below:

- **Swedish Leaf:** The Swedish Leaf dataset contains 1125 images belonging to 15 Swedish tree species. Each of these species has 75 images. Every image in the dataset is composed of an isolated leaf scanned on a plain white background.
- **Flavia:** The Flavia dataset contains 1907 images of leaves belonging to common plants found in the Yangtze Delta, China. The images in this dataset belong to 32 different species. Each image in the dataset is obtained by scanning individual leaves on a plain white background.
- **Leafsnap:** Leafsnap is composed of images from 185 tree species native to the Northeastern United States. This dataset has two parts: Lab and Field. The 23,147 lab images are acquired from Smithsonian Collections and are of high quality. Leaves in these images are pressed and pictured in a well-lit environment. The remaining 7719 field images are collected by using mobile devices in outdoor environments. In both these parts, the leaf is placed on a uniform white background during image acquisition.
- **MK Leaf:** The MalayaKew (MK) Leaf dataset consists of 44 plant species found at the Royal Botanic Gardens, Kew, England. Two variants of the dataset are available, D1 and D2. D1 contains leaf images and D2 is composed of patches created by manual cropping of leaf images from D1. D2 contains 34,672 patches for training and 8800 patches for testing. The D2 variant of the dataset is used for experimentation in our work.
- **MEW:** The Middle European Woods (MEW) dataset contains leaf images belonging to plants and shrubs of Central Europe. It has two variants: MEW-2012 and MEW-2014. MEW-2012 contains 9745 images from 151 species (153 classes), whereas MEW-2014 contains 15,074 images from 201 species. All the images are obtained by scanning the leaves on a white background.

3 Computer Vision for Plant Recognition

Computer vision and machine learning are extensively used for solving real-world problems. In this section, we explain the different methods that were employed and experiments that were conducted to solve the plant species classification problem. The first subsection describes the methods that were used in detail. The second subsection lists all the experiments that were carried out along with the experimental parameters. This is followed by a discussion on the experimental results.

3.1 Methods

Convolutional neural networks (CNNs) have become state-of-the-art solutions for many of the computer vision problems because of their efficacy. Among all the CNN architectures present, it was ascertained that the classification ability of ResNet-based architectures performs better than its forerunners allowing deeper networks to be built. For the baseline, we use VGG-16, which is a simple feed-forward network with no skip connections compared with existing residual networks. Cross-entropy is utilized as the loss function for all the networks. After the completion of the training process, Grad-CAM [25] is employed on these networks, to visually understand the classifications made by the aforementioned methods.

3.1.1 VGG-16

VGG-16 [26] is a feed-forward convolutional neural network with 16 weight layers. This network is characterized by its simplicity for using convolutional filters with a receptive field of 3×3 in every layer. Convolutional layers in the network are followed by two fully connected layers and a softmax classifier. Due to its known efficacy in classification tasks, we use VGG-16 as our baseline model.

3.1.2 ResNet

Residual networks (ResNets) [11] are feed-forward neural networks that use skip connections in their architecture. ResNet-based architectures outrank their predecessors [2] in classification ability since they do not suffer from the vanishing gradient problem. This enables us to build deeper ResNets. We use ResNets of 18, 34, 50, 101, and 152 layers in our work. All of them have similar architectures with a single convolutional layer that takes a $224 \times 224 \times 3$ image as an input. This convolutional layer is followed by four parent blocks. A block or a basic block represents stacked convolutional layers, as shown in Fig. 5a. Each parent block contains multiple basic blocks, and their number varies based on the position of the block and the depth of the ResNet. Each basic block in ResNet-18 and ResNet-34 has two convolutional layers, while each block in ResNet-50, ResNet-101, and ResNet-152 has three convolutional layers. Table 1 explains the detailed architecture of different ResNets.

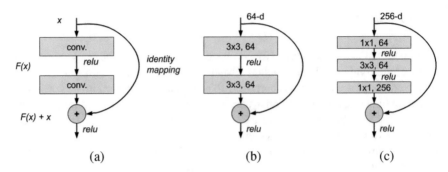

Fig. 5 Various building blocks for residual learning[11]. Left (**a**): Basic building block. Centre (**b**): Building block for ResNet-18 and ResNet-34. Right (**c**): Building block for ResNet-50, ResNet-101, and ResNet-152

3.1.3 Grad-CAM

Convolutional neural networks were considered a black box due to the lack of methods to provide insight into the working of these networks. With the recent growth in deep learning research, the contents of these black boxes are unveiled by using visualization methods. These methods present the working of CNNs in a human-interpretable form; they use filters and activation maps to create visualizations.

Gradient-weighted Class Activation Mapping (Grad-CAM) [25] uses the gradients of any target class, flowing into the final convolutional layer, to produce a coarse localization map. This results in a coarse heatmap of the same size as the convolutional feature maps (14×14 in the case of the last convolutional layers of VGG-16), highlighting the important regions in the image for predicting the target class. This heatmap($L^c_{\text{Grad-CAM}}$) is given by

$$L^c_{\text{Grad-CAM}} = ReLU \underbrace{\left(\sum_k \alpha^c_k A^k \right)}_{\text{linear combination}} \tag{1}$$

where A^k is the kth feature map of a convolutional layer and α^c_k is the importance weight for the feature map for any class c and is defined as

$$\alpha^c_k = \overbrace{\frac{1}{Z} \sum_i \sum_j}^{\text{global average pooling}} \underbrace{\frac{\partial y^c}{\partial A^k_{ij}}}_{\text{gradients via backprop}} \tag{2}$$

Table 1 Different ResNet architectures with stacked building blocks [11]. Column 1 displays the names of the parent blocks. Column 2 shows the size of the output of the block. Columns 3–8 specify the size, depth, and number of filters and blocks

Layer	Output size	ResNet-18	ResNet-34	ResNet-50	ResNet-101	ResNet-152
conv1	112×112	7×7, 64, stride 2				
		3×3 max pool, stride 2				
conv2_x	56×56	$\begin{bmatrix} 3\times3,\,64 \\ 3\times3,\,64 \end{bmatrix}\times2$	$\begin{bmatrix} 3\times3,\,64 \\ 3\times3,\,64 \end{bmatrix}\times3$	$\begin{bmatrix} 1\times1,\,64 \\ 3\times3,\,64 \\ 1\times1,\,256 \end{bmatrix}\times3$	$\begin{bmatrix} 1\times1,\,64 \\ 3\times3,\,64 \\ 1\times1,\,256 \end{bmatrix}\times3$	$\begin{bmatrix} 1\times1,\,64 \\ 3\times3,\,64 \\ 1\times1,\,256 \end{bmatrix}\times3$
conv3_x	28×28	$\begin{bmatrix} 3\times3,\,128 \\ 3\times3,\,128 \end{bmatrix}\times2$	$\begin{bmatrix} 3\times3,\,128 \\ 3\times3,\,128 \end{bmatrix}\times4$	$\begin{bmatrix} 1\times1,\,128 \\ 3\times3,\,128 \\ 1\times1,\,512 \end{bmatrix}\times4$	$\begin{bmatrix} 1\times1,\,128 \\ 3\times3,\,128 \\ 1\times1,\,512 \end{bmatrix}\times4$	$\begin{bmatrix} 1\times1,\,128 \\ 3\times3,\,128 \\ 1\times1,\,512 \end{bmatrix}\times8$
conv4_x	14×14	$\begin{bmatrix} 3\times3,\,256 \\ 3\times3,\,256 \end{bmatrix}\times2$	$\begin{bmatrix} 3\times3,\,256 \\ 3\times3,\,256 \end{bmatrix}\times6$	$\begin{bmatrix} 1\times1,\,256 \\ 3\times3,\,256 \\ 1\times1,\,1024 \end{bmatrix}\times6$	$\begin{bmatrix} 1\times1,\,256 \\ 3\times3,\,256 \\ 1\times1,\,1024 \end{bmatrix}\times23$	$\begin{bmatrix} 1\times1,\,256 \\ 3\times3,\,256 \\ 1\times1,\,1024 \end{bmatrix}\times36$
conv5_x	7×7	$\begin{bmatrix} 3\times3,\,512 \\ 3\times3,\,512 \end{bmatrix}\times2$	$\begin{bmatrix} 3\times3,\,512 \\ 3\times3,\,512 \end{bmatrix}\times3$	$\begin{bmatrix} 1\times1,\,512 \\ 3\times3,\,512 \\ 1\times1,\,1024 \end{bmatrix}\times3$	$\begin{bmatrix} 1\times1,\,512 \\ 3\times3,\,512 \\ 1\times1,\,2048 \end{bmatrix}\times3$	$\begin{bmatrix} 1\times1,\,512 \\ 3\times3,\,512 \\ 1\times1,\,2048 \end{bmatrix}\times3$
	1×1	Average-pool, fc, softmax				

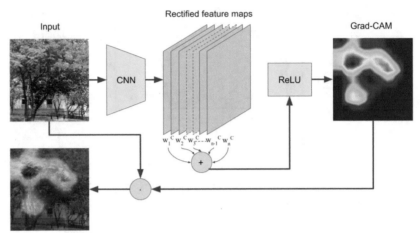

Grad-CAM: "Senna auriculata"

Fig. 6 Grad-CAM overview: input image is propagated through the convolutional layers of the model. Softmax score is calculated, and gradients are set to 1 for the specified class. For the remaining classes, the gradients are set to zero. When this signal is sent to rectified feature maps that are of interest, they are combined to compute Grad-CAM localization, a heatmap that indicates the areas in the image where the model has looked to make the specified classification. This heatmap is upscaled and pointwise multiplied with the input image for better visualization

To compute the neuron importance weights for an activation map for class c, we first compute the gradient of the score y^c (before the softmax) for class c with respect to feature maps A^k of a convolutional layer, that is, $\frac{\partial y^c}{\partial A^k}$. These weights are then substituted in Eq. (1) to obtain the class-discriminative localization map Grad-CAM($L^c_{\text{Grad-CAM}}$). This entire overview is clearly shown in Fig. 6. Grad-CAM is very generic and can be used to visualize any activation in a deep network. But in this work, we visualize the last convolutional layers of the networks.

3.2   Experiments, Results, and Discussion

In this section, we explain the experiments conducted and present the results obtained. In addition, we provide visual explanations for these classification results. We then analyse and discuss the obtained results in detail. We use Precision@K (P@K) to measure the effectiveness of our classification models. P@K can be defined as the number of true positives in the top-K predicted classes for a given sample. For each test sample of our task, this value is either 1 if the expected class is present in the top-k values or 0 if it is not present. Tables 2 and 5 show the averaged P@K values obtained on test data.

3.2.1 Data Augmentation

Data augmentation is a crucial strategy employed to improve the diversity of the data available for training the networks. It improves the performance of the networks by making them robust to variance in new data. During the training phase, we used random vertical–horizontal flipping, rotation, and greyscale conversion. The smaller side of the image is then resized to 672 pixels, followed by the cropping of the central 560×560 patch. A 448×448 region from this patch is then randomly cropped. This region is resized to 224×224 pixels to be used as an input to the networks.

3.2.2 Experimental Setup

All the convolutional neural networks used in our work are pre-trained on the ImageNet dataset. Each network is fine-tuned on the Indic-Leaf dataset. The dataset is split into train, validation, and test sets in the order of 60:20:20. The batch size is set to 100. Stochastic gradient descent (SGD) with a momentum of 0.9 is used for optimization. The momentum [29] helps in having a stable update of weights since it partially uses the direction of the previous batch along with the gradient of the current one to make the update. All the networks have been trained for 100 epochs with an initial learning rate of 0.01. It is decayed by a factor of 0.5 when there is no reduction in validation loss for three consecutive epochs. The fine-tuned networks are used by Grad-CAM to obtain visual explanations for the classification task on test data.

We evaluate the ResNet-18, ResNet-34, ResNet-50, ResNet-101, ResNet-152, and VGG-16 models on our dataset. Each one of these models is trained and tested on two configurations of the dataset and three colour spaces. Each species in the Indic-Leaf dataset is categorized into levels as mentioned in Sect. 2. Images in different *levels* vary in the type of visible features they contain. This information is used to create two different data configurations for experimentation. In the first configuration (*cfg1*), all the images belonging to a species are considered one training class (*label=specie*). In the second configuration (*cfg2*), each *level* of a species is considered a training class (*label=specie_level*). If there are s species and each has a maximum of l levels, then *cfg1* will have s classes, whereas *cfg2* will have a maximum of $s \times l$ classes in the softmax layer.

3.2.3 Results

To find a convolutional network that performs best on the Indic-Leaf dataset, a series of experiments have been conducted. Table 2 shows the exhaustive set of quantitative experiments performed on the dataset. The first column shows the name of the model and the second column shows the configuration. The third, fourth, and fifth columns show Precision@K for $K = 1, 3, 5$, respectively. Each column has

Table 2 P@K values obtained by all the models on test data for $K = 1, 3, 5$ in YCbCr, RGB, and HSV colour spaces

Model	Cfg	P@1			P@3			P@5		
		YCbCr	RGB	HSV	YCbCr	RGB	HSV	YCbCr	RGB	HSV
VGG-16	cfg1	88.49	89.30	88.99	94.43	94.82	94.93	96.34	96.54	96.29
	cfg2	85.47	85.21	86.08	93.07	93.39	93.48	95.08	95.24	95.28
ResNet-18	cfg1	86.97	85.90	86.50	93.64	92.85	93.57	95.24	94.67	95.38
	cfg2	82.63	82.95	82.46	91.62	91.70	91.26	93.83	93.66	93.63
ResNet-34	cfg1	86.99	86.92	87.24	93.48	93.20	93.70	94.93	94.99	95.37
	cfg2	83.98	84.35	84.11	92.31	92.53	92.71	94.79	94.90	94.93
ResNet-50	cfg1	89.85	88.84	89.43	95.35	94.40	95.15	96.62	95.90	96.80
	cfg2	86.05	86.50	86.50	93.43	93.45	94.10	95.22	95.46	95.95
ResNet-101	cfg1	89.45	**90.08**	89.94	95.11	95.35	**95.51**	96.71	**96.90**	96.74
	cfg2	86.75	87.39	86.92	94.30	94.28	94.28	96.25	95.96	96.49
ResNet-152	cfg1	89.25	89.65	89.11	94.79	94.79	95.00	96.24	96.49	96.49
	cfg2	87.21	87.20	86.72	94.41	94.40	94.17	96.22	96.00	95.80

The maximum P@1, P@3, P@5 achieved are represented by bold text

three sub-columns showing P@K values obtained in different colour spaces of the dataset. Each row displays these P@K values by a model in different colour spaces. Each of these rows has two sub-rows, one for each configuration. The first sub-row displays the results from *cfg1* and the second from *cfg2*. As seen in Table 2, ResNet-101 *cfg1* in the RBG colour space outperforms other models with P@1 of 90.08. Our baseline VGG-16 achieves P@1 of 89.30, outperforming ResNet-18, ResNet-34, and ResNet-50 architectures. It can be observed that models using images in the RGB colour space outperform models using images in other colour spaces.

From Table 2, it can be observed that in each colour space, models trained in *cfg1* outperform the models trained in *cfg2*. This is expected as the models in *cfg2* have more than three times the number of classes compared to those in *cfg1* in their softmax layer and low inter-class difference due to the split of each species into multiple levels. To test this hypothesis, the best-performing model in *cfg2* is made to predict species (*label=specie*) from the test data. We noticed an increase in P@1 value from 87.39 to 89.47. This significant change in P@1 supports our hypothesis. Figures 7 and 8 show P@1 and loss curves obtained on validation data during the training phase of the models from Table 2.

We use the confusion matrices obtained on the testing set by *cfg2* models from Table 2 to better understand the division of the Indic-Leaf dataset into different levels. These matrices are presented in Table 3. The first row (a, b) shows the confusion matrix for ResNet-101, while the second row (c, d) shows the confusion matrix obtained by averaging the individual confusion matrices of models from Table 2. The first column (a, c) shows the matrices obtained in species agnostic configuration, while the second column (b, d) shows the matrices obtained in species non-agnostic configuration. In species agnostic configuration, if the predicted class and ground-truth class of a test sample have the same *level*, we count it as a positive

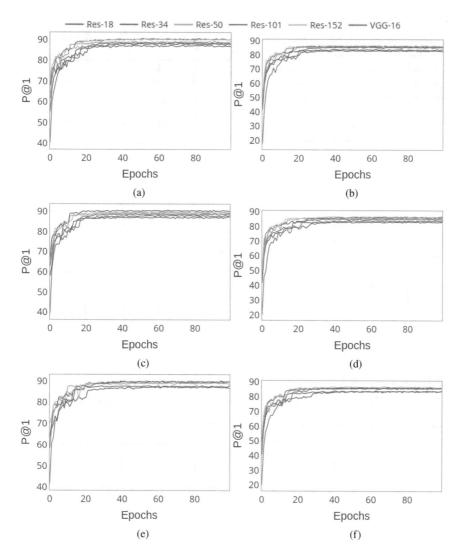

Fig. 7 P@1 of validation data plotted against epochs for different models in multiple colour spaces. The left column (**a**, **c**, **e**) shows P@1 from *cfg1* models and the right column (**b**, **d**, **f**) shows P@1 from *cfg2*. The first row (**a**, **b**) shows P@1 for models trained on the YCbCr colour space, the second row (**c**, **d**) for the RGB colour space, and the third row (**e**, **f**) for the HSV colour space

prediction. In species non-agnostic configuration, the predicted class and ground-truth class need to belong to the same species and be in the same *level*. Otherwise, they are counted as belonging to "other" class as shown in the fifth column of Table 3(b) and (d). It can be observed that the confusion between levels is minimal when the models are made to predict the species of the test sample along with the *level* in non-agnostic mode.

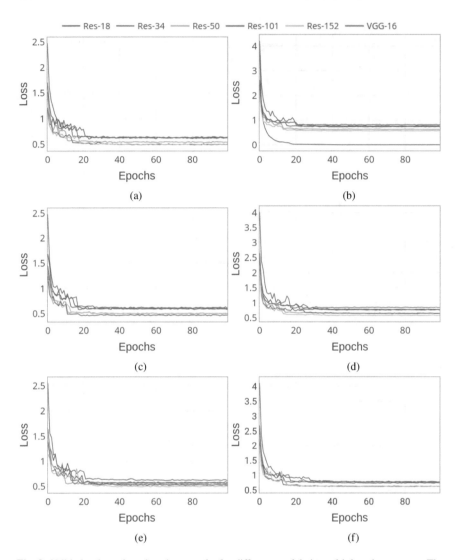

Fig. 8 Validation loss plotted against epochs for different models in multiple colour spaces. The left column (**a, c, e**) shows loss from *cfg1* models and the right column (**b, d, f**) shows loss from *cfg2*. The first row (**a, b**) shows loss for models trained on the YCbCr colour space, the second row (**c, d**) for the RGB colour space, and the third row (**e, f**) for the HSV colour space

To ascertain the significance of different *levels* in the dataset, a series of experiments were conducted by constraining the training set to contain only specific levels [20]. The best-performing model from Table 2, along with the baseline VGG-16, is used to analyse the impact of different levels on the test set from Table 2. The ResNet-18 architecture is used to understand the impact of depth in the obtained predictions. The results are presented in Table 4.

Table 3 The confusion matrices obtained for the *cfg2* models. The first row (a, b) shows the confusion matrix for the ResNet-101 model from Table 2. The second row (c, d) shows the confusion matrix obtained by averaging the individual confusion matrices of models from Table 2. The first column (a, c) shows the matrices obtained in species agnostic configuration, while the second column (b, d) shows the matrices obtained in species non-agnostic configuration

(a) Species agnostic confusion matrix for ResNet-101

gt	pred			
	1-0	1-1	1-2	1-3
1-0	1.000	0	0	0
1-1	0	0.990	0.010	0
1-2	0	0.019	0.981	0
1-3	0	0	0	1.000

(b) Species non-agnostic confusion matrix for ResNet-101

gt	pred				
	1-0	1-1	1-2	1-3	Other
1-0	1.000	0	0	0	0
1-1	0	0.990	0.010	0	0
1-2	0	0.009	0.981	0	0.010
1-3	0	0	0	0.991	0.009

(c) Species agnostic confusion matrix

gt	pred			
	1-0	1-1	1-2	1-3
1-0	1.000	0	0	0
1-1	0	0.987	0.013	0
1-2	0	0.023	0.966	0.011
1-3	0	0	0.016	0.984

(d) Species non-agnostic confusion matrix

gt	pred				
	1-0	1-1	1-2	1-3	Other
1-0	1.000	0	0	0	0
1-1	0	0.970	0.013	0	0.017
1-2	0	0.014	0.959	0.008	0.019
1-3	0	0	0.013	0.979	0.008

Table 4 The P@1 values of different models when the training set is constrained to specific *levels*. The header of each column specifies the *levels* used for training the specified model in each row [20]

Model	Levels							
	0, 3	1, 3	1, 2	2, 3	0, 1, 2	0, 1, 3	0, 2, 3	1, 2, 3
VGG-16	44.73	61.89	54.65	56.39	61.06	68.80	68.10	68.60
ResNet-18	45.25	60.36	54.20	57.31	60.21	67.12	66.64	66.99
ResNet-101	48.07	64.09	56.75	60.41	63.24	69.54	69.70	69.90

Table 5 P@1 values obtained by the ResNet-101 model on different leaf datasets

Model	Precision	Swedish	Flavia	Leafsnap	MK Leaf	MEW-2012	MEW-2014
ResNet-101	P@1	98.67	99.74	97.19	99.91	97.74	98.61
	P@3	100	100	99.69	99.98	99.49	99.70
	P@5	100	100	99.84	99.98	99.64	99.90

To observe the complex nature of the Indic-Leaf dataset, we experimented on the existing leaf datasets mentioned in Sect. 2.4. We picked the best-performing architecture from Table 2 and fine-tuned it on these datasets from the ImageNet pre-trained model. The classification results obtained can be seen in Table 5. The Flavia and MalayaKew Leaf datasets obtain P@1 above 99.5%, whereas the Swedish Leaf and Middle European Woods (2014) datasets obtain P@1 of 98.67% and 98.61%, respectively. We achieve P@1 of 97.74% on the Middle European Woods (2012) dataset. It can be observed that P@3 for all the datasets is above 99%. Overall, it

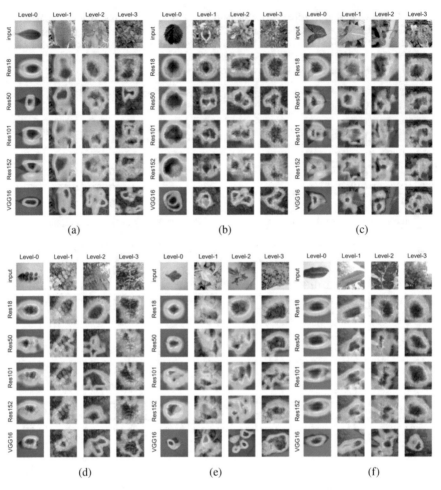

Fig. 9 Visual explanations for the classification task: Grad-CAM is used to find the regions in the images supporting the target class. Each sub-figure contains the images from a particular species across different levels, and visual explanations for the target class from different classification models are provided for these images. (**a**) *Anacardium occidentale* L. (**b**) *Acalypha wilkesiana.* (**c**) *Syngonium podophyllum.* (**d**) *Tecoma capensis.* (**e**) *Sphagneticola trilobata.* (**f**) *Kigelia africana*

can be observed that ResNet-101 achieves Top 1 accuracy above 97% on all the datasets.

After the neural networks have been trained, Grad-CAM is employed to visually inspect the areas of an image that support the classification. Figure 9 shows the visual explanations for images from the test data. Each sub-figure contains images from the same species. Each column has an image from a different *level*, and each row shows visual explanations from a convolutional neural network model on these images. These visual explanations are obtained by employing *cfg1* models of the RGB colour space from Table 2.

3.3 Discussion

In both the experimental configurations, we observe that the best-performing models use data in the RGB colour space. We find ResNet-101 achieving P@1 of 90.08% to be the best trade-off between model capacity and optimization difficulty. The increase in P@1 for the ResNet-101 *cfg2* model (*label=specie_level*) when made to predict species (*label=specie*) implies an accurate prediction of species when compared to the prediction of species made along with the *level* by the model. Moreover, the models in *cfg2* have lower P@K values than their *cfg1* counterparts, suggesting the complex nature of the *cfg2* variant of the dataset. This trend can also be noticed in Table 3. The division between *levels* does not cause a significant reduction in P@1 values of the models since the division between them is fairly acceptable. It can be further noted that the confusion between levels is minimal even when the models are made to predict the species of the test sample along with the *level* in non-agnostic mode. From another set of experiments made to focus on the significance of the division of the dataset into multiple *levels*, it is evident that the higher the number of *levels* in the training process, the better the performance of the model. It can also be deduced from the second column of Table 4 that higher inter-level variance provides for better performance of the models.

It can be observed from Table 5 that the ResNet-101 model achieves an almost perfect leaf classification above 99.7% on the Flavia and MK Leaf datasets. Although high accuracy is achieved, the class and image variance in datasets should be considered during its interpretation. For a constrained task such as leaf classification, the available datasets have a low number of classes and images. The Swedish Leaf dataset with 15 classes can be considered as one such example. The 98.61% P@1 achieved on MEW-2014 with 201 classes can be considered more informative than the 98.67% P@1 achieved on the Swedish Leaf dataset. Similarly, P@1 values of Leafsnap with 185 and MEW-2012 with 153 classes should be considered while evaluating the performance of classification models on these datasets. ResNet-101 that achieves the highest P@1 of 90.08 on the Indic-Leaf dataset achieves Top 1 accuracy above 97% on these datasets. This essentially validates the complex nature of the Indic-Leaf dataset.

The heatmaps generated by Grad-CAM provide an insight into the decision-making process of the networks. It can be observed that ResNet-18 generates heatmaps that are spread out covering the entire leaf and have a single peak. Contrarily, VGG-16 generates heatmaps that are relatively smaller, do not cover the entire object, and have multiple peaks. These generated heatmaps can be interpreted as the ability of the network to identify only the parts of the image that are needed for a high classification rate. They may be used to segment individual leaves from the image. The heatmaps generated by the rest of the ResNet networks do not follow a specific pattern that can be assessed.

4 Applications

Applications harnessing computer vision technologies are not uncommon. Recent trends show that such technologies need a significant amount of data for further improvement. The developed applications should also be accessible to the general public. In this section, we look into such applications that were developed over the course of this project. The first is a web-based application where users can access the catalogue of species, add new observations, and revise existing data. The second application is a mobile application that can be used to identify the plant species by capturing an image.

4.1 Web Application: Community Collaborative Approach

Community collaborative approaches for creating digital catalogues have been gaining significant traction in recent times. Crowdsourcing is a recent phenomenon that enables a computer vision researcher to collect data more swiftly. With widespread and accessible Internet connectivity, a web-based application will be an ideal platform for such tasks. Keeping this in view, we created a web application with two main goals: the creation of a catalogue on Indian plant species and the creation of a dataset to be used in computer vision tasks. Instead of relying on unregulated crowdsourced platforms like Amazon Mechanical Turk, our approach relies on creating a network of experts and harnessing their domain knowledge in expanding the portal. The obtained data can be used to improve plant recognition. In this subsection, we explain the flow of the web portal along with the functionalities of the various modules involved.

The dashboard is the first component of our web portal accessible to the user upon visiting. It contains various statistics related to plant species to help understand their distribution in the database. Apart from that, there are three other parts of the dashboard: a catalogue module, a tagging module, and an annotation module as shown in Fig. 10a. The catalogue module provides the user with a complete list of plant species by querying the database. The user will be provided with a few images of the species along with its details, as shown in Fig. 10c. Using the tagging module, users can provide missing details or edit existing ones about any plant species. The annotation module lets users annotate the images by drawing bounding boxes to mark the important regions in the images. Figure 10d shows this module.

The catalogue is accessible to every user of the web portal. But to access other functionalities that provide a gateway to the database, users have to register on the portal. The web portal contains multiple levels of users ranging from normal, to

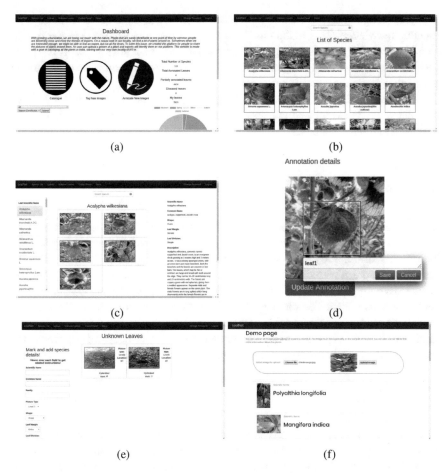

Fig. 10 Different components of the web application. (**a**) Dashboard showing catalogue, tagging, and annotation modules. (**b**) Catalogue module displaying a list of plant species with a search bar. The search bar supports multilanguage querying. (**c**) Catalogue module displaying details of *Acalypha wilkesiana*. (**d**) Annotation module: Users can annotate plant parts in an image. (**e**) Images tagged as unknown. (**f**) A demo application that users can use to identify the plant species in the image. It can be seen that *Mangifera indica* (ground truth) is predicted to be the second likely species in the queried image

experts, to administrators. New users will be assigned a level upon completion of the registration process. The accessibility to different functionalities of the web portal depends on the particular level a user falls under. Any registered user can add new entries to the database using the portal. For any image being added to the portal, the user will be asked to fill the details of the plant species captured in the image. These details are explained in Sect. 2. If any plant-specific details cannot be provided, users can simply mark the entry as unknown. After the data is submitted to the portal, the metadata of the images is extracted and recorded for further analysis.

Every image submitted by regular users is validated by a set of experts with domain knowledge. This maintains the quality of the data accessed in the portal. Experts can access the data tagged as "unknown" as shown in Fig. 10e. If the plant species captured in these images are identified by the experts, they are added to the portal along with the relevant information.

Our web application is built by integrating multiple technologies. It uses AngularJS for the front end and NodeJS for the back end. MongoDB is used to build and maintain databases.

4.2 Mobile Adaptation

In the past decade, the mobile phone industry has undergone rapid and significant improvements. Its hardware technology has advanced enough to support the deployment of complex software solutions for everyday problems. These devices provide an unprecedented gateway for developed software applications to reach the masses. Keeping this penetration of mobile phones in view, we developed a mobile application that identifies plant species through image acquisition. Considering market demographics, this application is designed to work on the Android platform. Images obtained as queries while the application is being operated are stored for further analysis. In this subsection, we explain the flow of our mobile application.

4.2.1 Implementation

Client–server architecture is very common across mobile applications that require the processing of an image. They provide more flexibility and mobility to mobile-based clients. Our Android application is designed to run on versions 5.0 and above to account for the maximum market coverage without compromising the required features. The application is also designed to be standalone and work without a network connection. All the required resource files are packaged with the application installation file. They include a trained neural network model for classification, images, and annotation data for plant species in our dataset. Upon installation of the application, they are saved to the internal memory of the mobile phone and are loaded into RAM when needed. The complete pipeline for the mobile application created is shown in Fig. 11.

The application is intuitive with a simple user interface. At the start of the application, the user has to obtain an image either by using the *Camera* button that provides access to the built-in camera or the *Load* button that provides access to the picture library. This can be seen in Fig. 12a and b. Users can further select the area of the image containing the plant to be identified in case there are multiple plants, as shown in Fig. 12c. Once the selection is confirmed, the image is sent for further processing. The application, by default, will send the image to a web server and receive classification results. If there is substandard Internet connectivity, the neural

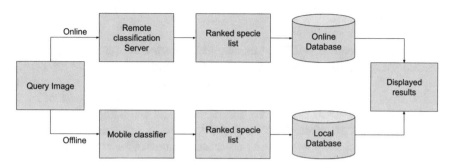

Fig. 11 The working pipeline of our mobile app. When the query image is captured, the application selects either an online mode or an offline mode based on the mobile network connectivity. In both modes, the application receives a list of species ranked based on the similarity to the species of the queried image. In online mode with no space restrictions, the whole database is used for identifying the species of the queried image. This is not the case in offline mode, since it is designed to operate with a truncated version of the online database integrated with the application

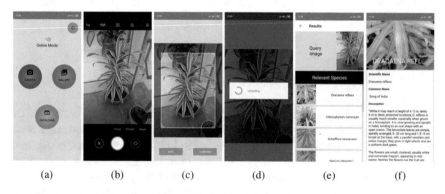

Fig. 12 The different screens of the mobile application. (**a**) The home screen where a user can select the query image. (**b**) Using the camera application to capture the image. (**c**) Selecting a region of interest from the captured image. (**d**) App querying the server to identify the plant. (**e**) Displaying a sorted list of species based on their similarity to the plant species in the queried image. (**f**) Details about the selected plant species from the list

network model is loaded into RAM from internal memory to obtain classification results. The obtained results are sorted based on the similarity to the queried image and are displayed in a list format, as can be seen in Fig. 12e. Each item in the list contains the scientific name of the species along with an image of the leaf. When an item on the list is clicked, relevant information about the species is loaded onto the screen from the database. This can be seen in Fig. 12f.

4.2.2 Quantization

In Sect. 3, we detail the different models that were trained for the task of plant species classification. These models are computationally complex to effectively deploy on the mobile platform. To adapt them to the mobile environment without making any significant reductions in accuracy, post-training quantization is performed. This process reduces the size of the model while improving hardware accelerator and CPU latency with a slight decrease in its accuracy. We use the TensorFlow Lite library to perform post-training quantization for quantization of weights.

The weights of a neural network are usually represented by a 32-bit floating point. But deep neural networks can also work with smaller data types such as 8-bit integers with a reduction in precision [14]. If the weights are quantized to 8 bits, there is $4\times$ reduction in memory. Quantized models will take up less storage space during deployment and less cache space during the functioning of the application. This will allow for more data to be in the cache, hence reducing the frequency of accessing the objects from RAM.

5   Conclusion

In this work, we aimed to create a plant species recognition system to automate the manual identification process. To aid the same, we created the Indic-Leaf dataset composed of 27K images. These images belong to 112 Indian plant species captured in the wild. Each of these species is divided into further levels to help understand the features of the plants in different scales. State-of-the-art convolutional neural networks are used to conduct a quantitative and qualitative analysis of our dataset. We experimented with different colour spaces and observed that models using image data in the RGB colour space outperform other models using the image data in other colour spaces by a narrow margin. We also provided the results from a different set of experiments to showcase the significance of the division of the dataset into different *levels* on the overall performance of the models. To remove any ambiguity regarding the inter-level confusion of the models over the accuracy, we conducted a series of experiments to show that such a case is minimal and can be omitted considering the compelling positive contribution of these *levels* to the accuracy of the models.

We used the ResNet-101 architecture that outperforms other models achieving P@1 of 90.08 on the Indic-Leaf dataset to train five different existing leaf datasets for classification. We observed that ResNet-101 achieves P@1 of above 97% on all these datasets, hence validating the complex nature of the Indic-Leaf dataset. Further, to understand the classification decisions of the models, we employed Grad-CAM to generate visual explanations for the testing data. The generated heatmaps provide a unique insight into the working of the models employed for classification. To improve the performance of these models and to utilize them to a greater extent, more data is required. A web portal is created for this purpose. This web portal acts as a platform for the experts and amateur botanists to contribute information related to different plant species. The integrity of the data uploaded into this portal is maintained by a network of users with hierarchical privilege and access to the web portal. This platform is designed to integrate additional modules such as the plant recognition system. To make this system more portable, we deployed the plant recognition system on smartphones by developing an application for Android devices. Different aspects of this application are described in detail, along with the quantization of convolutional neural networks that were integrated into the application. In summary, we explained an end-to-end pipeline for plant species recognition that can sustain itself with minimal effort by any individual user.

References

1. Agarwal, G., Belhumeur, P., Feiner, S., Jacobs, D., Kress, W.J., Ramamoorthi, R., Bourg, N.A., Dixit, N., Ling, H., Mahajan, D., et al.: First steps toward an electronic field guide for plants. Taxon (2006)
2. Alom, M.Z., Taha, T.M., Yakopcic, C., Westberg, S., Hasan, M., Van Esesn, B.C., Awwal, A.A.S., Asari, V.K.: The history began from AlexNet: a comprehensive survey on deep learning approaches (2018). Preprint, arXiv:1803.01164
3. Barré, P., Stöver, B.C., Müller, K.F., Steinhage, V.: Leafnet: a computer vision system for automatic plant species identification. Ecol. Inform. **40**, 50–56 (2017)
4. Beghin, T., Cope, J.S., Remagnino, P., Barman, S.: Shape and texture based plant leaf classification. In: International Conference on Advanced Concepts for Intelligent Vision Systems (2010)
5. Cerutti, G., Tougne, L., Mille, J., Vacavant, A., Coquin, D.: Understanding leaves in natural images–a model-based approach for tree species identification. Comput. Vis. Image Underst. **117**, 1482–1501 (2013)
6. Deng, J., Dong, W., Socher, R., Li, L.J., Li, K., Fei-Fei, L.: ImageNet: a large-scale hierarchical image database. In: Conference on CVPR09 (2009)
7. Farnsworth, E.J., Chu, M., Kress, W.J., Neill, A.K., Best, J.H., Pickering, J., Stevenson, R.D., Courtney, G.W., VanDyk, J.K., Ellison, A.M.: Next-generation field guides. BioScience **63**, 891–899 (2013)
8. Goeau, H., Bonnet, P., Joly, A.: Plant identification based on noisy web data: the amazing performance of deep learning (LifeCLEF 2017). In: CLEF 2017-Conference and Labs of the Evaluation Forum (2017)
9. Gu, X., Du, J.X., Wang, X.F.: Leaf recognition based on the combination of wavelet transform and Gaussian interpolation. In: Huang, D.S., Zhang, X.P., Huang, G.B. (eds.) Advances in Intelligent Computing. Springer, Berlin (2005)
10. Hang, S.T., Aono, M.: Open world plant image identification based on convolutional neural network. In: 2016 Asia-Pacific Signal and Information Processing Association Annual Summit and Conference (APSIPA) (2016)
11. He, K., Zhang, X., Ren, S., Sun, J.: Deep residual learning for image recognition. In: Proceedings of the IEEE Conference on Computer Vision and Pattern Recognition (2016)
12. Hopkins, G., Freckleton, R.P.: Declines in the numbers of amateur and professional taxonomists: implications for conservation. Anim. Conserv. Forum **5**, 245–249 (2002)
13. Husin, Z., Shakaff, A., Aziz, A., Farook, R., Jaafar, M., Hashim, U., Harun, A.: Embedded portable device for herb leaves recognition using image processing techniques and neural network algorithm. Comput. Electron. Agric. **89**, 18–29 (2012)

14. Jacob, B., Kligys, S., Chen, B., Zhu, M., Tang, M., Howard, A., Adam, H., Kalenichenko, D.: Quantization and training of neural networks for efficient integer-arithmetic-only inference. In: Proceedings of the IEEE Conference on Computer Vision and Pattern Recognition (2018)
15. Jamil, N., Hussin, N.A.C., Nordin, S., Awang, K.: Automatic plant identification: is shape the key feature? Procedia Comput. Sci. **76**, 436–442 (2015)
16. Joly, A., Goëau, H., Bonnet, P., Bakić, V., Barbe, J., Selmi, S., Yahiaoui, I., Carré, J., Mouysset, E., Molino, J.F., et al.: Interactive plant identification based on social image data (2014)
17. Kumar, N., Belhumeur, P.N., Biswas, A., Jacobs, D.W., Kress, W.J., Lopez, I.C., Soares, J.V.: Leafsnap: a computer vision system for automatic plant species identification. In: Computer Vision–ECCV 2012 (2012)
18. Larese, M.G., Namías, R., Craviotto, R.M., Arango, M.R., Gallo, C., Granitto, P.M.: Automatic classification of legumes using leaf vein image features. Pattern Recognit. **47**, 158–168 (2014)
19. Lee, K.B., Hong, K.S.: An implementation of leaf recognition system using leaf vein and shape. Int. J. Biosci. Biotechnol. **5**, 57–66 (2013)
20. Muthireddy, V., Jawahar, C.: Indian plant recognition in the wild. In: 7th National Conference on Computer Vision, Pattern Recognition, Image Processing and Graphics (NCVPRIPG 2019) (2019)
21. Novotný, P., Suk, T.: Leaf recognition of woody species in central Europe. Biosyst. Eng. **115**, 444–452 (2013)
22. Pimm, S.L., Jenkins, C.N., Abell, R., Brooks, T.M., Gittleman, J.L., Joppa, L.N., Raven, P.H., Roberts, C.M., Sexton, J.O.: The biodiversity of species and their rates of extinction, distribution, and protection. Science **344**, 1246752 (2014)
23. Sack, L., Dietrich, E.M., Streeter, C.M., Sánchez-Gómez, D., Holbrook, N.M.: Leaf palmate venation and vascular redundancy confer tolerance of hydraulic disruption. Proc. Natl. Acad. Sci. **105**, 1567–1572 (2008)
24. Scoffoni, C., Rawls, M., McKown, A., Cochard, H., Sack, L.: Decline of leaf hydraulic conductance with dehydration: relationship to leaf size and venation architecture. Plant Physiol. **156**, 832–843 (2011)
25. Selvaraju, R.R., Cogswell, M., Das, A., Vedantam, R., Parikh, D., Batra, D.: Grad-cam: visual explanations from deep networks via gradient-based localization. In: Proceedings of the IEEE International Conference on Computer Vision (2017)
26. Simonyan, K., Zisserman, A.: Very deep convolutional networks for large-scale image recognition (2014). Preprint, arXiv:1409.1556
27. Söderkvist, O.: Computer vision classification of leaves from Swedish trees (2001)
28. Sun, Y., Liu, Y., Wang, G., Zhang, H.: Deep learning for plant identification in natural environment. Comput. Intell. Neurosci. (2017). https://doi.org/10.1155/2017/7361042
29. Sutskever, I., Hinton, G.E., Krizhevsky, A.: Imagenet classification with deep convolutional neural networks. Adv. Neural Inf. Process. Syst. 1097–1105 (2012)
30. Wäldchen, J., Mäder, P.: Plant species identification using computer vision techniques: a systematic literature review. Arch. Comput. Methods Eng. **25**, 507–543 (2018)
31. Wu, S.G., Bao, F.S., Xu, E.Y., Wang, Y.X., Chang, Y.F., Xiang, Q.L.: A leaf recognition algorithm for plant classification using probabilistic neural network. In: 2007 IEEE International Symposium on Signal Processing and Information Technology (2007)

Printed in the United States
by Baker & Taylor Publisher Services